Brutal
Journey

Brutal
Journey

Holt Paperbacks
Henry Holt and Company, LLC
Publishers since 1866
175 Fifth Avenue
New York, New York 10010
www.henryholt.com

A Holt Paperback® and ® are registered trademarks of Henry Holt and Company, LLC.

Distributed in Canada by H. B. Fenn and Company Ltd.

Library of Congress Cataloging-in-Publication Data

Schneider, Paul, 1962–
    Brutal journey : Cabeza de Vaca and the epic first crossing of North America / Paul
Schneider.—1st ed.
        p.   cm.
    Includes bibiliographical references and index.
    ISBN-13: 978-0-8050-8320-0
    ISBN-10: 0-8050-8320-0
    1. Narvâêz, Pânfilo de, d. 1528.   2. Nââez Cabeza de Vaca, Alvar, 16th cent.   3. America—
Discovery and exploration—Spanish.   4. Florida—Discovery and exploration—Spanish.
5. Explorers—America—Biography.   6. Explorers—Spain—Biography.   7. America—
Description and travel.   8. Florida—Description and travel.   9. Indians of North America—
History—16th century.   10. Indians of North America—First contact with Europeans.
I. Title.

E125.N3S36   2006
973.1'6—dc22   2005050246

Henry Holt books are available for special promotions and premiums.
For details contact: Director, Special Markets.

Originally published in hardcover in 2006 by John Macrae / Henry Holt and Company

First Holt Paperbacks Edition 2007

Designed by Meryl Sussman Levavi

Printed in the United States of America

10 9 8 7 6 5 4 3 2

Cabeza de Vaca and the Epic
First Crossing of North America

Paul Schneider

A Holt Paperback
JOHN MACRAE / HENRY HOLT AND COMPANY
NEW YORK

For Nina,
and Natty

Contents

Brutal Journey

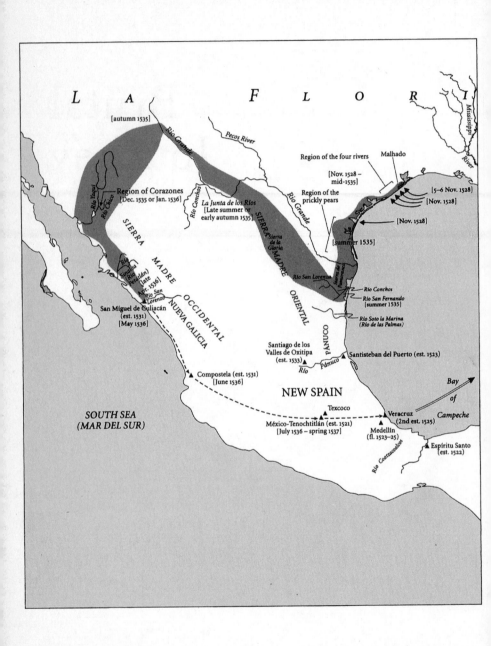

Approximate route of the Narváez survivors, 1528–36. (Courtesy of the University of Nebraska Press)

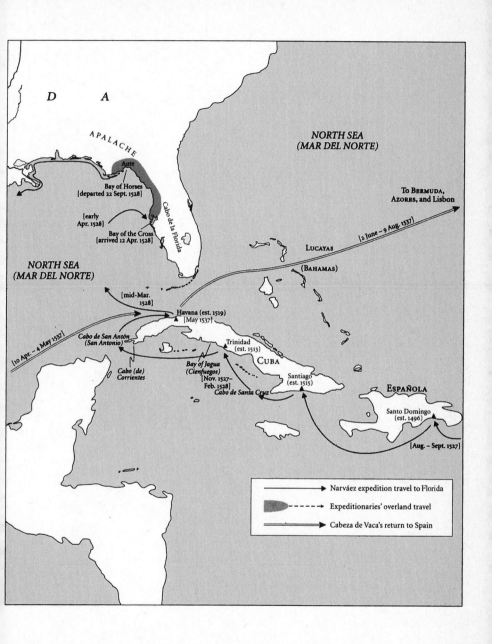

D A

APALACHE

NORTH SEA
(MAR DEL NORTE)

Aute

Bay of Horses
[departed 22 Sept. 1528]

Cabo de la Florida

[early
Apr. 1528]

Bay of the Cross
[arrived 12 Apr. 1528]

NORTH SEA
(MAR DEL NORTE)

[mid-Mar.
1528]

To Bermuda,
Azores, and Lisbon

[2 June – 9 Aug. 1537]

LUCAYAS

(Bahamas)

Havana (est. 1519)
[May 1537]

[10 Apr. – 4 May 1537]

Cabo de San Antón
(San Antonio)

Trinidad
(est. 1513)

Bay of Jagua
(Cienfuegos)
[Nov. 1527–
Feb. 1528]

CUBA

ESPAÑOLA

Cabo (de)
Corrientes

Cabo de Santa Cruz

Santiago
(est. 1515)

Santo Domingo
(est. 1496)

[Aug. – Sept. 1527]

→ Narváez expedition travel to Florida

- - -▶ Expeditionaries' overland travel

═▶ Cabeza de Vaca's return to Spain

Introduction

On Good Friday of 1528 an army of four hundred Spaniards, Africans, and Caribbean natives landed in the vicinity of Tampa Bay, Florida, under the command of a middle-aged conquistador with a last-chance license to conquer North America. They promptly disappeared without a trace into the swamps and, except for a small contingent that remained on board the ships, were soon assumed to be dead. But then, eight years and thousands of miles later, three Spaniards and a Moroccan wandered out of what is now the United States into what was then Cortés's gold-drenched Mexico.

They brought nothing back from their sojourn in the "unknown" north other than their story, for as one of them said later, "This alone is what a man who came away naked could carry out with him." But what a tale it was. Since leaving Tampa Bay, they and their dwindling company of comrades had become killers and cannibals, torturers and torture victims, slavers and enslaved. They became faith healers, arms dealers, canoe thieves, spider eaters, and finally, when there were only the four of them left trudging across the high Texas desert, they became itinerant messiahs. They became, in other words, whatever it took to stay alive long enough to inch their way across the continent toward Mexico, the only place they were certain they would find an outpost of the Spanish Empire.

Though well known to scholars of the European invasion of the New World, Pánfilo de Narváez's expedition to Florida is surprisingly unfamiliar to most North Americans. Part of the reason, no doubt, is the relative dearth of eyewitness accounts, a not-unexpected situation given the small number of survivors and the absence of even oral traditions reflecting the Native American perspective. There are only two firsthand narratives of the mission, both flawed in their own way and both European in origin. Best known is the astonishing personal memoir of the expedition's treasurer, Álvar Núñez Cabeza de Vaca, whose primary goal in writing was to convince the king that he deserved to be rewarded for his sufferings and services to the crown. The other is a shorter, official report that was prepared jointly by the survivors not long after their return; unfortunately, it exists only in a paraphrased form in an early Spanish history of the Indies.

Attempting to bring some possible version of the truth into focus through these two documents alone would be like trying to discern the craters of the moon through a telescope rigged out of two lenses salvaged from two different optical devices. It's a useful and theoretically possible exercise, but often more tantalizing in the questions it opens up than authoritative about some objective "reality." Fortunately, further details about the expedition can be inferred from the many other, better-documented Spanish intrusions into the region during the same period. Decisions made by Narváez can be compared and contrasted to those of his peers in similar situations, giving rise to a far more nuanced image of the commander than the traditional one of a bungling and vicious buffoon. Likewise, Cabeza de Vaca is not, in the end, quite as unerringly faithful and righteous as his own memory might suggest.

Hints about the lives and livelihoods of the various Native Americans encountered by the travelers surface in archeological reports and dissertations. What's been learned in the last fifty years about the original inhabitants of Florida, in particular, opens the door to a more even-handed image of the encounter between the conquistadors and the Indians. Likewise, high-tech research into the nature and volume of pre-Columbian trade within the Americas sheds new light on Cabeza de Vaca's temporary career as a peddler. In Texas and Mexico, meanwhile, a century of academic debates over the probable route of the survivors has finally coalesced into something resembling consensus.

And finally, for the interested person, the saw grass shallows of the Florida Panhandle are still there to wade out into. Thunderous downpours still roll in off the baked lands outside Laredo, Texas. Some of the plants may have changed, but the Sierra Madre remain.

The end result is a mosaic of pedigreed "facts" that when viewed as a whole bring a plausible rendering of the story to life. It's a daunting and occasionally frustrating undertaking; in a work of nonfiction there are always some tiles missing from the mosaic. Nonetheless, the story of the Narváez expedition is well worth the effort, and not only because the ordeal of the four who survived constitutes one of the greatest survival epics of all time. Or because they were arguably the first from the "Old World" to cross the continent of North America. Or that their journey and their stories inspired the better-known expeditions of De Soto and Coronado that followed them.

Beyond the day-to-day drama of the journey, what the Narváez survivors saw and said they saw provides a tantalizing glimpse of native North America in the moments before the waves of disease and dislocation began to change forever the human makeup of the continent. When fleshed out with what is known from other sources, the glimpse becomes something closer to a vision, and the journeyers—lost though they mostly were—become unintentional guides to a now lost New World.

It was a world populated by neither "noble savages" nor "bad Indians." As the survivors made their way from Florida to the Pacific, and then south, they met a dizzying array of peoples, some cruel enough to pluck men's beards out for pleasure, others kind enough to carry dying strangers to warm fires. Some were seemingly well off, dressed in fine furs and extravagant feather-work, others were desperately poor, their bellies bloated from hunger. And it wasn't just the residents of the New World that confronted the audacious newcomers; there were hurricanes and lightning, raging rivers, scorching deserts, and venomous vipers. This precontact North America—land, water, weather, and people—is the true protagonist of the story, against which the lives and dreams of the four hundred would-be conquerors are bent and twisted and, in all but a very few cases, extinguished.

For the expeditionaries setting out from Spain in 1527, North America began as an imagined place where they would find fabulous empires of gold: perhaps the seven lost cities supposedly settled by Portuguese bishops fleeing Muslim invaders in the early Middle Ages, or the fabled lands of the Amazon warriors, or even the fictional island of California. They would find nations of peoples waiting to be "liberated" from their heathen ways and ultimately thankful to be brought into the fold of "civilization," even if blood had to be spilled to convince them. In the process, the adventurers believed they would become wealthy beyond anything possible if they stayed home. Coming out of a seven-hundred-year tradition of privateer warfare against the Islamic Moors in Spain—the "reconquest"—they saw no conflict between fighting for their ideals and their pocketbooks at the same time. They were going to North America "to serve God and the king," as one of their contemporaries said, "and also to get rich."

As citizens of the strongest nation in Europe, an empire entering its golden age with a destiny ordained by the pope himself, the conquistadors had everything they needed to make it happen. They had the superior weapons, the legal structure, the philosophical framework, the experience, the private capital, and most of all they had the desire, hubris, and zeal. But in the end, on the ground in North America, for Narváez and his followers it wasn't enough. Even before they landed in Florida, reality slowly but methodically began stripping them of everything they thought they were and remaking them into something altogether strange and new. In the case of one of the survivors, the Moroccan slave Esteban, also called "the Black," the change was apparently irreversible.

All history is hindsight, of course, and in hindsight it's easy to say the hundreds who followed Narváez to their doom in the quagmire were fools following a fool. They probably were. But history also attempts to understand, and in 1527 there were plenty of reasons to leave the land of no-opportunity that was home and to believe in Narváez and join his mission to America. He was a seasoned and well-connected commander who had already played a major and bloody role in conquering the Caribbean, and had gotten rich doing so. More importantly to the rank and file, only seven years had passed since Cortés had conquered Montezuma's empire, and the fleets stuffed with treasure and rumor arriving from Mexico reignited the frenzy of interest in New World conquests that had flagged in the disappointing decades immediately following Columbus's discoveries. Where there was one such bonanza, there was sure to be another; and if Narváez and his army didn't go find it, others inevitably would. So the hundreds signed on to go to La Florida and told their loved ones not to worry.

Such historical "inevitabilities," driven as they are by great economic forces and social trends, are modern history's stock in trade. But in the end, they are only the stage on which real lives of pain and pleasure were played out, lives that were defined by various egos and varying abilities, and to some measure by chance. For Narváez himself, the connection to Cortés and Mexico was far more than simply inspirational. It was personal and direct, remembered with a wince each day whenever he put a hand up to his ruined eye socket. No, it was beyond personal; it was obsessive.

So the story begins not in Spain or in Florida, but in the Totonic city of Cempoallan, on the Gulf Coast of Mexico in the year 1520, not long after Cortés had placed Montezuma under house arrest up in Mexico City.

1

A Continent to Call His Own

I tell you that when you least expect it, he will be here and will kill you," said Tlacochcalcatl gravely.

Pánfilo de Narváez looked at the obese man before him and burst out laughing. He was ridiculous, this heathen chief of the Totonics, this "fat cacique" as Narváez and all the other Spaniards called him. They were in Cempoallan, the main city of the Totonics, a place of pyramids and town squares that was richer than anything Narváez had seen during his long career as a conqueror in Cuba, Jamaica, and Hispaniola. But even pyramids and town squares didn't make it easier for a civilized Christian like himself to take seriously someone who had a gold labret dangling from an immense hole in his lower lip, dragging it down so that his ugly, half-rotten bottom teeth and gums were exposed. It was hard to believe the man could talk at all.

Moreover, listen to what this Tlacochcalcatl was saying. He had previously warned Narváez and his officers to stay away from the gold and the pretty Indian women that Cortés had recently left behind in Cempoallan for safekeeping. That was funny enough, but this warning that Cortés would arrive from Mexico City at any minute and kill them all on this rainy day was downright hilarious. If anything, he, Narváez, would kill the little thief Cortés, who had stolen Mexico not only from Montezuma, but out from under Narváez and Governor Velázquez of Cuba as well. Killing Cortés and taking his rightful control of Mexico was precisely what Narváez had brought a fleet of seventeen ships and an army of nearly a thousand men all the way from Cuba to do. So he laughed his famously booming laugh, and standing beside him, his deputy Salvatierra laughed along with his commander.

They guffawed in the fat cacique's face, but just to be safe, Narváez mustered his troops and cavalry about a mile outside of town. They stood out there in the wet for hours, with their horses and cannon lined up and ready, waiting for Cortés and his traitorous rabble to appear out of the dripping jungle. The horses periodically whinnied their disapproval, while the soldiers shifted their weight from foot to foot, grumbling among themselves about how the gold and the girls always ended up in the officers' hands and beds.

But Cortés didn't appear, and eventually Narváez and his officers had had enough of the June drizzle. They put a few spies along the road and returned to the white-painted houses and heathen temples of Cempoallan's main square. Cursing the foolishness of Tlacochcalcatl, Narváez and his officers climbed back to the thatched shrine at the top of the town's largest pyramid, which they had appropriated as their living quarters. Of course Cortés wouldn't attack an army twice the size of his own; what did a heathen Indian know about anything?

Nonetheless, Narváez ordered that the pyramid be well guarded with artillery and cavalry. He stationed crossbowmen on a balcony above the temple where he and his officers were quartered and had his crier announce among the entire army that if Cortés attacked there would be two thousand pesos for the soldier who killed him. There would be two thousand as well for the soldier who killed the little thief's deputy, Sandoval. The password by which Narváez's soldiers would know each other was to be "Santa María, Santa María"— Holy Mary. The men cheered and went to bed.

A few hours later, near midnight, one of the advance spies from along the road into Cempoallan ran to the top of the pyramid and shook Narváez awake. The other spy had been captured, he reported, and Cortés's advancing army was now only moments away. In his later letters to Spain, Cortés estimated that he and his men arrived at Cempoallan about a half hour after the alarm had been sounded.

"When finally I came up to where Narváez was, all his men were already armed and mounted, with two hundred soldiers ready, posted to guard each building," he told the king. "We arrived so quietly, however, that when they at last perceived us and gave the call to arms I was already entering the courtyard of his lodging."

Narváez hardly had a chance to get out of his bed before he was swinging his broadsword in his bare feet and shouting instructions to his men. With a group of about thirty of his officers and guards, he battled furiously in the front rooms of the shrine at the top of the great pyramid without any way of knowing for certain what was going on in the squares below. What was going on was that his army was disintegrating. Whether because their saddle girths had been cut or their captains bribed, or both, his cavalry on the plaza was unable to slow Cortés's advance. The few who tried to mount and fight just fell off, though one witness said they were unhorsed. Whether because someone in Cortés's pay sabotaged the cannons' touchholes with wax, or because the powder was wet, Narváez's gunners only got off four shots before they were over-run. What's more, thanks to the captured spy, Cortés knew exactly where to look for Narváez. Sandoval simply pushed the guards at the top of the pyramid aside and attacked the temple.

It was against these fellow-Spaniards that Narváez now swung his big two-handed broadsword. Whatever his drawbacks as a commander, none of his contemporaries doubted Narváez's skill or daring once a battle began. "He defended himself like a gentleman," said one of Cortés's soldiers, Rodrigo de Castañeda. Out on the steps of the pyramid some of Narváez's guards also rallied from the initial surprise and fought hard and well against Cortés's men, who stabbed up at them with long pikes that they had purchased from their native allies. Inside the dark inner rooms of the shrine, where some of Cortés's men had penetrated, however, one of the pikes found its mark.

"Holy Mary protect me, they have killed me and destroyed my eye," a voice howled out, and everyone within earshot knew immediately that it was Narváez. In later legal wrangling over the events of the night, four witnesses particularly remembered the loud cries. His voice was distinctive, "very deep and hoarse as if it came from a vault," said one who knew him.

"We stood for some time fighting with our pikes which were very long," recalled one of Cortés's men who had rushed over to the pyramid to reinforce Sandoval, "and when I was least expecting it we heard shouts from Narváez."

Blood sprayed from Narváez's empty socket. Through the pain he heard Sandoval threatening to set fire to the thatched roof of the shrine if he didn't surrender immediately. In the square below, Cortés's men were already yelling "Victory, Victory, Narváez is dead." He paused to think, but there was no time. The room was rapidly filling with smoke and falling embers from the fire on the roof. Enraged, gasping, fully blinded now by thick smoke, Narváez and his men made a mad rush for the door.

"All the companions of Narváez came tumbling down the steps," remembered one witness. Narváez himself was thrown to the ground and clapped in irons. Someone, maybe Sandoval, ripped his commissions and other legal documents from under his shirt, which he protested to no avail. He asked for a doctor to attend to his ruined eye and his burned feet, but they just looked down at him, called him a traitor, and wouldn't do it.

By now the rain had stopped, and fireflies flickered eerily all over town as Cortés and his men mopped up the remnants of Narváez's army. Twice during the evening, Cortés himself went secretly into the room where Narváez lay in chains. The first time was only moments after the last pockets of resistance had been defeated, and Narváez never knew his archenemy had come into the chamber. Sandoval didn't need to be told how important it was that Narváez not escape, but Cortés reminded him nonetheless. Under no circumstances should the prisoner be left alone, he whispered, and then slipped back out. Sandoval added another set of chains to Narváez's legs.

The second time Cortés came into the room, Narváez learned he was there. He asked again for medical help, to which Cortés replied that he had already received much better than he deserved. But when Narváez begged in God's holy name for his life, Cortés told Sandoval to send for Narváez's personal surgeon to minister to his wounds.

Chained, filthy, and half-blind, Narváez nonetheless retained his sense of his own grandeur. "Jeering" and "haughty" were among the words used by one who knew him. "You should regard highly the good luck of having my person [as] prisoner," he said to Cortés once the doctor was at work.

Cortés replied that he really must thank God and his comrades for their help. Narváez, as a Catholic and a commander himself, understood. It was an appropriate thing for a man in Cortés's position to say. But the little thief didn't stop there. He sneered down at his prisoner lying on the floor in chains and told Narváez in front of all of his officers that capturing him was actually "one of the least important things he had done in New Spain."

Then he turned and walked out of the room, leaving Narváez to lie there with "two pairs of fetters on him" listening to the celebrations outside. An African soldier named Guidela was yelling absurdities about how "the Romans never accomplished such a feat" as Cortés had done by defeating Narváez. Others banged drums, clanged tambourines, and screeched on fifes.

Narváez lay there in chains, listening, while they yelled "Long live the King, long live the King, and in his Royal Name, Cortés, Cortés, Victory, Victory, for Narváez is dead!"

Only he wasn't dead, and as Narváez himself was just beginning to realize, he wasn't going to die from his wounds either. He was merely defeated, and would have to live with, or find a way to live down, the dishonor.

For nearly three years Narváez stayed imprisoned on the sweltering, bug-ridden coast of Mexico while virtually his entire army happily listened to Cortés's promises of easy gold and even easier native women and followed him back over the mountains to Tenochtitlan, the mysterious and fabulous Mexican capital. Back in Spain, during those same years, lawyers and lobbyists battled a war of bribes and briefs over who would end up controlling Mexico.

Narváez had reason to be hopeful about the legal effort. On paper, he and his patron Diego Velázquez, the governor of Cuba, had the better case: before Cortés sailed for Mexico, Narváez himself had spent nearly four years in Spain lining up the paperwork needed for a Mexican conquest led by Velázquez and himself. But Cortés had possession of both the prize and the deep pockets of Mexican treasure that came with it, and with the king up to his ears in debt from his successful campaign to get himself elected Holy Roman Emperor, money spoke the loudest. In the summer of 1522, Charles V returned to Spain from the Diet of Worms, where he had sworn to stamp out the heresy of Martin Luther, and put an end to the endless bickering over the spoils of Montezuma's empire. He gave Cortés the grandiose title of Marquis del Valle and ordered Narváez and Velázquez not to meddle any longer with affairs in Mexico.

It took another half a year for the news to reach Cortés, and then a few months more for him to decide that continuing to keep Narváez in jail could only do him more harm than good. Toward the end of 1523, in a gesture befitting his grand new rank, he released Narváez and sent him back across the Yucatan Channel to Cuba.

Embittered and angry is how Narváez's wife, María de Valenzuela, found her husband when at last he returned home. His eye had been poked out, which was bad, and his ego was damaged, which was worse. He was "entreating for justice and single combat," one of his friends remembered. In other words, Narváez wanted a formal duel with Cortés. Only then would the fraternity of conquistadors know which of them was the better man, which one was the greater warrior. But the opportunity to match arms with Cortés never materialized.

Narváez was not an entirely ruined man, however, thanks in large part to María de Valenzuela's efforts while he was away. Already once a widow before Narváez married her, she had spearheaded the legal effort to get Narváez released from prison alive. Mostly, though, she spent his absence forcing Native Americans and Africans to scrape and pan for

"The way they collect gold in the streams . . ." Engraving (after an original by Jaques Le Moyne) from Theodor De Bry's Americae, *part II, 1594.*

gold in the hills of her Cuban estates. She was a talented slave driver, as it turned out. "This is what he found," remembered Narváez's friend, the historian Gonzalo Oviedo. "Aside from finding his estate increased in value . . . she also had for him 13,000 or 14,000 gold pesos, which the woman had mined with their slaves and Indians."

It was not by any means a mountain of treasure like the one Cortés had stolen from Montezuma, and by extension from Velázquez and himself, but it should have been enough to keep a reasonable man happy. "I advised him as a friend to remain peacefully at home in the company of his wife and children and to give thanks to God since he had a place to live and the wherewithal to pass through this worldly vale so full of woes," said Oviedo.

But Narváez was in no mood to be thankful. Roughly fifty years old, he was admittedly not as young as he had been when he and Diego Velázquez had conquered Cuba. Or when he and Esquivel had subdued Jamaica. But unlike Velázquez, he was by no means ready to concede defeat, retire, recede, and die a rich but humiliated man. Velázquez had lasted barely a year after the town crier of Santiago, Cuba, had announced the horrifying news of Cortés's political victory back in Spain.

No, Narváez had the inklings of a new plan. If he couldn't get revenge on Cortés personally he would avenge his honor on the field of conquest. There was a whole continent of opportunities to the north of Mexico, just waiting for a man of ability to come and claim them for God and King. Less than a year after his return to Cuba, therefore, Narváez collected the gold his wife had saved and returned to Spain, arriving in Seville in mid-1525.

Some things had changed in the six years since he had last left Spain. In the first years of the 1520s, Charles V had overhauled the Council of Castile, his main administrative and advisory body for Spain, making it smaller and theoretically more professional. He had also created a new Council of the Indies to handle all issues relating to the growing empire in the Americas. Both actions were part of a general effort to streamline royal governance, a worthy project for an emperor whose holdings were scattered all over Europe and the New World.

In practice, however, getting a contract to conquer a chunk of the New World was still a matter of calling in favors, lining up contacts, and greasing palms in the clubby world of courtiers, bankers, priests, and generic sycophants that ran Spanish imperial policy. Charles might be trying to replace the older, more informal rule by verbal decree with a government of laws and paper, but at heart he was still an old school monarch, favoring an ad hoc, personal style of governance. He once famously (and perhaps apocryphally) called for a pen and paper, only to learn to his dismay that neither were to be found on the royal premises. During his reign there wasn't even a fixed place in Spain where a peti-tioner like Narváez could conduct his royal business. The seat of gov-ernment under Charles V was wherever Charles V happened to be sitting, and in the grand medieval style, he traveled constantly from city to city within his realm as business and whim took him. Not until 1561 did his son, Philip II, establish Madrid as the country's capitol.

Narváez caught up with the court in Toledo in the spring of 1525 and began lobbying in earnest. Like all petitioners, he submitted a legal brief detailing how much he had already done for his majesty in the past and suggesting what might be an appropriate way for the king to show his gratitude. But these *probanzas*, thousands of which are still stacked away in archives all over Spain and its former empire, were almost never read by the king himself. The real work of getting the desired payoff from the crown was therefore done much more infor-mally, over dinner or in private meetings with anyone closer to the center of power than one's self.

Before the Mexican fiasco, Narváez had served as an official repre-sentative of the colonists in Cuba and had been the number two man in the conquests of both that island and of Jamaica. So he knew plenty of people who might be interested in a piece of the North American action in exchange for a good word whispered in the right ear. For a while, however, his priorities were mixed, and he wasted his time com-plaining about Cortés. He was one of several who accused Cortés of killing his own wife, who had died mysteriously in the middle of the night after dinner, and of poisoning Governor Garay of Jamaica, who also died unexpectedly after dining with the new marquis. In some of his early petitions, Narváez went so far as to urge the execution of Cortés for treason.

By April of 1525, however, he quit pursuing Cortés and devoted himself to obtaining permission to undertake a new adventure in North America. This was only partly a recognition of political reality. Even supposing he could wrest some piece of Mexico from Cortés, which in all likelihood he could not have done, to take by legal maneuvers an already conquered empire would not have erased the ignominy of his earlier defeat at Cempoallan. The men of Narváez's generation and social class were obsessed with notions of honor and what one historian called "their love of great deeds for their own sake . . . this thirst for reputation." Narváez wanted his own conquest in order to restore his pride.

He had always been a deputy, serving under someone else's formal command, while people he considered his peers and quite a few he considered his inferiors had received islands and empires to conquer. Most grating of these, of course, was Cortés. But there was also Ponce de León in Puerto Rico and Florida, Esquivel in Jamaica, Velázquez in Cuba, Pedrarius in Panama. Even a meddlesome judge from Hispaniola named Lucas Vasquez de Ayllón, who had played a bit part in the Mexican fiasco, had come back to Spain while Narváez was rotting away in Cortés's jail, and gotten himself permission to settle a great stretch of the Atlantic coast of North America from northern Florida to the Carolinas.

Ayllón's interest in the North American mainland grew out of a slaving voyage in which he had invested. In 1521 he sent a ship on a *razzia*, or slave-hunting mission, to the Lucayos, as the Bahamas were then called. But when the ship arrived there, the captain found the islands already depopulated by the many slavers who had preceded him. Another Spanish slaver was also milling around the Bahamas complaining about how the easy pickings were gone, and the two captains decided to combine forces and sail to the northwest in search of the "Island of the Giants" that yet another Spanish slaver had reported finding seven years previously. They reached the mainland in June of 1521, most likely in what is now South Carolina, and after a brief squabble over which vessel's owner had the right to claim the territory, they went ashore and kidnapped sixty Indians. Most of these unfortunates died within a few years of being caught. One who lived a while longer was shipped to Venezuela and became a well-known pearl diver. Another, whom for reasons that are not clear they called Francisco "El Chicorano," became a personal servant of Judge Ayllón in Hispaniola.

El Chicorano could tell a good story. There were piles of enormous pearls to be had in the Carolinas, he informed Ayllón. There were also, he said, people with horses and "blond hair to their heels," led by a giant king named Datha. El Chicorano was an early practitioner in a long line of Native Americans who told their captors what they wanted to hear in order to finagle a ride back home; Ayllón became an early practitioner in the long line of Europeans who rose to the bait. Taking El Chicorano along with him to impress the emperor, he quickly returned to Spain and secured a contract to conquer the south Atlantic coast of North America.

Narváez was well aware of Ayllón's project, if only because it represented territory that was not currently available for conquest by himself. Early on in his lobbying effort he may even have tried to steal the contract out from under Ayllón, against whom he held a grudge: Ayllón received a royal letter shortly after Narváez arrived in Spain warning him that he if did not get his exploratory voyage underway soon, his contract would be awarded to an unnamed competitor. He quickly sent out the required ships in the summer of 1525, and a year later sailed for "New Andalusia" himself with a fleet of six ships and nearly six hundred Spanish, Caribbean, and African colonists.

With Ayllón's territory off the table, Narváez focused on other opportunities. Foremost among these were Juan Ponce de León's grant in Florida and Francisco de Garay's contract for the territory just to the north of Cortés's Mexican empire. Both of these were vacant because their proprietors were dead: Garay, who got his start when one of his Indian slaves on Hispaniola found a thirty-five-pound gold nugget, died as mentioned after dining with Cortés; Ponce de León succumbed to an arrow wound inflicted by the Floridians in 1521.

"I, Pánfilo Narváez, native of these your kingdoms, and resident of the island of Fernandina (Cuba), presented a petition to your very high Council in Toledo," Narváez reminded the king in a typical letter, "asking that the subjugation of the countries there are from the Rio de Palmas to Florida might be given me, where I would explore, conquer, populate and discover all there is to be found of Florida in those parts, at my cost."

Fortunately for Narváez, Charles V was anxious to replace Garay and Ponce de León. The mid-1520s were a time of intense speculation about North America in all of Europe. Much of this was due to Cortés's fabulous success in Mexico, of course. Add to that Ayllón's talk of a New Andalusia, complete with olive groves and vineyards. Also, in 1525 Esteban Gómez, a Portuguese pilot working for Spain, returned from a voyage along the coast from New England to Cape Breton and word got around that he had discovered cloves growing there. To some in Seville, cloves implied that a route to the spice-laden orient of

Columbus's dreams was found at last. The only problem was that what Gómez really said he had found was not *clavos* but *esclavos*, not cloves but slaves.

The emperor also worried about competition from other European kings. The pope's division of the globe between the crowns of Castile and Portugal did not amuse the other monarchs of Europe, and beginning officially with Cabot's voyage in search of the mythical island of Hi-Brasil in 1497, occasional English voyages out of Bristol had been creeping southward from Newfoundland. Even more alarming were the French: in 1522 a fleet of French privateers captured Cortés's second, and perhaps greatest, shipment of treasure meant for Charles V. Then in 1523 and 1524, Verrazano explored the east coast of North America from Georgia to New England. "I'd like to see the clause of Adam's will that excludes France from the division of the world," said his employer, the king of France.

Charles and his new Council of the Indies were not, therefore, inclined to trust England and France to abide forever by the pope's "gift" of the western hemisphere. Not when experienced Castilians were willing to raise and fund their own armies of conquest to go off in search of fabulous new heathen empires to bring into God's and Spain's fold. More than willing, Narváez felt positively entitled: "Consider that to other persons has been given more than I ask for, though they have not served as much as I have," he pointed out to the king. "Nor have they in their persons the qualities that I have, nor have they had, nor do they have as much wealth with which to serve, and it should be believed that if I did not intend to serve God and Your Majesty in these things, I would not put myself to so much expense and danger."

For a year and a half, Narváez followed the court around Spain, periodically tweaking his petitions in ways that he hoped would improve his chances of success, but never changing his basic proposal "to serve Your Majesty by the exploration, conquest and populating of certain lands in the Ocean Sea, asking that the subjugation of the countries there are from the Rio de Palmas to Florida might be given me . . . for me, my heirs and successors."

Finally, at Granada, on December 11, 1526, the emperor gave Narváez a license to conquer and subdivide all the territory between those areas already claimed by his old adversaries Cortés and Ayllón—everything, that is, from New Spain to New Andalusia. By combining old claims of Garay and Ponce de León, the new grant encompassed the entire Gulf Coast of what would one day become the United States. In terms of geography, it was exactly what Narváez had asked for. It was his own private manifest destiny that went, as his contract stated, "from one sea to the other."

All he had to do was go and take it.

2

The Company Gathers

The first six months of 1527 slipped by in a blur of meetings and paperwork. Narváez's contract gave him exactly one year to gather an initial army of at least several hundred men and leave Spain. According to its terms, the force had to be big enough to found at least two towns with a hundred persons each, and to garrison two more fortresses along the coast wherever he saw fit. He was also expected to establish trade with the Indians and provide for their peaceful conversion to Christianity, though he was granted the traditional loopholes allowing him to enslave anyone who resisted conversion, engaged in sodomy, dined on human flesh, or who had been previously enslaved by other Indians.

All of this was to be achieved without any direct assistance from the emperor. This wasn't unusual. Queen Isabella had invested personally in

Columbus's voyages, but after that, the Spanish conquest of America was almost entirely funded by the conquistadors themselves, with help from whatever private investors they could lure into their projects. Narváez tried in his petition to slip in a payback clause: "I ask Your Majesty that all I shall expend in exploring, subjugating and populating, be ordered to be paid me out of the royal revenue from those lands." But the Council of the Indies brushed him off. "This is not proper," it responded in a memorandum, "the King will grant him other favors for what he will expend in this."

All he got from the king upfront were a few tax breaks and a promise to recognize Narváez's authority over the new lands. He was granted the positions of governor, captain-general, chief justice, and *adelantado*, which was a largely honorific title left over from Spain's long war with the Moors. The first two came with a good salary of 250,000 *maravedís*, but even this was more like a stock option, as it was only to be paid out of revenues from the conquest. The latter two titles were unpaid, but unlike the former were granted to him and his heirs in perpetuity. It was a boilerplate contract for the period: on the same day that it was issued a colleague of Narváez's named Francisco de Montejo received a nearly identical commission to "pacify" Cozumel and the Yucatan.

Despite his wife's substantial savings, Narváez was not so rich that he could outfit an army of the sort required entirely out of his own pocket. No figures regarding Narváez's financing have been discovered, but Ayllón's similar-sized expedition was reputed to cost more than 100,000 gold ducats. That may well have been an exaggeration: by contrast, the king's twenty percent cut of all income generated in the Indies in 1518 was only 122,600 ducats. Whatever the real figure, Ayllón mortgaged most of his sizable fortune in order to raise it, and Narváez likewise got money wherever he could.

Many of the earliest voyages to the new world, including those of Columbus, were bankrolled by Italian sources. But with the accession of the Hapsburg Charles V to the Spanish throne in 1516, German bankers became much more important. The Fugger and the Welser houses, in particular, were well positioned to get in on the action. They had largely financed the 850,000 florins in bribes and soft money that secured Charles his election as leader of the Holy Roman Empire, a loose affiliation of mostly German principalities that Voltaire called "neither holy, nor Roman, nor an Empire." By the end of his reign, Charles's entire income from the New World was pledged to the foreign lenders who underwrote his European ambitions.

On a far smaller scale, Narváez met in Seville and elsewhere with brocade-wearing representatives of the various lending houses. He probably mortgaged his Cuban holdings, and most likely signed away his promised salaries as well. He called in what debts were owed him and tried to get out of paying those that he owed, successfully petitioning the king to refund six hundred pesos that he'd paid in a fine that grew out of the old affair with Cortés in Mexico. Every ducat counted when there were ships to purchase and outfit, captains and crews to hire, provisions and trade goods to stockpile. Mostly, though, he secured outside investors with fabricated promises about the wealth of his new domain.

As grating as it was for him personally, Narváez was happy that the news and rumors from the Indies were still dominated by Cortés's fabulous cities of gold. Such tales softened bankers' hearts and loosened their wallets. What's more, in order to have any reasonable hope of fulfilling the terms of his contract with the emperor, he needed to recruit at least four hundred people, preferably several hundred more, and the more good news they heard about the New World, the better. So though Narváez the plaintiff had earlier called for suppression of Cortés's letters on the grounds that they unduly damaged his reputation, Narváez the recruiter happily led his listeners to believe that Mexico was just a warm-up to the gold-encrusted country to which he was going.

"Narváez, and other captains who want them, find people like this in numbers more than they need, because poverty in some, avarice in others, and lunacy in most, prevents them from understanding what they do, or knowing whom they follow," his friend Oviedo said of the recruitment process. "Once dispatched from Court, he comes to Seville with less money than he likes, and sends out for the one part, a drummer, and a friar or two and some priests, who adhere to him at once, under color of conversion of the Indians, and turn the minds of others to go by promising riches of which they know nothing."

The Seville of 1526, in which Narváez did most of his fundraising and recruiting, was a remarkably cosmopolitan place. Despite the forced conversions and expulsions of both the Jewish and Moorish populations at the turn of the fifteenth century, and the continuing madness of the Inquisition, Spanish society remained the most multicultural in Europe. Nowhere was this more evident than Seville. With its royal monopoly on all business with the Indies, by the 1520s it was not a novelty to see natives of the New World—both free and enslaved—in the streets of the old Moorish capital. The trade with the Americas also brought others to town, and not just the German bankers already mentioned. Merchants from Charles's domains in northern Europe and Italy were setting up shop in order to service the growing transatlantic trade.

There were also more slaves from various parts of the "Old World" in Seville than in any other Spanish city. Most of these were still the light brown or olive-complexioned peoples from around the Mediterranean, all of whom had been enslaving each other for centuries. (Some of the Spaniards who signed on with Narváez may themselves have spent a portion of their lives indentured on the North African coast.) There were enslaved white Russians in the mix, as well as other fair-skinned peoples from the Balkans. In recent decades, however, the Portuguese had been developing the sub-Saharan slave trade, and black slaves were becoming more common.

But Narváez wasn't particularly interested in attracting slaves and merchants to the expedition. Instead, he and his agents culled most of their recruits from the steady stream of in-migration to Seville from northern and central Spain. During the summer of 1527 Narváez sent word north to his family and neighbors in the smaller towns along the Duero River and its tributaries that another of their local boys was about to lead a glorious mission in the Indies. Recruiters also banged the drums in the streets of Extremadura, the down-at-heel province along the border with Portugal that produced many conquistadors. But most of the recruits had already come to Seville on their own accord. A full-blown demographic shift from north to south was underway in the country, a process that ballooned the city's population from around 50,000 in Narváez's time to nearly three times that number a generation later.

The call for volunteers was typically answered by the younger sons and nephews of lesser gentry, boys and men who sought opportunity in the New World because their father's estates were not legally divisible. Or, just as often, because their grandfather's estate had not been divisible. Known as caballeros and, slightly below them on the social ladder, hidalgos, they could preface their name with the honorific "Don" but were otherwise untitled. More to the point, they were caught in an economic bind. Their code of military honor prevented them from working the land like peasants, or working with their hands like converted Jewish and Muslim tradesmen. Even commerce and international trade was frowned upon if it was more than a hobby.

Meanwhile the end of the seven-hundred-year "reconquest" of

Spain from the Moors in 1492 had dried up the military opportunities at home, leaving the hidalgos and caballeros as a declining middle class in an economy and political structure that no longer needed them. Except, that is, as privateer soldiers in the now transatlantic march of Christian civilization. They signed on in great numbers, filling most of the leadership roles in Narváez's and other expeditions. Typical of this group was a young man named Andrés Dorantes, who signed on with Narváez sometime that winter. He was originally from Béjar, on the border of Extremadura and Castilla y León, where his father was prominent enough to get him a recommendation from the local duke. As frequently happened, he didn't propose to go off to the New World alone; two of his cousins, Diego Dorantes and Pedro de Valdivieso, decided that this was their great moment of epic opportunity too.

The prevalence of minor "gentlemen" like the Dorantes cousins in the usual accounts of the Spanish conquistadors often masks the far more diverse nature of the companies of Narváez and his contemporaries. For instance, in addition to his poorer cousins, Andrés Dorantes also brought with him at least one slave, who was to play a major role in the adventure to come. His name was Esteban, and he was a "black Moor" from the Atlantic coast of Morocco. How he came to be in Dorantes's possession is unknown, but slaves were captured by the Spanish and Portuguese in many small, privately financed battles for control or loot along the Moroccan coast during the first decades of the 1500s. In particular there had been a battle in Esteban's hometown of Azemmour in 1513, during which an ambitious young officer named Ferdinand Magellan was wounded.

Likewise, Esteban's religious status at the time he left for America is debatable. The fact that he spoke Arabic and was from Morocco certainly implies (to modern ears especially) that he was a Muslim by birth. His Christian name, Esteban or Steven, however, suggests he had been converted either by choice or by force, and one of the surviving accounts of the expedition explicitly describes him as a Christian. There were plenty of reasons, however, why Dorantes would want his slave to be described as a Christian. In 1502 all Muslims who refused to renounce their religion were told to leave Castile, and most had converted to Christianity at that time, becoming known thereafter as Moriscos. Furthermore, all African slaves sent to the New World were required to be Christian and if they were not born in Spain required a special permit as well. Whatever his original faith, therefore, Esteban was definitely not attending a mosque at the time his master signed him on to go to America. Nor was it likely that he bathed regularly, which Christian Spaniards of the time were certain was a suspicious, vaguely sexual habit of reprobate infidels.

There were other indentured Africans on the expedition, though their names have been forgotten. Some may not have been traveling with their masters; slaves were sometimes sent on consignment to the New World by absentee owners. The evidence from other expeditions suggests there may also have been free Africans in the company. A free man of African origin traveled with Columbus in 1492, possibly as the pilot of the *Niña*, and at least one free black was likely among the company on the admiral's second voyage as well. Closer to Narváez's own time, a man named Juan Garrido accompanied Cortés to Mexico. Garrido had also gone with Ponce de León to Puerto Rico in 1508 and possibly to Florida in 1513 as well. There were two free Africans on that voyage of Ponce de León's, as well as at least one light-skinned slave who was probably from Greece or Russia.

Far more common than either free blacks or enslaved whites on expeditions like Narváez's were formerly Jewish Spaniards who decided to put the ocean between themselves and the notorious Inquisition. Even before Judaism was banned outright in Spain in 1492, the Holy

Office was ferreting out converted Jews, or conversos, who showed the least signs of backsliding. In the severest cases, those who refused to confess were burnt at the stake. Those who confessed were hung first to spare them the pain of the fire, after which their corpses were burned. Victims who escaped by fleeing were burnt in effigy for the entertainment of the crowd. It was officially illegal for New Christians to go to the Indies, but conversos were well represented on every major voyage to the New World. By one estimate, conversos made up five to eight percent of those who went to Mexico with Cortés and Narváez. Not all of them were foot soldiers either: Judge Ayllón, already mentioned, was a converso.

Identifying converted Jews is as unscientific now as it ever was. One member of Narváez's new expedition who superficially has some of the characteristics often associated with conversos of the period was Captain Alonso del Castillo. Many Spanish Jews changed their surnames when they converted, commonly selecting a geographical description as a new identity. Though the surname del Castillo translates literally to "of the castle," it's obviously quite close to "del Castilla" or "of Castile,"* and there were moriscos and conversos of both those surnames who were persecuted by the Inquisition. Of more specific relevance is that Castillo's father was a doctor from the university town of Salamanca. Certain professions were closely associated with Jews and conversos: finance, trade, academia, law, and especially medicine. In several cases the Inquisition itself wound up in the embarrassing position of having to hire converso doctors to care for the victims in its prisons because there were no "old Christians" with the right training to be found. Two of Castillo's uncles were judges, another profession associated with conversos.

---

* Castile got its name from the many castles dotting its landscape.

None of these circumstantial associations proves anything, of course, and a perfectly strong case can be made that Castillo was an "old Christian," with "pure blood."* But he's an interesting member of the expedition for plenty of other reasons, not the least of which being he was one of the very few who survived. Suffice it to say that Narváez didn't question closely the religious background of anyone willing to invest heavily in the expedition, and Castillo mortgaged part of his estate to pay for supplies.

In meeting after meeting, Narváez and his agents asked everyone the same questions. What do you have? What can you bring? What can you invest? The returns would be a hundredfold or more, they promised. "And thus the poor volunteer gives the little money that remains to him," wrote Oviedo, who knew the process well. "And if this snare is well handled he will sell his cape and his coat, and go in his shirt, because he thinks that when he comes to the tropics he will arrive well dressed, and may await, as a favor, for what has been promised him."

Not everyone who signed up was a caballero or hidalgo with enough money to own a horse. As always, the majority of the Spaniards would be men who fought on foot with swords, pikes, crossbows, or the primitive muskets known as harquebuses. There might be a few who operated heavier artillery as well.

Nor were they all from Spain. Beginning in 1526, the old regulation prohibiting non-Castilians from crossing to the Indies was changed to allow anyone from Charles's Hapsburg domains in Europe to go. It was a regulation that had been routinely ignored anyway, and Narváez signed up at least one Greek and probably several other

---

* The fact that Castillo was a member in good standing of the caballero class does not preclude the possibility of a converso background: according to the 1553 *Summa nobilitatis*, "the standard treatise on nobility" in Spain, converted Jews and Muslims could "without discrimination be admitted on equal terms to the rank and immunities of nobility."

non-Spaniards as well. There was even a Mexican prince who came along with the contingent of six priests. His name was Tlaxclachelton, which the Spanish shortened to Don Pedro.

The only members of the expedition that Narváez could not squeeze for investments were his fellow royal appointees. The most important of these was the treasurer, Álvar Núñez Cabeza de Vaca. He was to be the king's eyes and ears on the ground during the expedition, ensuring that Charles V got his five percent of any gold and precious stones that Narváez came across. And that he got his salt tax, his import duty, and whatever else Cabeza de Vaca could think of that might conceivably go to the king: "other dues belonging to us on all and every kind of exchange that has been or shall hereafter be made in that land, as well slaves and guanines, as pearls, precious stones and the other articles whatsoever they may be, upon which should be duty of any sort." The treasurer had a few nonmonetary duties, including seeing to it that the natives were well treated. But mostly, he was the taxman. Once the gold and silver started flowing out of the mines of La Florida, "the reporting . . . must come very long and in great detail," said the king.

Cabeza de Vaca, who lived to write the most detailed account of the expedition, got his job the same way Narváez had, which is to say he followed the court around and called in favors. He, too, had many contacts. His paternal grandfather, Pedro de Vera, was a hero of the wars of conquest in the Canary Islands and against the Moors in Granada. He took his surname, however, from his mother's family, which was not an unusual thing to do in Spain at that time. Despite the humorous literal meaning of their name—"cow's head"*—for at least

---

* The apocryphal story is that in 1212, an ancestor had been given the name after marking a secret pass through the mountains with a cow's skull, allowing Christian forces to surprise and overwhelm the Moors in the battle of Las Navas de Tolosa.

three hundred years the Cabeza de Vacas were a leading family in the treasurer's hometown of Jerez de la Frontera, near the Andalusian coast south of Seville. The extended family included various dukes, marquises, and other *ricoshombres,* or "rich men," of the realm. A relative had been one of Charles V's tutors, and one of the original members of the Council of the Indies, which certainly helped Cabeza de Vaca's case.

An even better connection was his previous employer. Starting when he was a teenager, Cabeza de Vaca had served off and on in the service of the great ducal house of Medina Sidonia, working his way up from some sort of page boy to a position of extreme confidence within the family. His trustworthiness became clear in the delicate matter of the mentally challenged fifth duke, whose wife wanted an annulment in order to marry her husband's younger brother, who had taken over as the sixth duke. Mental incompetence wasn't sufficient grounds for an annulment but sexual incompetence was, and Cabeza de Vaca escorted three beautiful women to the deposed man's bedroom with instructions to prove once and for all that the fifth duke couldn't fulfill his marital duties. Whether the women were brought singly or together is not known, but the annulment was approved.

The duke of Medina Sidonia ranked only behind the lord high constable and the admiral of Castile in the rigid etiquette of the court: he could even wear his hat in the presence of the king. In terms of real influence, he could open any door he chose for his trusty steward, after which in the usual fashion Cabeza de Vaca recited all the services he had performed for the king over the years. He had fought and been wounded in various military campaigns against the French and others in Italy, including the 1512 battle of Ravenna, in which 20,000 soldiers from all over Europe were slaughtered by their fellow Christians. More recently, he had assisted in the violent suppression of the "revolt of the *comuneros,*" a rebellion by some of the nobility against the growing power and foreign connections of the king.

What Narváez thought of Cabeza de Vaca's appointment as treasurer in February of 1527 is hard to say, though later relations between the two suggest he was unimpressed. At about forty years of age, Cabeza de Vaca was a decade younger than Narváez and had never been to the New World. He had seen some war, which was good as far as it went. But to an old Indies hand like Narváez, he was just a fussy courtier obsessed with honor and rules, neither of which went very far in the jungles of the New World. But on paper, Cabeza de Vaca was to be the second most powerful person on the expedition, and there was nothing Narváez could do about it. He was a necessary annoyance; not to be disrespected but not to be altogether trusted either.

Nor could Narváez say much about the selection of the royal inspector of mines, Alonso de Solís, the comptroller, Alonso Enríquez, or the religious contingent led by Father Juan Suárez. He was at least happy that the priests were Franciscans rather than Dominicans. In the interests of peace on earth, the two orders were generally kept separated in the New World, and the Dominicans had a reputation for worrying out loud about the treatment of the Indians. Narváez's own former chaplain during the conquest of Cuba, the Dominican Bartolomé de Las Casas, had become the loudest voice of all, in part because of what he had witnessed during that campaign. The Franciscans, Narváez thought, showed more humility.

By late spring of 1527 nearly six hundred people had signed up to accompany Narváez to La Florida. Some four hundred and fifty of these were troops, officers and slaves. Another hundred were the sailors and officers of the five ships he had purchased. There were a dozen or more wives of recruits: married men were not permitted to travel to the

Indies without their spouses unless they secured special permission from the Council of the Indies. A few single women may have been in the group, as well, though only if they were daughters or servants of married couples who were going. All had theoretically proven they were not heretics and had secured their passports from the Council of the Indies. And all were told by Narváez or his agents to be in the port of Sanlúcar de Barrameda at the mouth of the Guadalquivir River, prepared to board ship and sail, by the middle of June.

3

Across the Ocean Sea

On June 17, 1527, Narváez stood on the quarterdeck of a flagship with a fleet of vessels and an army of conquest under his command. For weeks he and his deputies had been checking lists, counting barrels, collecting money promised to them in order to pay it to others to whom it was promised. Finally, though, the day had arrived and heralds were in the streets rounding up the stragglers.

It had been a long time coming, and not all of it fun, but from the perspective of the quarterdeck it was worth the wait. His ships were a little older than he might have wanted, the men a little greener. He was a little deeper in debt than he liked, but he was almost on his way, bound again for the Indies, where he had first gone some thirty years before in the heady initial decade of the New World. And this time, he had a contract of his own from the imperial majesty to conquer and settle a great stretch of the unknown northern continent. Tall, strong, red-haired, and one-eyed, he surveyed his fleet and the crowds gathered on the dock to wish it off. Narváez was in a fine mood.

All ships bound to and from the Indies were technically required to depart and arrive through the port of Seville. But that meant a twenty-league voyage up the winding and silty Guadalquivir River, so in practice many fleets, including Narváez's, made their final preparations and departure from the port of Sanlúcar de Barrameda at the river's mouth. It was a busy place, choked with ships and boats of all sizes. Voyages to and from the Americas were no longer the novelties they had been when Narváez was a youth; there are official records of nearly three thousand ships of various tonnage sailing from Seville or other authorized ports to the Americas between 1504 and 1555, and no doubt many others left no record. Added to these boxy square-riggers were smaller lateen-rigged vessels coming and going to Seville from elsewhere in Europe with trade goods to supply the American voyages. Cloth from Flanders, beads from Italy, and increasingly, slaves from Portugal's colonies in Africa were constantly being loaded and off-loaded. Along the waterfront were the usual industries that serviced vessels and mariners in the age of sail—shipwrights, sail lofts, chandlers, and warehouses. It all made for a harbor full of masts, streets full of sailors and out-of-work adventurers, and the usual associated ribaldry.

Nevertheless, in a time when most news traveled by mule, the departure of a large new expedition of conquest remained an occasion of some note. And it wasn't only Narváez's fleet setting off from Sanlúcar on that day. Francisco de Montejo had four ships and 258 men heading out to "pacify" the Yucatan Peninsula and the island of Cozumel. There were probably a few other ships making ready as well. The Spanish practice of crossing the Atlantic in great convoys was not formalized until twenty years later, when the trickle of gold and silver from the Americas had grown to a river. But already the fear of piracy, and of the crossing in general, resulted in ships banding together. The threat was greater on the return voyage, when the holds would hopefully be filled with gold, but the previous year had seen the Caribbean full of French and English corsairs nipping like beach flies at any exposed morsel of the Spanish Empire. Any merchantmen headed west welcomed the chance to sail with Narváez and Montejo's armed fleets.

On the docks in the hours before departure, the six hundred people who were to sail with Narváez made their farewells, some of them tearful. Everyone both on board and on shore knew that for every Cortés or Narváez who came back from the Indies a rich and powerful man, there were many more who never returned. Most remembered the return to Seville only five years before of eighteen ragged survivors out of the 276 who had sailed off with Magellan.

Some who came down to the ships carried letters, hoping to get them delivered to friends and relatives in the New World. "Many letters come from ignorant mothers and wives," said the conquistador-turned-historian Oviedo. He was sympathetic to the impulse though not optimistic about the chance of delivery. They "seek to write to their sons and husbands, and to other relatives, addressed only 'To my beloved son, Pedro Rodriguez, in the Indies, which amounts to saying, 'To my son, Mahomet, in Africa,' or 'To Juan Martínez, in Europe.'"

But departures of fleets for the Indies were not sorrowful occasions. More often there was a celebratory feel to the goings on, usually accompanied by a band of hired musicians on the dock. After all, these were not official soldiers being sent by their government to defend entrenched or crumbling colonial or economic interests far from home. They were young entrepreneurs, certain of the superiority of both their culture and their weapons. Even the prophet Isaiah had predicted that

Caravels making ready to cross the Atlantic, from De Bry's Americae, *part XIV, 1594.*

this conquest would be undertaken by Tarshish, which everyone knew
was Spain:

> *Why, the coasts and islands put their hopes in Me*
> *And the vessels of Tarshish take the lead*

In bringing your children from far away
And their silver and gold with them
For the sake of the name of Yahweh your God.

Their country had been ascendant for only a generation, but Spain was approaching its grandest century and the young on board Narváez's ships could feel it in their bones. Not only had their God driven the Moor from Spain, he had opened an almost unimaginably vast New World to them. Every returning convoy brought more news and treasure from the new lands, along with rumors of even greater things to come. It was a decade that the historian J. H. Elliot described as "the first intoxicating years of Charles' imperialism."

"To be young in the Hispanic Peninsula during this period of human experience was to have faith in the impossible," is how another influential historian, Irving Leonard, described the first third of the 1500s. "An enormously enlarged world teemed with possibilities of adventure and romance in which one's wildest dreams and fondest hopes of fame and fortune could be fulfilled. Life had a zest."

On Narváez's ships, hundreds of these zestful souls were now staking out their few square feet on deck, or in the dark and stuffy spaces below. Never mind that one of the few women on board was telling people she had a bad feeling about the future, that a Moorish clairvoyant in the town of Hornachos had warned her of impending doom. And never mind either that the vessels were crowded and not exactly new: "old and worn out ships which have arrived there through the mercy of God and by force of double pumping" is how Oviedo described them. The expeditionaries had made up their minds and made their peace, and they were ready to go across the ocean and get rich. They were ecstatic to be almost underway.

When at last the moment arrived and the order was given to raise anchors and unmoor from docks, sailors in canvas pants hauled away at ropes, calling out in unison. Sails rose, timbers creaked, and slowly at first the vessels moved off and away. Once clear of the dangerous bar at the mouth of the harbor, more sails were raised, and as they filled with wind, the ships picked up speed until one by one they disappeared from the view of the stragglers going home from the docks. The pilots set a course to the southwest, bound for the Canary Islands. This was the route pioneered by Columbus on his first voyage, and it was never really improved upon as a method of sailing square-riggers from Spain to the New World.

The 850-mile passage to the islands rarely took much longer than a week, but the shortness of the crossing belied its potential for unpleasantness. The conquistadors nicknamed it the "Sea of Mares" because so many of their mounts died crossing it. Fortunately for the few horses suspended in great slings in the holds of Narváez's ships—he planned to purchase more in Hispaniola and Cuba—this time the Sea of Mares behaved, and near the end of June the boy in the masthead sung out that he could see the great volcanic cone of Tenerife rising on the horizon.

No one was more interested in the view as the ships made their way to the port of Las Palmas than the treasurer, Cabeza de Vaca. From antiquity until 1492 the Canary Islands had been considered by Europeans to be the western limit of the world, vaguely associated with the mythical "fortunate islands" or Elysian Fields of the classical Greeks. They had been periodically "discovered" and then forgotten by various Arabic-speaking explorers during the Middle Ages, and then again by Genoese pilots in the employ of Portugal. In 1404, a Norman adventurer named Jean de Béthencourt set himself up as king of the islands and paid homage to the court of Castile in exchange for recognition as such. But the final subjugation of the local Guanche peoples didn't begin in earnest until 1480 when Cabeza de Vaca's paternal grandfather, Pedro de Vera, arrived on a mission to pacify Grand Canary.

De Vera was already a violent man before he left Spain, having once removed his glove to yank out the tongue of a man he had just killed for insulting the king, and in the Canaries he carried out a massacre of almost biblical proportions. It was done to impress an extravagantly beautiful and cruel woman named Beatriz Bobadilla, who is most often remembered by history for having romanced Columbus during his various stays there. She had come to the islands in a rather singular way after losing her job as King Ferdinand's favorite among Queen Isabella's honor maids. The ever-practical Isabella, when she noticed the king's misplaced attentions, offered Bobadilla to an army captain who had been accused of murder. If he would take the lovely maid back to the Canary island of Gomera and keep her there, said the Queen, he could have the girl for his wife and the island for his fief. The little matter of the murder, meanwhile, would be conveniently forgotten.

The plan worked well until even Beatriz's attractions failed to satisfy the captain's manly urges and he raped a young native girl, setting off a rebellion in which he was killed. This was when Cabeza de Vaca's grandfather hurried over from a neighboring island and, by various gruesome means, executed all Guanche males over the age of fifteen. Most of the remaining native population he exported to the slave markets of North Africa and Andalusia.*

Cabeza de Vaca was only about ten when de Vera died, but he grew up in a household full of slaves from the islands, and he almost

---

* The local bishop was outraged, and in the ensuing scandal, de Vera was forced to refund those in Castile who bought female Canary Islanders, who were to be set free. He was recalled to Spain and sent to fight the Moors, against whom blood thirst was always considered less morally ambiguous as they had had centuries of opportunity to recognize the true faith and change their evil ways.

certainly regaled his fellow passengers with stories of the conquest as Narváez's ships approached the islands. "The son of Francisco de Vera and the grandson of Pedro de Vera who won the Canary Islands" is how he sometimes proudly described himself. Even the over-leveraged Narváez may have been amused to hear from his treasurer how old Pedro de Vera had once pawned two of his own sons, Cabeza de Vaca's father and uncle, into slavery under the commander of Muslim forces in Malaga as a bond for funds for the Canary project.

Since Pedro de Vera's time, the town of Las Palmas had grown with the transatlantic trade into a substantial supply port, and while Cabeza de Vaca wandered around sightseeing, the sailors, slaves, and those of lesser rank in the expedition were put to work preparing for the long crossing ahead. Water and wine supplies were topped off, as was firewood. Fresh meat, some of it still on the hoof, salt cod, and bacon were brought aboard. Bananas and other available fruit were purchased. Gomera cheese kept particularly well and was loaded aboard almost all ships bound across the Atlantic.

The islands were also the last chance to make any significant repairs or alterations to the ships themselves. Columbus replaced the rudder of the Pinta there and converted the *Niña* from a lateen rig to a square rig, which was better for catching the steady westward trades. Magellan took on a load of caulking pitch when he stopped by in 1519. Given Oviedo's dour assessment of Narváez's fleet, it's likely his carpenters also found enough work to fill their time until once again the order was given to raise anchors and sails. The last view of the Old World was the great cone of Tenerife sinking below the horizon as the fleet made its way southwest for a few more days in order to get more fully into the trade winds, after which the pilots pointed the prows due west for the New World.

For many on board, the following weeks out of sight of land were excruciating, particularly when they stretched inexorably into a month and then, in the case of Narváez's fleet, even a little more. Ships of the period were generally under a hundred feet in length and chronically overloaded.

"A ship is a very narrow and stout prison from which no one can flee," remembered Father de la Torre, a missionary who sailed on a similar voyage a decade and a half later. "Closely compressed into its narrow confines, heat and suffocation are unbearable. The deck floor is usually one's bed and, though some brought good mats, ours were small, hard and poor, thinly stuffed with dog hair; our bed covering was extremely wretched blankets of goatskin. . . . On top of this, when one feels well enough, there's no place where one can study or withdraw to himself a little on shipboard; one remains eternally seated for there is no place to walk."

What bothered Father de la Torre the most were the various vermin—rats, roaches, and the like—and the smells that even the warm trade winds couldn't fully dispel. "An infinite number of lice eat one alive, and clothing cannot be washed because seawater shrinks it. And bad odors pervade everywhere, especially below deck, and the whole ship becomes intolerable when the ship pump is working, which varies according to whether the ship is sailing well or not. It goes at least four or five times a day in order to pump out of the hold the water that has leaked in, and this smells very foul indeed."

There wasn't much to break the monotony. Prayers were sung every morning and again at vespers, usually by the ship's boy. The boy also turned the half-hour glass, by which the pilots attempted log progress, and announced the changing of the watch every four hours. On sunny middays there was an attempt to get the correct local time by placing a pin in the center of the compass and watching for its shadow to point north. Though most of this went unseen by the passengers, rumors filtered across the decks as to their possible location on the Ocean Sea, as the Spaniards called the Atlantic, and their progress across it. There was gossip about whether the clouds portended storms, whether other vessels spotted were hostile, and whether the supplies would run out. The sailors got their daily quart of wine and the passengers got whatever they had been able to bring for themselves.

Even food was hardly something to look forward to as the ships crawled across the hot middle of the Atlantic. "No one has any desire to eat and can hardly face anything sweet," remembered de la Torre. "The thirst one endures is unbelievable and is increased by the hardtack and salt beef constituting our fare."

Another passenger of the period, Alonzo Enríquez de Guzmán, remembered one better day at sea: "There are fish that they call flying fish, which fly for twenty paces, more or less, and sometimes fall on board the ship. I saw and ate some, which had a smoky taste." But flying fish were not something you could count on, and Guzmán's overall memory was of "eight hundred leagues over the sea, suffering hunger and thirst, and seeing no land."

Some played card games to while away the endless hours. Though often prohibited, cards were so popular among Spaniards that by the 1550s the crown tried to make a little money with a royal monopoly on their production. Occasionally the passengers on transatlantic voyages also staged informal cockfights between the residents of the larder. On Father Torre's ship the cockfights lasted until the last bird—or, more accurately, the next to the last bird—had become someone's dinner. Singing was a sailor's art. But mostly, there was the newest craze, pulp fiction.

Spaniards of the age of conquest were infatuated with romantic novels full of chivalrous knights, snorting dragons, distressed damsels, and hordes of golden treasure. The first printing press in the country began operation in 1473, and the first romances appeared in the 1490s. But the first blockbuster was the 1508 book *Amadis of Gaul*, an involved tale about a knight who falls in love with a twelve-year-old girl, then has to slay monsters and visit enchanted islands to win her. In a formula that proved durable, he got the girl in the end.

As befitting the first bestseller, *Amadis* was followed shortly by the first hastily written sequels and the first flood of shameless knockoffs. Fifty fat page-turners appeared in its wake, and any moderately successful book was reprinted almost indefinitely throughout the century. The genre only went out of favor after the 1605 publication of Cervantes's crushing satire, in which the book-mad "and valorous Don Quixote had . . . the terrifying and never before imagined adventure of the windmills." But in the 1520s, when Narváez's army sailed, romantic fiction was a full-blown literary craze. The emperor himself was a fan, as was Columbus's son Ferdinand. The founder of the Jesuit order, Ignatius Loyola, didn't ask for a Bible to get him through his life-altering war wounds, but for "vayne treatises," and Saint Theresa of Avila conspired with her mother to keep their shared addiction to reading secret from her father.

Not surprisingly, disapproving fathers, priests, politicians, and other morally confident types railed and legislated against the perceived effects on the manners, attitudes, and even the slang of youth. The new books and music had too much violence, said one critic: "One hero kills twenty men, another thirty and another, riddled with six hundred wounds and left for dead, promptly recovers." And too much sex, said another, the mere thought of which might have the truly horrifying effect of arousing young women: "Young men are just the same . . . for with their natural desires inflamed by evil reading, their one thought now is to dishonor young women and to shame matrons. All of which is the result of reading these books, and would to God that, for the good of their souls, those who have it in their power would prohibit them!"

The tirades were to little avail. Those who saw themselves as intellectuals preferred to discuss the new works of Erasmus, which were also popular, but everyone else talked about fictional places with names like California, Patagonia, the Antilles, or the land of the Amazon. In the minds of would-be conquerors like those on Narváez's ships, these were places that might well turn out to exist after all. The Amazons were repeatedly discovered, or at least heard tell of in the Americas. And, of course, lest anyone doubt, there was Montezuma's fabulous and altogether real city of Tenochtitlan. "We were amazed and said that it was like the enchantments they tell of in the legend of Amadis," is how Bernal Díaz remembered his first impression of Mexico City. If Cortés had found one enchanted city, the readers on board told themselves as the weeks passed at sea, there surely must be another for them to find.

The first sign that land was near was usually a sighting of birds, but the spontaneous cheer didn't go up until the call came from the crow's nest that terra firma was, in fact, on the horizon. Unless they had drifted far off the usual course, it was Guadeloupe or the small island of Désirade, off its eastern coast. Passing into the Caribbean, the fleet made its way along the inside of the leeward islands. They passed Puerto Rico and finally, sometime in the middle of September, reached Hispaniola and the port of Santo Domingo in what is now the Dominican Republic.

For Cabeza de Vaca, Andrés Dorantes, Esteban the Black, and the many others for whom it was the first trip to the Indies, it was a thrilling moment. They had crossed the Ocean Sea and were at last in the New World, where they would have grand adventures conquering cities and making great fortunes.

To the handful of others in the fleet who were veterans of earlier conquests—Castillo, Father Suárez, Don Pedro the Mexican prince— the arrival in port was somewhat less exciting. But it was always good to have the crossing behind one, and there was the possibility in Santo Domingo of seeing old friends or hearing news of old comrades and new conquests. "What news? What news is there in the land?" one passenger to Hispaniola a quarter century before recalled the sailors shouting out as they arrived in Santo Domingo. The answer at that time was "Good news, good news! There is much gold! A nugget was found weighing many pounds—and there is a war with the Indians, so there will be plenty of slaves."

By the summer of 1527, however, the gold rush in Hispaniola was long over. There were a few signs of an emerging new economy to come along Santo Domingo's muddy streets and in the hinterland: sugar mills manned mostly by African slaves and often owned by Italian and German bankers were opening, and that very year the crown had issued a royal license to "a house for public women . . . in a suitable place, because there is a need for it in order to avoid (worse) harm." Still, there was no mistaking that Santo Domingo was a former boomtown whose time at the center of the New World was past. Smallpox had wiped out much of the native population in 1519, and conquests elsewhere had drawn away the most ambitious Spaniards, who usually took their slaves with them.

For Narváez, standing once more on the quarterdeck, none of this mattered. The city had come down in the world economically, but it was still the official capital of the Indies, and his arrival there at the head of a new fleet of conquest was a vindication of the first order. Santo Domingo was where he and virtually all the other conquistadors of his generation had started their careers some thirty years earlier. It was the seat of a royal panel of judges that had been a major thorn in his side during the Mexican fiasco. Now here he was with papers from the king making him the future governor of a stretch of territory far bigger than Hispaniola and Cuba combined! What he couldn't see from the deck of his ship, however, was that the slow unraveling of all of his plans and dreams was about to begin.

⚮

Santo Domingo was crawling with hustlers looking to sign up adventurers with lies about the pearls in Venezuela or the gold in Amazonia, and within days of their arrival in town, Narváez began losing his hard-won recruits. The first desertions didn't much bother him: his previous record as a commander suggests he was only vaguely aware of what was going on outside his inner circle, and a handful of bad apples was to be expected out of a barrel of six hundred. But after a week or two it became clear it wasn't just the bad apples he was losing: he was hemorrhaging men.

Part of the problem was that it was much harder for Narváez to keep telling his own lies about the riches that lay waiting for his men in La Florida when there were grizzled sailors and burnt-out Indies hands hanging around the docks and public houses saying they had actually been to those coasts in search of slaves and had seen nothing that would make them go back. The recruiters for other bosses reminded Narváez's greenhorns that Ponce de León came back from La Florida with nothing to show for his efforts but a fatal arrow wound. Better to go where there actually is gold, like Mexico. Or to stay here, marry a sweet widow, and make sweet sugar.

Nor did it help Narváez that the news all over the Indies was that Ayllón's recent expedition to North America had ended in an even greater disaster than Ponce de León's. Trouble had started before they landed, when their flagship ran aground off the coast of South Carolina and most of their supplies were lost. Then, instead of the promised New Andalusia of olive groves, vineyards, and giant blondes, the remaining colonists found themselves surrounded by miles of deserted pine barrens. Autumn brought starvation, then sickness, and finally death. Ayllón himself succumbed on October 18, 1526, and after an ugly succession squabble, the survivors tried to sail back to Hispaniola, towing his corpse in a small boat behind one of the ships. There was nothing to eat on board, nothing to drink, and it was bitterly cold; a man took off his frozen pants and looked down to see that much of the frostbitten flesh from his legs had come off with the clothing. By the time the ships limped separately into various Caribbean ports, only a hundred and fifty out of six hundred were still alive.

Even Narváez's own enthusiasm must have been tested by the sight of Ayllón's widow, Ana Bezerra, with her five young children, in the process of selling her fine home on Hispaniola to ward off her dead husband's creditors. By the time a month had passed in Santo Domingo and nearly a hundred of his men had gone missing, he was desperate to get away from the temptations of the place. But there was still much to do on the island, so he rushed from vendor to vendor with his royal letter announcing that he was "acting under the king's banner" and requesting their cooperation.

He was shopping for another ship or two, looking for a small brigantine, or a pinnace that could be used for exploring coasts and rivers. He also bought cassava bread, baked to a level of dryness that allowed it to keep for many months. Pigs had arrived in the New World with Columbus, and by 1508 Hispaniola was overrun with feral swine, making for cheap salt pork that Narváez bought by the barrel. He had brought live pigs from Jamaica to Cuba during the conquest of that island in 1512, but there's no mention of livestock this time. His plan was for his army to live mostly off the land. Or, more accurately, off the Indians who lived off the land. The niceties of colonization—domesticated animals and European women—could come later.

Narváez did want horses, however. The horse originally evolved on the great plains of prehistoric North America and crossed to Asia on the thousand-mile-wide "land bridge" that appeared in the Bering Strait during periodic ice ages. For reasons that are unclear, not long (geologically) after humans made the reverse journey from Asia to North America, horses disappeared from the Western Hemisphere and were therefore unknown to Native Americans until the arrival of the Spanish. They are often cited as one of the Europeans' primary military advantages, but due to their extreme cost, they didn't play a conspicuous part in the early conquests of the Caribbean Islands. That changed, at least in the perception of conquistadors and historians, with Cortés's invasion of Mexico. He had only sixteen animals, but he said of them in his well-publicized second letter to the emperor that "our whole safety lay (after God) in the horses."

Narváez was painfully familiar with that letter, and he bought as many horses as he could afford on Hispaniola, which was not nearly as many animals as he wanted. The supply was growing in the Caribbean as local gold rushes dwindled and colonists turned to sugar and ranching. But demand from places like Mexico and Panama had more than kept pace and prices had not dropped that much from what they had been seven years before when Bernal Díaz reported that "horses and Negroes were worth their weight in gold, and that is the reason why more horses were not taken, for there were none to be bought."*

When, at last, Narváez had accomplished all he could in Hispaniola, he decided to move his base of operations to Cuba. This was an

---

* The situation was the same on the other side of the Atlantic; in African slave markets at that time, a single Arabian horse bought anywhere from six to twenty human beings.

easy decision: not only was Cuba where his wife and children were living, he knew he could collect more horses and supplies from his many
friends and neighbors. Though he wasn't supposed to raid the existing
manpower of the islands, he also planned to pick up some recruits to
replace the deserters. Best of all, given the relative isolation of the
island, the rate of desertions should decrease. The fleet, enlarged by
the one ship Narváez had managed to purchase, arrived in the port of
Santiago de Cuba toward the end of September.

Santiago had been founded only fifteen years before and was in
the process of transforming itself from a military outpost into a colonial
town. There were a few stone buildings under construction, but for the
most part the houses were built of wood and thatch and the streets were
full of a ripe mixture of human and animal waste. For the less experienced members of the expedition, who had thought Santo Domingo a
rustic place, the scruffy capital of Cuba was a noticeable step closer to
the frontier. For Narváez, though, it was good to be home where, as he
expected, many of his old associates were happy to invest in the new
adventure. His mentor, the governor, was dead, but the Velázquez family was still the wealthiest in Cuba, and at least one young Velázquez
signed on to go to La Florida and others almost certainly contributed
money and horses.

Narváez was also particularly pleased to find Vasco Porcallo in
town. Porcallo is one of the men whose reputation for brutality gave
rise to what became known as the "Black Legend" of Spanish atrocities
in the Americas. He is said to have stymied a planned mass suicide by a
group of "his" Indians by threatening to follow the desperate victims
into the afterlife and carry on tormenting them there. More verifiably,
he was investigated in 1522 for castrating slaves and forcing them to
eat their own genitals. Another victim was compelled to castrate himself. Porcallo's defense was not that the incidents didn't happen, but

that they were the only way to prevent his chattel from eating dirt, a common method of slave suicide. The outcome of the investigation is unclear, but it didn't affect Porcallo's wealth or reputation. He was, said Cabeza de Vaca, "a prominent gentleman," an assessment echoed a dozen years later by the De Soto chroniclers, one of whom called him "a very rich and splendid cavalier."

Nor did the unpleasant affair have any effect on his friendship with Narváez, who had himself been accused of excessive violence during the conquest of Cuba. Porcallo was a comrade from those days, and over a glass or two of wine in Santiago, the old warriors reminisced about past opportunities and strategized about Narváez's new one. There were still hundreds of decisions to be made. Should Narváez send a ship up to North America to try to kidnap a few natives who could act as translators, as Ponce de León and Ayllón had done? He decided against it. Should he send his horses overland to Havana on the island's northwest coast, thus sparing them the potentially deadly thousand-mile voyage around the island as Cortés had done? He decided against that as well. And who should he take with him from Cuba?

Porcallo briefly considered joining the expedition himself; a decade later he got swept up in the glamour of De Soto and went briefly to Florida with a great retinue of slaves and servants only to return home at the first sign of trouble. Perhaps because he had seen Narváez in action in Mexico, he decided to stay home. He did offer his old friend some horses and other supplies from his estates in Trinidad, a port town 150 miles to the west along Cuba's southern coast that he and Narváez had founded together in 1514. After a stay in Santiago of less than a week, therefore, the fleet set off for Trinidad, taking Porcallo with them.

Halfway there Narváez divided the fleet, telling Cabeza de Vaca and an officer named Pantoja to take Porcallo and two of the ships on to Trinidad to collect the promised supplies. He and the other four ships would wait for them in the nearby Gulf of Guacanayabo, a region he had conquered many years before. The reasons for the decision are murky, though he probably had leads on additional horses and supplies available in the area.

The weather was also showing signs of deteriorating. The Spanish had been in the Caribbean long enough to know that late summer and fall was the season of the great storms the Taino Indians of Hispaniola called "hurricanes." As early as 1502 Columbus, on his third voyage, predicted the hurricane that destroyed the fleet of his persecutor Ovando and wrecked Santo Domingo, resulting in a famine that killed about a thousand colonists. And just the year before Narváez's expedition, in October of 1526, a hurricane leveled several sugar mills on Hispaniola. Perhaps his sailors now sensed a change in the air, or saw a great stripe of cloud across the sky, one of the tentacles of an approaching hurricane. Trinidad was a lousy port to be in during a major storm, especially one that came out of the south, but a good sailor could always hope to find a lee shore somewhere in the great curving Gulf of Guacanayabo. Why send all your ships to Trinidad, they asked, if you only need to send one or two? And Narváez agreed.

Cabeza de Vaca outranked Porcallo, but Narváez sent him along as something of a backup. "He ordered a captain [named] Pantoja to go to Trinidad with his ship, and for greater security, he ordered me to go with him," said Cabeza de Vaca later. Pantoja was one of Narváez's closest confidants, and as a fellow old Cuba hand, was an appropriate agent to close the deal on Porcallo's horses and other items. When the two ships reached the port, therefore, Cabeza de Vaca remained on board and Pantoja climbed into the small ship's boat to head ashore with Porcallo and about fifteen others. It was the ninth of November, or thereabouts, 1527, and the weather was definitely worsening.

As the shore party pulled away from the ships, the two pilots yelled to Pantoja not to dawdle. The sooner he was back, the sooner the ships could sail away to deeper water or a safer harbor. Nodding, he told the men to pull hard on the oars, and the worried sailors watched the small boat make its way to the beach. Night fell, but the wind did not.

Rain began in the early hours of the following day, and by midmorning, a strong north wind had kicked the sea up into a froth. It wasn't so rough yet that small boats couldn't navigate the harbor, however, and one of the sailors on deck called out that a canoe was approaching. One of its passengers had a letter for Cabeza de Vaca, "beseeching me to go there, and offering to give me such supplies as they had and were needful for us." Why the letter writer couldn't do his business with Pantoja, who was already in town, was unclear, and Cabeza de Vaca refused to go, saying piously that it was his duty to stay with the ships.

The wind was thankfully still from the north, meaning they were somewhat in the lee in the south-facing harbor, but the sailors didn't like the look of things. The rain wasn't so much falling now as spraying horizontally into eyes and faces. As the storm strengthened they talked of taking the vessels out of Trinidad to run before the storm. "They greatly feared that the ships would be lost if they stayed there for long," said Cabeza de Vaca. But there was no sign of Pantoja.

Around noon, the canoe again appeared and despite the rising seas made its way laboriously out to the ships. The message was the same, though this time the bearer told Cabeza de Vaca that there was a horse on shore for him to ride into town. And this time his own sailors encouraged him to go, if only to find Pantoja and Porcallo and tell them in no uncertain terms to "hasten to bring the supplies as soon as possible so that we could leave quickly."

He asked for companions, but no one wanted to go with him,

complaining that it was too cold and wet. They would come ashore tomorrow, they promised, in order to attend mass in the rustic chapel in town. Cabeza de Vaca could have ordered them ashore, but as there was only the single horse he relented and descended the bucking rope ladder to the waiting canoe. Before setting off, he told the ships' masters to use their own judgment about the storm. But if the wind began to come around to the south, he said, they were not to try to save the vessels but should "drive the ships onshore in a place where the men and horses would be saved." Then he got in the canoe and surfed ashore.

Within the hour, the seas of the harbor became too rough for small boats. There was no chance, either, of driving the ships onto the beach, as the wind was still howling straight off the shore. So while the landlubbers huddled beneath the creaking decks and the horses wailed and snorted in their swinging slings, the sailors checked their ropes and checked their knots and pumped their bilge and rode it out in the harbor through that night and Sunday as well.

Cabeza de Vaca, who left the only account of the storm, doesn't mention the eye of it per se, but he says there were "two contrary winds," suggesting the center of the hurricane passed quite near them. At around dusk on Sunday the buildings in the little town began to fall apart. The roofs went first, whole panels of thatch torn off and hurled away. Then the walls came tumbling down. In the dark he managed to find seven or eight other people and they all linked their arms together as they wandered around in the storm all through that night. "As we walked among the trees we were no less frightened, fearing that, as they were falling too, we would be killed underneath them," he remembered later. The storm peaked in the early hours of the morning, with a strange, almost demonic symphony of noise: "a mighty crashing and sound of voices, and loud sounds of bells and tambourines and other instruments, which lasted until morning when the storm abated."

By dawn's exhausted light, the stunned colonists poked disconsolately among the rubble for what remained of their lives or wandered the countryside in search of what remained of their livestock. Cabeza de Vaca and Pantoja meanwhile had managed to find each other and rushed to the harbor to look for the ships. But all that remained were buoys showing where the anchors lay.

For an optimistic moment, Cabeza de Vaca imagined that the ship's masters had managed at the last minute to cut the hawsers and run out before the storm, but in their hearts he and Pantoja both knew the truth: "We realized they were lost." Out of the ninety who had come in the two ships to Trinidad, some thirty had gone ashore before the storm reached its apex. Pantoja now took fifteen of these and went down the coast one way in search of survivors; Cabeza de Vaca did the same and went the other direction. Half a mile back from shore he found one of the ship's boats in the top of a wrecked palm tree. Elsewhere a few articles of clothing—a cape and a coverlet—and pieces of packing crates turned up along the beach. Finally, nearly thirty miles down the beach they came across the mangled and smashed bodies of two crewmen from Cabeza de Vaca's ship.

Narváez's grand expedition had not even officially set off for La Florida and already sixty men were dead. A quarter of his ships were sunk, and a fifth of the horses he had worked so hard to find and to pay for were drowned in their slings. Even the additional supplies promised by Vasco Porcallo were gone, as the entire region was now a disaster area, with winter coming on and not even enough provisions to feed the local population. When Narváez finally arrived five days later with his four remaining ships, which had found safe harbor somewhere to the east, even the thirty survivors on the beach were at the point of starvation, having "suffered great trials and hunger . . . because the supplies and subsistence the town possessed had been lost."

His entire company was in a state of shock, nearly mutinous, begging him to postpone any further activity until spring. Porcallo and the other townspeople also advised him to delay and regroup.

Narváez's own thoughts as he surveyed the ruined town and listened to the pathetic pleadings of his army can only be imagined, though it's possible to identify a few things that he was certain of as he considered his options. He knew, for instance, that less than twenty years before he had conquered the entire thousand-mile island of Cuba with a force only a quarter the size of this suddenly timid collection of greenhorns. He knew that every day of delay cost him more money than it cost them. He knew that Cortés had written smugly in his letters to the emperor that "fortune favors the brave."

But Narváez also surely suspected by now that it was the unhappiness and disloyalty of his own army in Mexico—twice the size of the current force—that had cost him an empire and landed him in Cortés's stinking jail. He knew this was his last chance at glory, a chance not to be squandered by haste. God was forcing his hand.

They would stay the winter in Cuba, he announced.

The only question was where? They couldn't remain where they were, with its lack of even basic food supplies and its substandard harbor. Nor would he send his wind-shocked troops back to the relative bustle of Santiago de Cuba, where they might once again begin to succumb to better, or at least less dangerous, offers of employment. The same was even truer of Havana, which was even less developed than Santiago de Cuba but was a regular stopover for ships traveling between Mexico and Spain.

That left Jagua (now Cienfuegos), further west along the southern coast of Cuba; its superbly protected bay had an opening that was only "a crossbow shot in width." Narváez knew the place well, having spent Christmas of 1513 camped out there in the company of

Velázquez, the meddlesome priest Las Casas, and three casks of wine. Jagua had the additional, albeit somewhat symbolic benefit of being closer to the Yucatan Channel, through which the fleet would eventually have to pass into the Gulf of Mexico. It was therefore arguably a small advance toward La Florida rather than a tactical retreat.

What Jagua wasn't likely to provide in 1527 was the opportunity to replace the lost ships and other supplies. For those, Narváez would have better luck in Havana or Santiago. He therefore put Cabeza de Vaca in charge of the ships and men and sent them on their way up the coast toward Jagua. His confidence in his treasurer's ability to handle the assignment is intriguing in light of both the later antipathy between the two officers and the fact that Cabeza de Vaca's first assignment had so recently resulted in the loss of two ships and sixty men. If Cabeza de Vaca had only ordered the men ashore before it was too late . . . If he had ordered the ships to run before the storm . . .

But shipwrecks were a regular part of doing business in the Indies, and Narváez didn't blame the treasurer for the unfortunate turn of events. Had he wished to leave the army in the hands of someone else, he could easily have said that he needed the treasurer's assistance back in Santiago, though the presence of meddlesome royal eyes and ears as he made still more promises and struck still more financing deals was probably something he wished to avoid. They parted company in the middle of November, Narváez by land and Cabeza de Vaca and the army by sea.

4

Into the Gulf

On February 20th of 1528 Narváez arrived in Jagua to collect his army. During the intervening three months, he had purchased and outfitted two ships to replace those that were lost in the hurricane. He had picked up a few more recruits as well, though there is no evidence of the kind of a groundswell of enthusiasm for his expedition that there had been for his mission to arrest Cortés eight years earlier or that there would be a decade later for De Soto's expedition to Florida. The hurricane didn't help: "Because there was a feeling that this expedition was ill-starred," wrote I. A. Wright in her history of the early years on the island, "there was no stampede in Cuba to Narváez's banner."

He came in one of the newly acquired (though not new) ships, a two-masted vessel known as a brigantine that he purchased in

Trinidad. The other ship, with forty men and twelve horses on board, he had sent to Havana with orders to wait there for the rest of the fleet. Havana, which Narváez founded on the south shore of Cuba in the Gulf of Batabanó in 1514, had by now moved to its current location on the north coast facing the Gulf of Mexico. Though still essentially an outpost, this new position at the mouth of the Straits of Florida, through which the Gulf Stream carried all the great treasure fleets from Mexico, had already resulted in it becoming an important port. Now reunited with the four ships at Jagua, Narváez planned to sail around the western tip of Cuba to Havana where they could replace the food and other supplies that had been depleted during the winter layover.

Cabeza de Vaca was expecting his arrival and had already broken down the winter camp and repacked the ships. Only the horses had been left ashore until the last possible moment, and these were hastily loaded back into their dismal slings below deck. Only two days after Narváez sailed through the needlelike entrance to Jagua harbor, therefore, the other four ships were ready to follow him back out of it, and on February 22 the order was given to raise anchors. Once again, this time with four hundred men and eighty horses, the expedition to conquer La Florida was on its way.

Over the winter Narváez had hired a master pilot to lead the fleet. His name was Miruelo, and according to Cabeza de Vaca, he got the job "because they said that he knew and had been in the Rio de las Palmas and was a very good pilot of the entire north coast." Such knowledge would have been immensely valuable to Narváez given that "the entire northern coast" was precisely the territory he aimed to conquer. But just who this Miruelo was and what he really knew about the Gulf of Mexico is not at all clear.

The debate is centuries old. Garcilaso de la Vega, writing in the 1590s, thought Narváez's Miruelo was the nephew of another sailor of the same name who "while trading among the Indians was blown by a storm to the coast of Florida," where he had been well treated by the locals and even given some gold. Ponce de León, on his way home from "discovering" Florida, met a slaver in the Bahamas who some think was named Miruelo. Another potential Miruelo is said to have traded up and down the west coast of Florida in 1516, bringing back rumors of gold, riches, and new harbors. Some historians suggest he was a pilot named Morillo, who had sailed with Governor Garay of Jamaica to Mexico in 1523, or that his name was really Mirnedo, or . . .

Obviously more important than who Narváez's Miruelo was, is what he might actually have known about the geography of the Gulf of Mexico. There were several ways he might have become acquainted with the western end of Narváez's paper empire, but if indeed he was "a very good pilot of the entire north coast," as he claimed, the best place for him to have gained such comprehensive knowledge would have been as a member of the 1519 Pineda expedition. Pineda reconnoitered the coast north of Mexico as part of an effort by Governor Garay of Jamaica to establish a claim there. He may have been searching specifi-cally for a water route into the recently discovered "Southern Sea," as the Spaniards called the Pacific Ocean, or for a passage around Florida, which everyone thought was an island. He obviously didn't find either of those, but he and a fleet of four ships worked their way east from Florida along the entire Gulf shore to Mexico. They were probably the first Europeans to see the mouth of the Mississippi and may have been the first to notice the mouth of the Rio Grande as well.

Most importantly for Narváez and company, Pineda produced the first moderately accurate map of the Gulf of Mexico. Back in Seville, Narváez and his officers had studied it extensively and may have been given a copy of it, though it was information that was only released by the crown on a "need to know" basis, lest it fall into French or English hands. Among other things, it clearly showed Tampa and Charlotte harbors, the Mississippi, and the Rio de las Palmas.

But whatever this Miruelo knew about the Gulf Coast of North America, his knowledge of the far more familiar southern coast of Cuba turned out to be less than optimal. Only two days after leaving Jagua on what was supposed to be an easy week's cruise around the western tip of the island to Havana, he ran the entire fleet aground on the Canarreos shoals. These sandy ship traps are in the Bay of Batanabó between Cuba and the relatively large Isle of Pines, which lies thirty-five miles off its southwestern coast. The unpredictable and unforgiving nature of the bay was one of the reasons Havana was moved, something both Narváez and Miruelo certainly should have known. Nonetheless, one after another of Narváez's vessels lurched to a stop, stuck in the silty shallows.

In fairness to Miruelo, the Canarreos shoals are notoriously difficult to navigate due to their shifty nature. The problem of finding a channel is compounded by unusually colorful and murky water, caused by dark and light sediments of the bottom getting churned up by the tides. When Columbus found himself stuck in the same area on his second voyage as he was attempting to determine if Cuba was an island or mainland Asia, his sailors got downright spooked by the water that was alternately white as milk and then dark as tar. And if you tried to land, Columbus remembered later, the mangroves were "so thick a cat couldn't get ashore."

For at least two weeks and possibly three, Narváez's ships made no progress. There were occasional moments of hope, when high tide or good luck freed a vessel temporarily from one shoal. But with no way to read the water, such momentary relief was always followed by the wrenching feel of another sandbar under the keel. It was stop, and go, and stop again for days on end, and it felt more like purgatory than like progress. Supplies, already low from the winter layover, diminished further. Morale, which had been momentarily high as they left Jagua, waned anew. On deck the sun roasted the skin, and in the stifling spaces below deck, the horses in their slings began to weaken. When the animals began to die, the taste of fresh meat was bitter consolation; conquistadors didn't relish horsemeat, but they didn't turn it down either.

Nothing the sailors and pilots did seemed to make any lasting difference to the situation. Only when a storm out of the south—an event that normally would not have been looked upon as a blessing—blew enough water up against the coast of Cuba to lift the fleet off the sand did they at last get free. Such a wind had the potential to drive the ships onto the shore, and Cabeza de Vaca says it was "not without much danger" that they finally escaped the shoals sometime toward the second week of March.

Their troubles weren't over, however, as the stormy blessing in disguise soon became too much of a good thing. The Gulf Stream is formed by the warming and expanding of water bottled up in the Caribbean behind the chain of Greater and Lesser Antilles Islands. This warm water spills through the Yucatan Channel between Cuba and Mexico into the Gulf of Mexico where it expands still more and is ejected around the tip of Florida and up past the Bahamas into the Atlantic. Gales from the north in late winter or early spring colliding with the current from the south can pile up enormous seas in the Yucatan Channel. At Guaniguanico and again at Cape Corrientes, both near Cuba's western tip, Narváez's fleet ran into such storms. For three days they battled the wind and the towering swells. In the hold, more horses perished.

At last the storm abated enough to allow them to beat their way around Cape San Antonio, at Cuba's extreme western tip, and then eastward along the north coast of the island toward Havana. The pilots announced they were only thirty-five miles from the harbor; they would be there in the morning. Everyone was on deck as the ships made their way toward the port in the dawn light. The wind was kicking up a bit out of the south, but they could see the masts of anchored vessels. They could almost smell and taste the food. When the wind kicked up a bit more, the mate called out orders to the sailors who echoed them back as they scrambled to the lines to reef sails.

The sailors knew the truth long before the landlubbers, who looked to them for reassurance when they first noticed that the green coastline no longer appeared to be getting nearer. A shake of the head or an averted glance was enough to send some of Narváez's would-be conquerors back below to keep company with the dying horses. Those who stayed above watched the coast of Cuba inexorably disappear below the frothy grey horizon line.

Once more, Narváez faced a decision he had not intended to have to make. With his fleet now blown into the unknown middle of the Gulf of Mexico, the question was where to go from here? Riding out the blow and attempting to return to Havana as originally planned wasn't a serious option; most of his company would desert if given half a chance. Why wouldn't they? So no, there would be no more delays or backtracking. They would go forward and establish a base in his new territory to the north. Only when that was done would he send for the ship they were supposed to meet in Havana.

In the cramped captain's quarters of his flagship, Narváez and Miruelo looked at their charts and discussed where in the vast hypothetical empire they should go. Narváez's first choice was the mouth of the Rio de las Palmas, in northern Mexico. For several reasons, Narváez always planned to begin his conquest of North America at the western end of his territory and work his way east toward La Florida.

Rio de las Palmas was close to the Mexican bonanza, which could wishfully be interpreted to mean there was a good chance of finding gold in the mountains inland. It was presumably within the Aztec sphere of knowledge, and he had in his company the Mexican prince, Don Pedro, who might serve as a translator and diplomat. Most of all, though, a western start would ensure that Cortés would not creep northward into his turf. They could be there in a week if they were lucky, or at most a fortnight.

For a full month they fought the sea, trying to beat their way west against unfavorable winds and the eastward pull of the nascent Gulf Stream. Hourly, they tossed the log lines over the stern and counted the knots as the rope played out behind the ships in the hope that some indication of their speed might be deduced. They moved the pegs on the traverse boards. They watched their compasses, and on clear nights and noons observed the declination of the North Star and the sun. It was all basically guesswork. There would be no good way to do more than estimate a ship's longitude until the invention of accurate timepieces in the nineteenth century, and they had only a vague idea of the dimensions of the Gulf.

Finally, on April 7th, land was sighted. But it wasn't off to the west, as it would be if they were near the mouth of the Rio de las Palmas. Instead, a long, low coastline running north and south lay to their east. Some scholars have recently suggested that Narváez and company believed throughout the entire month in the Gulf that they were progressing toward Mexico. It's not impossible. Though their skills at dead reckoning were extraordinary, the currents off Cuba could confound their best attempts to measure speed, and weather could prevent even rudimentary consultation with heavenly bodies. What's more, Miruelo and his fellow pilots may have been incompetent even by the standards of the day. But if they thought they were approaching the Rio de las

Palmas, the appearance of land to the east was a rude surprise. No matter who Miruelo was, he and Narváez both knew that the Rio de las Palmas flowed out of a north-south trending coast lying at the western end of the Gulf. They knew the sun didn't rise over the coast of Pánuco and Rio de las Palmas.

Far more likely, therefore, the call from the masthead that land lay to the east was the expected and welcome result of an earlier decision to reverse course and make for Florida. After weeks in the storm-tossed Gulf, the dead reckoning of Miruelo was good enough to tell Narváez that he wasn't making any progress westward toward the Rio de las Palmas. The dead horses down in the hold, meanwhile, told him he'd better quit trying. When they left Jagua, they expected to reach Havana in a week, or two at the most. Instead, they had now not touched land in nearly two months, long enough to have sailed all the way to Spain and part way back. The only reason there were any stores at all remaining on board when Florida was sighted is that their precious horses were now dying at a rate of one or more a day.

With land in sight, Miruelo turned the fleet south, keeping the low green shoreline as close as seemed prudent off the port side. For two days they scudded along a featureless coast, which showed no sign of veering significantly from its north-south orientation. Traveling along a landmass like this to determine its primary orientation was an established method of estimating location: Ponce de León found himself off an unknown coast in 1513 and concluded it was the north shore of Cuba primarily because "Cuba ran east-west like it." The course wasn't only to confirm where they were, however. Miruelo announced he knew of a fine harbor along that coast, one "that entered seven or eight leagues inland" and would be an auspicious place to found the colony. The entrance, he said, was somewhere to the south of them.

Then suddenly, instead of five ships sailing down the unchanging coast of Florida, there were only four. Nothing is known of the circumstances of the wreck except for a single, parenthetical fragment of a sentence from Cabeza de Vaca offered not in chronological order, but as an afterthought near the very end of his memoir. He says nothing about survivors or salvage efforts, or even if they witnessed the event. "The other [ship] had been lost on the rugged coast" is all Cabeza de Vaca says.

In the wake of this latest disaster, someone spotted a small opening in the beach, not much more than a hundred yards wide. Behind it was not Miruelo's great harbor, just "a shallow bay," but Narváez had had enough. When the tide was rising strongly, he ordered the ships to make their way through the narrow cut, which is known today as John's Pass. They slid on the current into Boca Ciega Bay, just north of the entrance to Tampa Bay proper and got their first glimpse of the people they had come so far to conquer.

On the far shore there was a collection of round structures, at least one of them quite large. Some of the buildings were perched atop sizable earthen mounds that were not quite pyramids, but were nonetheless impressive and hopeful signs of a relatively advanced culture. Whatever other wealth these people had, it was obvious they had plenty of fresh water and fresh food. And grass for the remaining horses. Narváez nodded, giving the order, and the anchors dropped with a splash. He called to Alonso Enríquez, the comptroller of the expedition, and told him to prepare to go ashore.

While sailors scrambled to ready one of the ship's boats, Enríquez and a small contingent of soldiers strapped on their cotton-lined helmets and put on shirts of iron mail. Once they were in the boat, someone handed down a small supply of trade goods: bluish beads, brass bells, iron chisels, pieces of cloth, and other trinkets, and the men pulled at the oars. Enríquez directed them toward a small deserted island within hailing distance of the village, where he got out. He held up his hands in a gesture of peace to the people they could now see standing on the beach in front of their houses. "And he called to the Indians," remembered Cabeza de Vaca, "who came and were with him a considerable amount of time."

They were healthy, well-fed looking people, larger than Enríquez and his men. He determined immediately that they were not Taino or Arawak or any other people that the Spanish were familiar with from the Caribbean. Nor were they like the Mexicans, who had cotton cloth and gold jewelry. By European standards, these Floridians were virtually naked, the men in breechclouts and the women in skirts woven of Spanish moss. Their bodies, however, were elaborately tattooed, particularly on their arms. One soldier in the De Soto expedition later described the bodies of Florida Indians as "decorated." Judging from items found by archeologists in nearby burial sites, some wore fire-darkened pearls in bands around their biceps, and beads of bone and shell around their necks. Some pierced their ears and other body parts, and the most powerful among them wore copper ear-spools and pendants, brought via trade networks from the far north and intricately decorated with embossed markings and perforations

Enríquez held out a sample of gold and some corn, attempting to find out if the Indians knew where more of either might be found, and they responded with hand signs that they had neither item. They had plenty of fish, which they caught with nets woven from fibrous plants, and venison, taken with great longbows as tall as themselves. They were happy to trade good quantities of both of these for the glass beads, and perhaps a brass bell or two, and Enríquez loaded his boat with fresh food.

Unidentified Floridian Indians, by John White, circa 1590, showing the size of the long-bow and the extent of tattoos. (Courtesy of the Trustees of the British Museum)

Back on board the ships that evening, he reported to Narváez that there was no obvious sign of great wealth among the people who had come out to trade. But they seemed peaceful, and the food was a cause for celebration in itself for those few who got to eat some of it. All in all, it was an auspicious beginning. Or so it seemed to Narváez and his officers as they discussed their plans into the night. Gold, they reminded themselves, was never on the coast, but was always up in the mountains inland. The gold would come in good time.

For the people who had come out from shore, however, the arrival of the four enormous ships in their home waters was anything but auspicious. It was instead a startling and ominous turn of events, though it was not as if unknown gods or demons had descended from the sky. These were not, after all, the first Spaniards to arrive off Florida, or even the first to visit the Tampa Bay region, as Pineda's map attests. Indeed Narváez's fleet had probably been observed working its way down from the north in the days before entering the bay: in the same area a dozen years later, the De Soto expedition reported seeing smoke signals announcing their arrival "along the whole coast." It's safe to say that the Indians of Boca Ciega already knew a thing or two about the sort of people who traveled in such tall ships, even if it was mostly by rumor and hearsay.

The official European discoverer of Florida was, of course, Juan Ponce de León. He made his first voyage there with three ships in 1513 and, according to the main source on the voyage, "called it La Florida, because it presented a beautiful vista of many blossoming trees and was low and flat; and also because they discovered it during the time of Easter." That holiday, in Spanish, is called Pascua florida, or the feast of flowers. Ponce de León gets the credit, but no one disputes that there were other Europeans who preceded him. Two years before he even sailed for La Florida, there were published accounts in Europe of "marvelous lands and marvelous countries that have been found" north of Cuba.

The marvelous finders in question were primarily illicit slavers who sailed up from the already conquered Caribbean Islands either with no permission at all, or with a wink and a nod from the colonial authorities. In the decades after Columbus's first voyage, royal policy went back and forth on the legitimacy of slaving in the New World, though there was always a list of conditions under which enslaving Indians might be considered the Christian thing to do. It was a cosmic version of plausible deniability that allowed the king to get the guilt-free sleep he needed while the mines and plantations of Cuba and Hispaniola got the wage-free labor they needed.

How many slaving raids were made to Florida in the years before Narváez's arrival cannot be known; smugglers don't keep records. What is known is that by 1511 the Bahamas were entirely depopulated and the slave hunters were nosing around the mainland. According to Narváez's old chaplain Las Casas, that year a group of investors sent several ships to the Bahamas where they searched "many of them very thoroughly" with no luck before deciding to head northwest. "It is certain that this was the land and coastline that now we call Florida," said Las Casas of the place where the slavers filled their irons with native necks and ankles. That particular voyage touched on the Atlantic coast of Florida rather than anywhere near Narváez's landing place in the vicinity of Tampa Bay, but it is safe to assume that with the chronic labor shortages in the Caribbean, other slavers did explore the peninsula's west coast.

Ponce de León never got to Tampa Bay either. This "bastard son of the best-known family in Seville" had became one of the richest men in the Americas when gold was discovered on Puerto Rico, which he had conquered in 1506. But Boriquén, as Puerto Rico was originally called, belonged to the Columbus family by virtue of its "discovery" by the admiral, and Ponce de León was part of the anti-Columbus faction in the new colonies. In 1512, after lending the king ten thousand ducats to help him get elected Holy Roman Emperor, the discoverer's son, Diego Colon, was returned to power in the Indies and promptly took the government of Puerto Rico away from Ponce de León. As a consolation prize, the king gave Ponce de León permission to explore to the north, where everyone knew, but didn't officially admit, there was a lot of territory waiting to be claimed.

What role the famous Fountain of Youth actually played in his plans is not clear, but Spaniards of the period sincerely believed in all manner of possibilities in the New World: Cortés, for instance, was specifically instructed to keep an eye out for "people with large, broad ears and others with faces like dogs . . . and also where and in what direction are the Amazons." Most such rumors originated in Old World mythology, but the idea of the Fountain of Youth came as much from Native American sources, and contemporaries of Ponce de León insisted that he was in fact looking for it: "his vain belief in the nonsense he heard from the Indians," Oviedo called it. Recent scholars, however, tend to discount the fountain as a motive, though some have suggested it wasn't a Fountain of Youth the aging conquistador sought but a Fountain of Viagra. At any rate, he didn't find either one.

He did, however, notice the Gulf Stream. While sailing south along the Atlantic coast from an initial landfall somewhere in the vicinity of Daytona Beach, one of his ships was dragged out of sight of the others, despite the fact that it was a clear, blue day with plenty of wind to fill the sails. The fleet eventually reunited, and continued past Miami and along the Florida Keys, which he named "the Martyrs" because "from a distance the rocks that stuck up looked like men who were suffering." They worked their way up the Gulf Coast of Florida to the vicinity of Charlotte Harbor where, on June 4, 1513, they met an Indian who spoke Spanish.

To Americans raised on the persistent myth of the trackless wilderness and the dusky savage, this idea that the first European to officially set foot in what became the continental United States was greeted by a Spanish-speaking Indian is astonishing. (It was bad enough that the first Indian met by the Pilgrims in Massachusetts a century later spoke English.) To Ponce de León and the other members of his expedition, however, a Spanish-speaking native was only mildly unexpected. The main source for the voyage notes rather blandly that the polyglot "was believed to be a native of Española or some other island inhabited by Castilians." In other words, he was a refugee or a runaway slave who had fled to Florida in a canoe, bringing with him news of the devastation that followed the bearded men in metal hats.

The people of the Caribbean were spectacular long-distance canoeists, capable of crossing regularly from the mainland to the islands and back. In the Bahamas, not long after his first landfall, Columbus wrote in his journal that "it is from the northwest that strangers come to fight and capture the people here," and then added the next day, "I believe that people from the mainland come here to take them as slaves." Slaves, that is, and wives. According to Martyr, "the women of the Lucayan islands (the Bahamas) are so beautiful that numerous inhabitants of the neighboring countries, charmed by their beauty, abandon their homes, and for love of them settle in their country." Martyr also reported that the Floridians canoed regularly to the Bahamas to hunt pigeons.

Columbus described the boats he saw in the Bahamas as "made from a tree-trunk, like a long boat, all of a piece, wonderfully shaped in the way of this land, some big enough to carry forty or fifty men." The natives called them "canoa," he said, and the Europeans took to calling them that as well. In Cuba, Columbus saw a canoe that could carry 150 people, which was eight times as many as his own vessel, *Niña*. But the best evidence of the navigational abilities of the Caribbean peoples came on his second voyage, when Indians who had accompanied him to Spain and back piloted his fleet all the way up the lesser Antilles Islands, along the Virgin Islands, and then along the southern coast of Puerto Rico. These were all new places to Columbus, and when these Arawak pilots announced that they had reached Hispaniola, he was skeptical about their identification of the island. The land before them was low and flat, and his memory of Hispaniola was that it was mountainous.

But as they traveled along the coast, mountains appeared and it was soon clear that the Arawaks were correct, and it was the admiral of the Ocean Sea who didn't know where in the New World he was.

So it was no great surprise to Ponce de León and his men to find refugees from the islands in Florida. For his part, the Spanish-speaking Indian in Charlotte Harbor appeared to know his Spaniards pretty well. He came out in a canoe to within hailing distance of the flagship and told Ponce de León to wait where he was, because the chief of the local Calusa Indians had some gold to trade. Naturally Ponce de León waited, but instead of the chief and his gold, twenty large canoes full of Calusa warriors soon surrounded the ships and showered arrows over the gunnels. Others paddled to the anchor lines and tried to cut them in order to pull or drive the boats ashore. All were finally driven off by the guns of the Spaniards on board but returned the next day in even larger numbers. Once again they inflicted little damage, but Ponce de León got the message and sailed home.

Only after the news of Mexico eight years later, when "the name of Hernando Cortés was on everybody's lips and his fame was great," did Ponce de León again feel the urge to wager his life and what remained of his fortune on his claim to North America. The location of this 1521 colony was probably again the vicinity of Charlotte Harbor, but wherever it was, it wasn't welcome. Within six months the colonists were overrun by local insurgents. The survivors fled in their ships, some to Mexico to join up with Cortés, others to Havana, where Ponce de León himself soon died from a festering wound he'd received in his thigh.

Whether the people of Boca Ciega Bay who greeted Narváez and his men seven years later knew of Ponce de León's misadventures is impossible to say. At that time Charlotte Harbor was a boundary between the Calusa peoples of the southern tip of Florida and a people archeologists have come to call the Safety Harbor culture of Tampa Bay, to which the village at Boca Ciega belonged. Though both cultures had diverged from a common predecessor around 900 A.D., by the time Narváez arrived the Calusa and the Safety Harbor peoples learned of each other's doings primarily through trading prisoners of war.

But even if no specific details of Ponce's invasions were known in Boca Ciega, which is by no means a given, there were other means by which they could have learned a thing or two about Spanish ways before the arrival of Narváez. For one thing, the slaving raids continued: Ponce de León himself complained to the king that Narváez's old employer, Diego Velázquez of Cuba, had "scandalized all the land of Bimini and Florida by taking 300 head from there!" In addition to Pineda's voyage and the various rumored voyages of Miruelo, known visits to Florida's west coast include a stop by Francisco Hernández de Córdoba on his way back to Cuba from the Yucatan in 1517. "These Indians carried very long bows and good arrows and lances, and some weapons like swords, and they were clad in deerskins and were very big men," remembered one member of that expedition.

Finally, the people who greeted Narváez's fleet could have learned of the Spanish from the vessels that periodically wrecked along the Gulf shore, as one of Narváez's had just done. This was particularly true after the treasure started flowing from Mexico out through the Gulf Stream toward Spain. These wrecks occasionally produced European survivors, as well as artifacts that archeologists now know made their way into the native economy, where they were traded and treasured.

In the village of post-and-thatch buildings at the back of the little bay, everything that was known and imagined of the metal-clad strangers and their ways was discussed with urgency the night after the tall ships appeared. Cabeza de Vaca remembered one building in the town at the back of Boca Ciega that was big enough to hold three hundred people, and it's easy to imagine the entire population gathered there to pass around the wondrous square-edged tubular Nuevo Cadiz beads and other gewgaws that the bearded men had given in exchange for food. Hushed children listened in the back as their elders debated the options. Some said fight, some said flee, others said wait and see. Some asked what level of risk the chance to collect a few more beads was worth? And at last, in the dark, they came to a consensus about a course of action.

It's a nice image, but it's also quite possible that there was no such egalitarian town meeting. In Safety Harbor burial mounds, "status" goods like beads are usually concentrated near the bones of a few privileged individuals rather than spread among the population, suggesting to archeologists that there was a powerful elite that controlled the economy and political structure. The presence of the mounds themselves also indicates a high degree of social planning and division of labor, and later visitors to Safety Harbor towns noticed that high chiefs were always greeted with a special salute by more plebian members of the group. In other words, the townspeople's opinion about what to do in response to the Spaniards' arrival may have been neither asked for nor welcome.

The decision may even have been made by a regional authority somewhere else entirely. Though the various chiefdoms around the bay occasionally made war on one another and may not have all spoken the same dialect, there is also some evidence of political integration among the Indians of the Tampa Bay region. De Soto's 1539 expedition to the same area noticed that smaller villages paid tribute, both materially and politically, to a powerful inland leader named Paracoxi. Similarly, a cacique named Tocobaga told a Spanish delegation in the 1560s that he couldn't make any important decisions without consulting his allies. He then rapidly assembled a hundred chiefs and fifteen hundred warriors from as far as three days' travel away, whereupon the leader of the Spanish delegation, who had originally wished to see the allies in question, quickly asked Tocobaga to send them home again.

As soon as Narváez's ships appeared, therefore, runners may have gone out from the village carrying the news and seeking advice. And one way or another, by consensus or command, a decision was arrived at in the course of the first night. Under cover of darkness, the men and women of the town at the back of Boca Ciega Bay loaded their canoes. Silently, they pushed out from shore. Others, carrying their loads on their backs, moved along well-worn paths through the forest. And in the morning when Narváez, Cabeza de Vaca, and as many men as the ship's boats could carry rowed ashore, there was not a local man, woman, or child to be found anywhere in town.

5

The Requirement

It was good to stand again on dry land with the weight of a helmet on his head and chain mail on his chest, good to strap on his sword. Almost ten years had passed since Cortés had stolen Mexico; eight years since his eye was poked out trying to get it back; five since his release from jail; nearly a year since leaving Spain. But it was at last that "tomorrow," which had been put off so many times. It was Good Friday of 1528, and Narváez was there on the beach. His beach. His king's beach. His God's beach. It was good.

With the residents gone into hiding, or up the bay to the next village, or to wherever, the forty conquistadors who went ashore with Narváez were free to rummage around the abandoned town. There was the single large building already mentioned and an unknown number of smaller houses. Cabeza de Vaca called them *buhíos*, a native term from the Caribbean that meant a "dwelling with an open shed attached," but it's not at all clear that Safety Harbor houses actually fit that description. Archeological sites are scattered all over Florida's Gulf Coast, but other than some post holes that no one was able to make much sense of, nothing has been discovered about Safety Harbor domestic architecture. All there is to go on, therefore, is a single description of a town by a member of De Soto's expedition through the region a dozen years after Narváez and company. "The town was of seven or eight houses," remembered the Gentleman of Elvas, "built of timber, and covered with palm-leaves. The chief's house stood near the beach, upon a very high mount made by hand for defense; at the other end of the town was a temple."

As its name implies, the "Narváez Midden," across Boca Ciega Bay from John's Pass, is the place where popular (and some scholarly) opinion has located the arrival of the expedition in 1528. These days the mound is not as big as some of the pink mansions nearby, but there's still a solemn quality about the place. The portion of it open to the public is covered with great-girthed oaks hung with Spanish moss, and smooth-skinned gumbo-limbos. Everything droops mysteriously, and when one of the ancient trees falls, local archeology buffs hear about it through the grapevine and drive across the endless suburban sprawl of the bay area to the mound to seek among the upended roots for artifacts.

This is a reversal of the way the place appeared to Narváez and his officers as they prowled around their Safety Harbor village, poking at any left-behind belongings with their sword tips. At that time Safety Harbor towns were tiny patches of development in a seemingly endless moss-hung forest through which people from smaller fishing villages traveled on shady paths to attend religious ceremonies and political meetings. The mound itself was a treeless piece of landscape architecture, topped with the house of a powerful family. From one of its longer sides, an earthen ramp descended to a cleared plaza that was always kept meticulously clean of debris. There was a long shell midden running parallel to the shore, on top of which most of the houses of the general population were built to protect them from high water, and not far away there was usually another mound, this one filled with graves and topped with a house of the dead that was adorned with carvings.

No one knows for sure that the Narváez Midden is the actual place, that "Narváez Was Here," so to speak. A few Spanish artifacts have been found at the site: some shards of olive jars, in which the Spanish carried all manner of perishables, a few nails, an iron chisel and possibly a few sword-blade fragments. But nothing that archeologists can definitively connect only with early-fifteenth-century Spanish culture has been found.

What's more, the maddeningly brief descriptions of the landing place by Narváez survivors don't conjure an image of the "major town with a large ceremonial temple mound" that archeologists think existed at the site. Though Safety Harbor peoples were not as skilled ceramicists as some of their predecessors in Tampa Bay, they produced distinctive pottery covered with curvilinear and geometric designs pressed into the wet clay before firing. They carved stone and wood into effigies of animals important to their traditions, especially birds, frogs, and deer. But neither Narváez source mentions seeing any of these as they rummaged through the abandoned town. Other than the single large building and the *buhios*, all that they reported seeing were two things: "many fishing nets, and among them they found a gold disk."

A single piece of gold. Cabeza de Vaca remembered it as a rattle rather than a disk, but either way, gold was an odd thing to find among the fishing nets. The few gold and silver items that have turned up in

Safety Harbor archeological sites are small personal ornaments associated with high-status individuals. Ironically, given Narváez's Mexican fiasco, virtually all the gold owned by Florida Indians appears to have originated from Spanish ships wrecked on their way from Mexico to Spain. In other words, the rattle in the fishing nets was most likely a scrap of treasure that Narváez's rival, Cortés, had lost and long since forgotten about. But unless Don Pedro, the Mexican prince traveling with the expedition, recognized it as the work of his countrymen, Narváez had no way of knowing that the gold came from anywhere other than Florida. One rattle was not a bonanza, to be sure, but it was not a bad sign either, and Narváez decided he would begin his conquest here.

That night on board the ships, his sea-weary company was in high spirits, not so much because of the tiny finding of gold but because they knew the decision had at last been made. After all the storm-tossed weeks at sea with a bunch of dying horses and diminishing rations, they were going to go ashore in the morning. Even the remaining horses could smell the land.

The first boats carried virtually the same company they had the previous day, which is to say Narváez and his principal officers and captains. Any royal officials who had not gone ashore on the first landing the previous day were not permitted to remain behind this time, and those who had commissions were reminded to bring their paperwork. The official scribe of the expedition, whose name was Alaniz, carried his writing equipment and seals as well. When you were appropriating a continent, or even an island, for his "Holy, Imperial, Catholic, Majesty," there was a certain amount of paperwork that had to be attended to on the beach.

As soon as all the important personnel were assembled on shore, flags were unfurled. Narváez read out his commission from the king and offered it around for display; Alaniz took note that the documents were

unanimously recognized as authentic. After so many years of disappointment, it was at last real: Narváez was now the royal governor of
La Florida.

In turn, Cabeza de Vaca and each of the other commissioned
royal officers of the expedition stepped up to Narváez and presented
their own credentials. The new governor made a show of pretending to
read the parchments, but everyone knew it was just a formality. The
mood may have been solemn and dignified, though more likely it was
somewhat jovial and perfunctory; a bit of legal theater in which everyone knew their parts and played them. In every case, however, Alaniz
took careful note that there were no disputed titles or positions. As the
historian Lewis Hanke wrote: "Spaniards were so accustomed to certifying every action they took that notaries were as indispensable to their
expeditions as friars and gunpowder."

With his government of North America duly in place, Narváez
ordered the rest of the company still on board the ships to begin disem-
barking. Back and forth the small boats went, ferrying olive jars, bales,
boxes, and people to the shore. Below the decks, the surviving horses
were released one at a time from their slings and led uneasily on weak
legs to a spot below the hatch. There they were again slung, blind-
folded, and hoisted up into the sunlight.

Meanwhile on the beach there was one more formality to attend
to; beginning in 1513, Spanish expeditions to the New World were
required to inform the Indians of their rights and duties under the new
regime and of the consequences if they resisted. The *requerimiento*, as
the document is called today, is a fascinating window into the imperial
mind-set of the Spaniards of 1528. But for the Indians themselves,
who had good reason to wonder about the motives of the strangers on
the beach, it was a long stream of gibberish. That is, if they heard it at
all. Except for a few spies in the nearby woods, the intended listeners

were not even within earshot when Narváez read it in his famously cavernous voice.

He began by introducing himself and giving a brief history of the world and its division into many nations:

On behalf of the Catholic Caesarean Majesty of Don Carlos, King of the Romans and Emperor ever Augustus, and Doña Juana his mother, Sovereigns of León and Castilla, Defenders of the Church, ever victors, never vanquished, and rulers of barbarous nations, I, Pánfilo de Narváez, his servant, messenger and captain, notify and cause you to know in the best manner I can, that God our Lord, one and eternal, created the heaven and the earth, and one man and one woman of whom we and you and all men in the world have come, are descendants.

While the crates and baskets were being unloaded onto the beach behind him, Narváez or his designated reader went on in the same floral fashion to tell the absent Indians that the land that their ancestors had occupied for the past twelve thousand years—roughly twice as long as the Christians believed the world had existed—did not, after all, belong to them. The pope, who Narváez explained was ordained by God "to judge and govern all people, Christians, Moors, Jews, Gentiles and whatever creed beside they might be," had given it all a few years back to the Spanish crown. If the Indians wanted to see the relevant paperwork, he read out, they were welcome to come and do so at any time.

As far as religion was concerned, Narváez was quite explicit in his reassurances to the surrounding trees and whoever might be hiding behind them. "You shall not be required to become Christians, except when, informed of the truth, you desire to be converted to our Holy Catholic Faith," he read out. If they did convert, he promised that "their Majesties and I, in their royal name, will receive you with love and charity, relinquishing in freedom your women, children and estates without service, that with them and yourselves you may do with perfect liberty all you wish and may deem well."

But as is often the case in such free choices formally announced by governments that perceive themselves to be both militarily and morally superior to all others, it was Narváez's duty to warn that if the Floridians made the wrong choice it wasn't going to be pretty. There had to be consequences.

> If you do not do this, and of malice you be dilatory, I protest to you, that, with the help of Our Lord, I will enter with force, making war upon you from all directions and in every manner that I may be able, [and] will subject you to obedience to the Church and the yoke of their Majesties; and I will take the persons of yourselves, your wives and your children to make slaves, sell and dispose of as Their Majesties shall think fit; and I will take your goods, doing you all the evil and injury that I am able, as to vassals who do not obey but reject their master, resist and deny him: and I declare to you that the deaths and damages that arise therefrom, will be your fault and not that of His Majesty, nor mine, nor of these cavaliers who come with me.

If the presentation and acceptance of the officer's commissions was a bit of legal theater, the reading of the *requerimiento* was a bit of legal theater-of-the-absurd, and even the Spaniards of the period knew it. The proclamation's principal author, a jurist named Palacios Rubios, said its purpose was to "calm the conscience of the Christians." Narváez's old chaplain Las Casas said he didn't know whether to laugh or to weep when he first read it. Narváez's contemporary, Oviedo, to whom it fell to read it to actual Indians for the first time, knew it was a joke from the minute he saw it. In Panama in 1514 he was sent out with three hundred men to find someone to read it to, but all they found were deserted towns.

"My Lords it appears to me that these Indians will not listen to the theology of this requirement," he said with a flourish at the end of the day, handing the parchment back to his commanding officer. "Would Your Honor be pleased to keep it until we have some one of these Indians in a cage, in order that he may learn it at his leisure and my Lord Bishop may explain it to him." Everyone laughed.

The most succinct statements of how the *requerimiento* really worked came from the two most successful conquerors of the entire Spanish invasion. Cortés, in his second letter to the king, said of Montezuma: "I promised your Majesty that I would bring him either dead or in chains if he would not submit himself subject to your Majesty's crown." And Cortés's cousin Pizarro, who conquered Peru, replied quite honestly when asked by a priest to take the time to convert the Indians: "I have not come for any such reasons. I have come to take away from them their gold."

There were some in Narváez's army who had reason to wince during the reading. The many native Caribbean slaves, if they knew what they were hearing as they carried barrels and cartons up the beach from the boats, could have thought of a few things to add. There was also the recently converted Don Pedro, once a prince in Montezuma's oppressive and blood-saturated empire, and now part of the religious contingent of a Spanish army in search of another Mexico to conquer. But the average Spanish soldier unloading the ships was, like Narváez himself, unencumbered by introspection. For seven hundred years, conversion and conquest, religion and real estate, had been inextricably intertwined in Spain. No less than the pope in Rome had instructed all Christians "to subdue Saracens, pagans, and other unbelievers inimical to Christ, to reduce their persons to perpetual slavery and then to transfer for ever their territory to the . . . Crown." The *requerimiento* was a formality, and the average Spaniard loved formalities.

"And so as I proclaim and require this," Narváez concluded, "I ask of the Notary here that he give me a certificate." He turned to Alaniz, who was expecting the request and had the document ready.

Out of earshot, safely hidden in the shadows at the edge of the forest, some of the owners of the village at the back of Boca Ciega Bay surely watched the great unloading operations. They saw the barrels and crates arriving on the beach and more and more people, until nearly 300 were ashore. Unknown animals were hoisted out over the side of the vessels and pulled ashore over the water, along stout lines that ran from the tops of the masts to a great tall tree near shore. If the ships were too far from shore for such an operation, the animals were swung out on a yard and lowered into the water and swum or rafted ashore. On land the creatures walked gingerly on atrophied legs, blinking in the sun to which they had grown unaccustomed.

The Indians of Boca Ciega Bay watched the strangers make fires in their fireplaces, make beds in their houses, post guards around their perimeter, and prepare to sleep on their land. It wasn't good, what was happening, and that evening they made a decision to go let these strange multicolored people with their one-eyed chief know that they weren't welcome.

The party that approached the Spanish camp the following morning was not warlike but was intended to be somewhat intimidating nonetheless. "Thanks to God they saw from afar as many as twenty Indians painted red (which is a certain red ointment that the Indians put on when they go to war or wish to make a fine appearance)" is how one of De Soto's men described a similar delegation a decade later, "and they wore many plumes and carried their bows and arrows."

Narváez no doubt called to the Mexican Don Pedro and to various enslaved Arawaks and Lucayans in the company to see if anyone could understand anything that the Floridians were trying to say, but it was useless. "Since we did not have an interpreter we did not understand them," remembered Cabeza de Vaca. Which isn't to say the delegation was unable to make itself clear. "But they made many signs and threatening gestures to us and it seemed to us that they were telling us to leave the land."

Whether Narváez chose to have the required proclamation read again to these Indians is unknown. Whether he laughed his cavernous laugh at their pathetic fulminations, as he had so many years ago in the face of the fat cacique of Cempoallan is also unsaid. All the sources report is that the townspeople eventually went away, that no violence ensued, and that Narváez simply ignored their request and told his men to keep at the work of unloading the ships.

6

In Tocobaga's Charnel House

In the coolness of the following morning, Narváez, Cabeza de Vaca, and some forty others strapped on their personal armor. Having taken formal possession of his empire, Narváez wanted to look around. Also in the company were the head priest, Juan Suárez, the inspector of mines, Alonso de Solís, and no doubt Alaniz, in case some decision or discovery needed to be notarized. The rest of the company is unnamed.

Everyone dressed according to their social position and job description, though some who considered themselves horsemen altered their gear selection as there were only six horses healthy enough to go along. Little wonder, really; after a month with their feet off the ground in the holds of the storm-tossed ships, the animals were now expected to carry not only a rider and his saddle, but somewhere in the neighborhood of fifty pounds of his personal armor. Narváez, Cabeza de Vaca, and the other four riders didn't wear the head-to-toe metal of their medieval forbearers, but they protected their midsections—front, back, and abdomen—with steel cuirasses. Or, if they preferred, one of their slaves or aides helped them into a shirt or vest of chain mail—up to thirty pounds of it. They pulled on gauntlets, with metal plates attached in appropriate places, to protect their hands and forearms. In one hand they carried a metal or leather and wood shield; in the other, a steel-tipped lance, nine to twelve feet long. Swords and daggers, strapped on at the waist, were of various designs, with hilts ornamented in proportion to personal wealth. On their feet were boots of Spanish leather, long enough to cover the thighs if need be, but usually rolled down to expose the knees. Finally, there were several varieties of helmet to choose from, though the most stylish had a ridge or keel along the top, and a brim that rose to a point in front and back. They were hot and heavy things, weighing as much as ten pounds.

Those who marched on foot generally chose somewhat lighter personal armor. These included a contingent of crossbowmen and a smaller number of musketeers with long, barreled matchlocks that they rested on a stick or post to fire. Others carried weapons of their own choosing: battle-axes, maces, or halberds, which were a cross of sorts between a spear and a battle-ax. In place of the cuirass, foot soldiers often wore brigandine, a heavy linen jacket to which metal plates had been riveted. Some, especially those who had been to Mexico, preferred Aztec-style quilted cotton coats, which were actually better protection against arrows than the brigandine. Those who couldn't afford a steel helmet wore leather instead. In short, there was no standard uniform, and men wore and fought in whatever they could afford to provide for themselves.

The armor didn't exactly glitter in the April sunshine. The Gentleman of Elvas, who was Portuguese, sniffed that most of the Castilians who tried to join the De Soto expedition a dozen years later "wore poor and rusty coats of mail, and all [wore] helmets and carried worthless and poor lances." And while De Soto was able to be choosy in his selection of comrades, and so rejected many of those whose weapons he felt were not up to snuff, Narváez took whoever he could get, especially after the desertions and drownings.

When everything was strapped on and cinched tight, they struck out into the shade, almost certainly following an established path worn clear by centuries of travel by the villagers whose homes they had so recently appropriated. There was no reason to hack a new way through the swampy land surrounding the bay. After all, they weren't looking for open, uninhabited land. They were looking for people, and a native road was most likely to lead to a population center. All day Narváez and his men marched through the flickering green without seeing anyone or anything memorable. Their bearing was north or northeast, and at dusk they finally trudged out of the woods onto the shore of an immense body of water that, when tasted, was salty. They had crossed the Pinellas Peninsula and were somewhere along the edge of Old Tampa Bay, the great northern arm of Tampa Bay proper.

Narváez was excited by the find. This could only be the safe harbor Miruelo had been promising, and the entrance to it must be somewhere in the vicinity. So even though they had not found food nor treasure, the two things they were seeking, Narváez wanted to return immediately to the ships and consult the pilots. But the men and horses were exhausted, and on the trail it was already almost pitch black under the thick cover of leaves and needles. They made camp on the beach, and in the buggy twilight ate their meager rations, posted sentries, and got what sleep they could.

The following morning Narváez hurried his men along as they retraced their steps. With no side explorations or stops, they made much

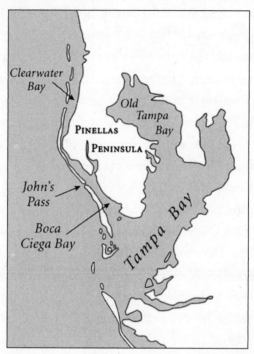

Detail of the Florida coast in the vicinity of the expedition's landing place. (Courtesy of the University of Nebraska Press)

better time returning and arrived back at the landing site in the early afternoon. Narváez immediately called for Miruelo and the other pilots and ships' masters, and described to them the bay, which they all agreed was indeed Miruelo's "good port." Miruelo himself argued further that the opening must be a short distance to the south of where they were currently camped, pointing out that they had already spent two days sailing down the coast to the north without finding any such opening.

This was sensible enough, and Narváez made a quick decision to send Miruelo with the brigantine south along the shore to the mouth of the bay. If and when he found it, his orders were to sail up into it and work his way along its shoreline, keeping the land close on his port side. This should theoretically bring him to where Narváez and the reconnaissance team had spent the previous night. That team, meanwhile, would return immediately to the shore of the bay and continue exploring. It was a long day of marching made for the sole purpose of giving Miruelo his sailing orders. But if all went according to plan, the land party would rendezvous with the brigantine on the coast of the newly discovered bay, and together they could then find a more suitable location than the camp at Boca Ciega for a permanent base of operations.

Specifically, Narváez wanted better anchorage for the ships than the shallow Boca Ciega Bay, having already lost two vessels in a bad harbor in Cuba. More important, he needed a population of Indians who grew enough food to feed four hundred uninvited guests. Once such a place was found, the brigantine could go back to the camp at Boca Ciega and collect the other ships and guide them to the safe harbor.

But when Narváez, Cabeza de Vaca, and the rest of the exploratory party arrived back at their campsite beside Old Tampa Bay there was no sign of the brigantine. This wasn't immediately disappointing, as there was no reason to assume that the ship would be there so soon. It would come, Narváez reassured himself, and gave the order to make camp. No sign of the brigantine in the morning was similarly dismissed: the men finished their light ration of salt pork and hard cassava bread and shouldered their loads.

Now keeping as close to the water as possible in the hope of spotting Miruelo's brigantine, they picked their way north along a coastline that was only intermittently what might be called dry land. Small, sandy crescents gave way to soggy mangrove points that had to be waded around if possible or cut behind. Out in the bay, strange-headed manatees lolled and dolphins cruised, but on the beach and in the muck just back from it, leather boots, already heavy, became heavier. Quilted-cotton armor, already hot, became hotter as the sun climbed higher. When the morning wore on with still no sign of the boat, Narváez tried not to worry. There was no sign either of people other than themselves, though at times the company gave up on hugging the coast and traveled on inland paths when the land was too broken up with lagoons and inlets.

Finally, after about ten miles of this, the vanguard encountered a small party of Indians, two or three of whom they immediately took prisoner. How this was done is not described, but the usual method was by trickery during a trade. Given the state of the horses and the dense nature of the coastline, they were certainly not chased down by the horsemen, which was a popular tactic in open lands. A decade later, De Soto carried a large supply of chains and neck irons for controlling captured Indians, and Narváez almost certainly did the same.

Tellingly, the first thing he and his men wanted from these new captives was not news of gold, but of food. "We showed them maize to see if they recognized it, because up to that point we had not seen any sign of it," recalled Cabeza de Vaca. They had been in Florida less than a week, but already Narváez and his officers were most concerned about their food supply, which had been so disastrously depleted by their misfortunes at sea. It wasn't an auspicious sign for the future of the mission: the Safety Harbor peoples of the central Gulf Coast of Florida were not great farmers.

Maize was developed as a crop by gardeners in central Mexico five to seven thousand years ago and gradually spread both north and south, reaching the southeastern United States around 200 A.D. The earliest "incontrovertible evidence" of corn in Florida are some charred kernels or cobs from the ninth century A.D. that archeologists found in the Panhandle region. In Tampa Bay, the ninth century is also roughly when an earlier people known as the Weeden Island culture began to lose ground to cultures more like the Safety Harbor people encountered by Narváez's army, and archeologists speculate that influences filtering down from the great corn-fed Mississippian societies to the north played a role in that transition. The large architectural mounds, for instance, are distinctly reminiscent of societies to the north. But the signature Mississippian trait—extensive corn cultivation and the resulting food surpluses—did not take hold: isotopes of carbon and nitrogen in Safety Harbor skeletons confirm that corn was not a large part of the local diet.

They did grow a very small amount of corn, however, and Narváez's new prisoners seemed to gesture that they knew where there was some to be had. They led the forty conquistadors along a well-used path to a town "at the back of the bay." This was probably Tocobaga, a large settlement located in the present village of Safety Harbor (from which, of course, the culture gets its modern name; "Tocobaga" is also sometimes used to describe all the Tampa Bay Indians.) There were impressive mounds overlooking the bay, and many well-made houses around the central plaza, and for a moment Narváez thought this might be the place for his base. But the fields were paltry, with nothing but "a small amount of corn that they had planted there." There wasn't nearly enough to feed his army. Worse, it wasn't even ripe.

The disappointed Spaniards wandered around the village in small groups, occasionally looking out at the bay for any sign of the brigantine. Tocobaga was just a much bigger version of the village at Boca Ciega: fishing nets, piles of shells, a few clever tools, pottery, and some second-rate furs. There was seemingly nothing of interest at all until one of the soldiers called out to Narváez to come and take a look at something strange. He had discovered a collection of large crates of the sort used by the merchants of Castile to pack trade goods bound to and from the Americas. There were also some fragments of European shoes, some iron, and some pieces of canvas and other fabrics, including some feather-work that looked like it was from Mexico. This was unexpected, but having so recently lost one of their own ships, the Spaniards assumed these items had been salvaged from some earlier wreck.

What was inside the crates was far more alarming. Each contained a corpse, carefully arranged and wrapped in a painted deerskin. Neither narrative mentions a building, but it's obvious to archeologists that Narváez and his men had entered a charnel house, probably perched at the top of a burial mound. The only existing eyewitness description of such a building is from a De Soto survivor, who said he saw "a temple, on the top of which perched a wooden fowl with gilded eyes."

The smell was ripe. As in many Native American societies, the proper care and veneration of deceased ancestors was a central part of Safety Harbor spiritual life. The bodies of the dead were stored in charnel houses until a mass interment in the mound could take place, either when a head chief died or when the charnel house became too full of bones to hold any more. Some of the corpses therefore were recently deceased, and others were in a state of moderate putrification. On most, however, the flesh had rotted enough that the bones had been ceremonially cleaned. In some southeastern cultures, trained bone-pickers known as a "buzzard men" did this grizzly job while mourners watched and sang. In the only known eyewitness account of the process among the Tocobaga, bodies were "broken" into pieces and stored in large jars for "two days until the flesh separates from the bones and they take the bones and they joine [sic] one bone with another until they mount the man as he was and they place him in a house that they have as a temple while they fast four days."

The resulting skeletons were bundled into tightly flexed positions and may, like the bodies in the Castilian crates, have been wrapped in painted deerskins. When fourteen hundred graves were removed from one of the Tocobaga mounds in the 1930s, many of the skeletons were still together, curled up with arms wrapped around knees or tucked to the chest in a fetal position. Others had been carefully disassembled and rearranged: a skull with a stockade of the long bones vertically around it, or a bed of horizontal long bones with a skull nestled among it.

Narváez, Cabeza de Vaca, and the other officers climbed to the top of the mound to the charnel house where, dizzy with the putrid smell, they looked at the chests with their enclosed corpses. Something about the scene—the sculpture-topped temple, the boxes, the bodies, the pierced and tattooed Indians, their skin quite red with ochre paint—gave the head priest a distinctly bad feeling. Friar Juan Suárez had been to Tenochtitlan very shortly after its fall to Cortés, and though the fabulous Mexican capital was by then in ruins, he had seen the great ossuaries there, stacked high with thousands of sacrificial human remains. This was nothing like that in scale, and there were no human sacrifices among the Florida Indians. Still, Suárez was confident he knew evil-doing when he saw it. These crates with their bodies in them set up on a mound in the middle of an unredeemed jungle were some kind of devilish idolatry, he told Narváez. They must be burned, he said, and the other friars nodded in agreement.

Torching the charnel house was not an action calculated to win friends among the Tocobaga. Most of what is known of the veneration with which Safety Harbor peoples viewed their ancestral remains comes from a member of the Narváez expedition named Juan Ortiz, who was later captured by a Tampa Bay cacique named Hirrihigua and lived among the Indians for a dozen years before being rescued by the De Soto expedition. Much of his captivity he spent as a night watchman at a charnel house, where wolves and Florida panthers visited regularly hoping to drag off an easy meal. The charnel house was also visited each dawn by relatives of the deceased, and Ortiz was certain that if he failed to protect the bodies of their relatives, his captors would execute him.

Further evidence that the people of Tampa Bay took their spiritual lives seriously came a generation later, when Pedro Menéndez de Avilés, the founder of Saint Augustine, Florida, visited Tocobaga in 1566. According to a member of the delegation, the cacique at that time thanked Menéndez for not killing his people and burning the town, and then went on to say "that his people had fled, and he had remained in the house of his gods, his house of prayer; that he would sooner die than forsake them."

The Tocobaga were not likely to be happy, therefore, when one of Narváez's soldiers brought a torch from a nearby cooking fire and put it to the crates. But there's nothing in the two eyewitness accounts to suggest that as the smoke of the burning bodies rose, so did the anger and resistance of the townspeople. It's possible the corpses in the crates were Christian shipwreck victims and that the Indians therefore didn't care about their loss: Cabeza de Vaca implied this, though readers in his own time wondered why Narváez and his men didn't bury the bodies if they were really Christian. A more likely scenario is the Tocobaga Indians did try to resist and learned a quick and bloody lesson from Narváez for their trouble.

There's no mention anywhere in the Narváez eyewitness accounts of the kind of violence associated with other sixteenth-century Spanish invasions. Unlike the chroniclers of De Soto's later expedition to Florida, for instance, who say offhand things like "this governor was very given to hunting and killing Indians," the Narváez survivors limit themselves to passive mentions of "taking" a few prisoners here or there. There is secondary evidence, however, that during this first week Narváez turned to his tried and true methods of shocking the Indians into quick

submission by loosing on them the horses, dogs, steel, and other awe-
some weapons of the Spanish Empire. (In Cuba, he famously sat stone
still on his horse while below him a great massacre of unarmed villagers
was carried out.) According to the sixteenth-century historian Garcilaso
de la Vega, in Florida Narváez sicced the attack dogs on the mother of
Hirrihigua, the same Tampa Bay chief who later captured Juan Ortiz.

This would have been an instant and gruesome death sentence for
the old woman, who wouldn't have gotten far if she tried to run, and
couldn't have lasted long if she tried to resist. "The reader must understand," said one of De Soto's men in reference to a similar dog attack, "that
to set the dogs on (an Indian) is to make the dogs eat them or kill them,
tearing the Indian to pieces." The old woman's children and neighbors
could only watch the carnage, and, indeed, the horrifying spectacle of
her death was precisely what was intended when the dogs were loosed.

The dogs used by the Spanish during their invasion of the Americas were incredibly strong and vicious. Narváez's old chaplain, Las
Casas, who had an eye (some say an imagination) for the egregious
outrage, said the beasts were often raised on human flesh in order to
develop a taste for it. "The dog charged like a mad horse and dragged
the Spaniard behind him," he recalled of one incident in which a soldier lost control of his animal. "He was unable to hold his grasp and let
go of the leash. The dog jumped on the cacique and with his powerful
jaws tore at the man's stomach, pulling out the intestines as the cacique
staggered away."

The fact that neither of the Narváez survivors' accounts mentions
dogs means very little: those sources also don't mention harquebuses,
armor, mail, helmets, and pikes, all of which the army surely possessed.
Dogs were as standard as horses in the Spanish invasions: Cortés took
them to Mexico, Ponce de León took them to Puerto Rico. In Panama,
Balboa used dogs not just in battle but to enforce good Christian sexual

mores and dress codes: "The (native) king's brother and a number of other courtiers were dressed as women, and according to the accounts of the neighbors shared the same passion," recorded Peter Martyr. "Vasco ordered forty of them to be torn to pieces by dogs."

Narváez's peers would have thought him highly irresponsible not to bring dogs with him to Florida: as a De Soto survivor said, "The conquistadors in the Indies have always used greyhounds or fierce and valiant dogs in war."

Lest Hirrihigua forget his mother's grizzly end, when the dogs were done with their work, Garcilaso reports that Narváez ordered his men to slice off the chief's nose and hand it to him. Like the use of dogs, this sort of amputation was a common practice from Old World battles between Christians and Muslims that was quickly imported to the campaigns in the Americas. It was explicitly terroristic, intended not so much to punish the actual victim as to send a message to others. Las Casas saw Indians sent home with both their severed hands hanging around their neck by a string as "letters" to their leaders not to resist. Similarly Cortés cut off the hands or thumbs of seventeen Tlaxcalan "spies" and sent them back to their captain, and De Soto sent six prisoners back to their chief with "their right hands and their noses cut off, with the message, that, if he did not come to him to apologize and render obedience, he would go in pursuit." Hirrihigua's defacement was the one-eyed Narváez's forget-me-not.

Unfortunately for Juan Ortiz, Hirrihigua had a good memory. When Ortiz and two or three other members of the expedition were captured by his village a few months later, he forced them to run naked through the town plaza while his archers took turns potshotting at them. "But to delay further the death and increase the agonies of their victims, and at the same time to prolong and enliven their own festivity and enjoyment, they were to discharge only a few arrows at a time," reported Garcilaso. Around and around the naked conquistadors ran, trying to avoid the missiles until only Ortiz was still alive, begging for mercy from the noseless chief. The shooting only stopped when the daughters of Hirrihigua, joined by their mother, begged, Pocahontas-style, for Ortiz's life.

But Hirrihigua wasn't finished exacting his revenge. According to the De Soto survivors who later rescued him, Ortiz was put on a barbecue—a word the Spanish picked up from the Arawaks of Hispaniola—and cooked until he was "half-baked and blisters that looked like halves of oranges had formed on one of his sides. Some of these blisters burst and much blood ran from them so that they were painful to behold." He eventually escaped to a neighboring village, but one whole side of him was a massive scar. After his rescue, Ortiz became De Soto's translator and died in the winter of 1541–42, somewhere along the Arkansas River.

Quite coincidentally, the only remnants of a Safety Harbor channel house that archeologists have ever found were at a place not far from where Juan Ortiz was eventually rescued.* At a site called Parrish Mound 2, archeologists in the 1930s found the postholes of a trapezoidal building roughly twenty-five feet on a side. The posts were six to ten inches in diameter and were set side-by-side, stockade style, into four-foot-deep holes. In one corner the walls were double thick, and

---

* The story of Juan Ortiz is one of the enigmas in the occasionally murky record of the Narváez expedition because elements of his tale don't quite jibe with the selection of Boca Ciega Bay as the initial landing place. Ortiz was a crew member on one of Narváez's ships, possibly the brigantine, and told his rescuers he was taken prisoner in a village called Ucita where he and the others on board had expected to find traces of the expedition that had gone inland. They were lured ashore by "a cane sticking upright in the ground, with a split in the top, holding a letter, which they supposed [Narváez] had left there." The only logical places the ships might have expected to find such signs are the initial landing place, which is generally accepted to be Boca Ciega Bay north of the mouth of Tampa Bay proper, and the village where the crates were burned, which is usually assumed to be Tocobaga (Safety Harbor, Florida). The problem is that most students of the De Soto expedition are equally certain that Ortiz was rescued on the southern shore of Tampa Bay, just inside the opening (Bradenton, Florida).

there was an altar or a platform there, presumably for storing bones. There were also a few timbers lying across the space, most likely rafters from the collapsed roof.

In addition to providing the only physical clues to charnel house architecture, Parrish Mound 2 is also unusual in that it had all been burned to the ground. Most of the burials in it were cremations, which "deviates completely from normal burial practices" for Safety Harbor mortuary sites of that period. Especially in one corner, where archeologist Gordon Willey surmised there had been an altar, there was "a dense deposit of charred wood, ashes, and semi-burned human bone." As for the structure itself, Willey wrote in 1949 that "the destruction of the temple mortuary by fire may have been a purposeful act, or it may have been accidental or the result of warlike depredations. The results would have been much the same."

When archeologists today take note of the unusual nature of the site, they don't mention Narváez's burning of the crates as a possible cause.* A more likely explanation is a change in mortality and burial practices due to diseases brought to the area by later Europeans. Still, Parrish Mound 2, which is entirely gone now, is a curiosity. Several of the surrounding sites turned up a relative trove of Spanish artifacts both from the Narváez–De Soto period and later in the sixteenth century—eleven thousand seed beads at Parrish Mound 1, for instance. But there were almost no European items of any kind found at Parrish 2, suggesting that it burned before widespread contact with Europeans. Found in the mound were only three glass beads of an indeterminate age and a scrap of brass that two archeologists think might be "hardware of some type." In photographs it looks suspiciously like a fragment of a filigreed hinge.

* When traveling with De Soto a dozen years after Narváez, Vasco Porcallo also burned an entire village in the vicinity.

Leaving Safety Harbor

The charnel fire died down. The dogs were leashed. And with the Indians' attention now assured, the interrogation resumed. The lack of corn and gold was disappointing, but as the questioning went on, Narváez at last began to hear what he wanted to hear. From up on his horse, he looked down as his men held up corn to the faces of the terrorized Indians and gestured, pointed, and otherwise made themselves clear. *¿Donde?* Where? Where? And in response the Indians always pointed north and said "Apalache." Or was it "Apalachen"? Or "Palachen"? It didn't matter; it was north and, apparently, far away. But it was clearly there, and they had corn aplenty.

Even better, the Tocobaga said the same thing when Narváez ordered that they be shown gold. "They indicated to us by gestures that very far away from there, there was a province called Apalachen, in which there was much gold," remembered Cabeza de Vaca. In fact, anything the Spaniards held up and showed them, the Tocobaga were certain could be found in great plenty to the north.

Apalachee! It was a land of gold and plenty that would make Narváez richer than Cortés, and he was itching to get back to the main camp at Boca Ciega Bay and command the rest of his army to prepare to march north. But where were Miruelo and the brigantine? He decided to stay one more day in the vicinity of the bay, presumably to give the boat a chance to find them.

There was another, even more pressing, question to be answered as well. Gold a long way away was inconvenient but surmountable; Cortés's Tenochtitlan had lain far inland from the coast. On the other hand, food a long way away could spell disaster. If Apalachee was as powerful as it sounded, Narváez couldn't conquer it with half-starved troops. If it were as far away as the Tocobaga seemed to be saying, he might not even get there without more food. Before he could commit to an assault on Apalachee, he needed to know more. So, after someone put a cross and a letter in a prominent place near the beach, in case Miruelo and the missing brigantine should happen by, Narváez mustered his force and told them to make ready to march. Leaving the smoldering charnel house behind them, and with their four chained "guides" near the front, they slogged back into the shade of the forest. Their course was now north, away from the bay in the general direction of Apalachee.

It wasn't promising corn country, with water over the ankles as often as not and alligators sinking silently below the surface before the noisy column drew near enough to see them. Mile after mile of unbroken forest and swamp, with nothing to encourage them except the presence of the trail they were on. They carried on the next day through more of the same, and finally, after twenty-five or thirty miles of this, they entered another village. It was smaller than Tocobaga, only fifteen deserted houses set in a clearing. It may have been coincidence that the inhabitants were gone, but more likely runners up from Tocobaga had preceded them with the news that there were violent and powerful men on the way. In other words, the "letter" Narváez intended to send by cutting off Hirrihigua's nose had gotten through.

Narváez didn't care that the population was gone. He didn't need to see the heathens to learn what he wanted to know, which was that they grew more corn in the fields around this village than in the two previous towns. "A good-sized plot of sown maize that was ready to be harvested," recalled Cabeza de Vaca, and some more that was dried and stored. Once again, the grain wasn't enough in itself to replenish their supplies, but it represented a trend in the right direction. Every move north had brought more corn: more here than in Tocobaga, more in Tocobaga than at the landing place on Boca Ciega. It stood to reason, therefore, that they would find steadily more corn all the way north to Apalachee, where there would be more than they could eat while they counted their gold and converted their new labor force to Christianity. After two days in the village "without seeing a single Indian," but with full stomachs, Narváez and the reconnaissance team returned to the ships.

In his mind, and in conversations with Cabeza de Vaca and the other mounted officers as they traveled again along the shore of the great bay they had discovered a week before, Narváez examined the possible explanations for Miruelo's continuing absence. There was always the chance that something catastrophic had occurred, like the ship having been wrecked or attacked. But there had been no foul weather. What's more, he had chosen the brigantine for the mission precisely because it was designed for shallow-water navigation among shoals and the like. Brigantines were relatively small, only forty feet or less in length, and were rigged with lateen sails that allowed them to tack closer to the wind than the square-rigged or mixed-rigged larger vessels. And if the wind failed, or a river needed to be explored, they were fitted out with banks of great oars that could be pulled by one or two sailors each. If you were the type to assume the worst, you didn't set out to conquer continents, and Narváez didn't conclude that Miruelo's ship had been lost.

Instead, he figured that Miruelo hadn't found the opening to the large bay. This was considered a possibility even before the boat set off, and Miruelo's orders included the proviso that "in case [he] did not find the port, [he was] to travel to Havana and pick up Álvaro de la Cerda's ship." La Cerda was in command of the ship that had been waiting for them in Havana when they were blown off the coast of Cuba more than a month before. Accentuating the mounting concern about supplies, Miruelo was explicitly instructed that "both ships should get all the supplies they could and take them to where the Christians and the governor were waiting."

For the same reasons that he doubted Miruelo had wrecked—he had the brigantine and he had good weather—Narváez didn't believe that his chief pilot had navigated past the opening to Tampa Bay without seeing it. A better explanation, Narváez mused as they plodded their way back to the base camp, was that Miruelo had missed the opening because it wasn't there; that he was wrong, in other words, about the mouth of the bay being south of their landing point in the first place. "He had already miscalculated," as Cabeza de Vaca put it, "and he did not know where we were nor where the port was."

By the time the forty members of the reconnaissance team trudged out of the woods into the base camp on Boca Ciega Bay, the remaining three ships had been unloaded under the eye of the comp-troller, Alonso Enríquez. Collected on the beach, or up in the single large building in town, were the assorted barrels, baskets, casks, and large terra-cotta olive jars, in which the Spaniards transported most of their supplies. The thirty-six horses that had not gone with the exploring party were ashore by now as well, gaining strength with each passing day.

The total of their supplies looked even more meager collected together in one place, and the entire company was on short rations. Still, the 350 men and 10 or 11 women who were not a part of the reconnaissance team were relieved to be off the cramped ships at last. They were revived even more when the news trickled around camp of the great gold and riches waiting for them in the land of Apalachee off to the north. Despite all their earthly trials so far, a kingdom would in fact be theirs. It was the last day of April, 1528.

After a night's sleep, Narváez assembled his officers and announced that he planned to divide the army. The majority, some three hundred people in all, would march with him north toward Apalachee through the corn lands they had just discovered. The remaining hundred, including all of the women, would travel with the ships along the coast heading north "until they reached the harbor." It was, the pilots said, ten or fifteen leagues away at the most. There, the land party and the ships could reconvene.

There are multiple opinions among historians about what harbor Narváez thought his ships would find by heading north along the coast. Some have argued that the company was so disoriented at this point that the port they expected to find not far away "in the direction of Las Palmas" was Las Palmas itself or the settlement on the Rio Pánuco, both of which are on the coast of Mexico more than a thousand miles away. Others suggest that there was some entirely imagined port that they were seeking. But the explanation that most simply fits the expedition's stated belief that the harbor wasn't far, and the subsequent actions of the ships, is that Narváez was still looking for the opening to Tampa Bay, which is clearly shown on the maps from the period. If Miruelo hadn't found it to the south, he reasoned, it must be to the north.

Cabeza de Vaca was appalled by the plan to divide the company. When, purely as a legal formality, Narváez asked the opinion of the collected officials, the treasurer was adamant. "I responded that it seemed to me that by no means should he leave the ships without first assuring that they remained in a secure and inhabited port," he later recalled.

Cabeza de Vaca had a variety of reasons for his position and felt it was his duty to be frank. He pointed out that the pilots didn't all agree about where they were or what they would find up the coast. Furthermore, the horses were still all but useless, half-starved and wobbly from the weeks at sea. He worried that "we were traveling mute, that is, without interpreters, through an area where we could hardly make ourselves understood by the Indians or learn about the land what we desired to know, and that we were entering into a land about which we had no information, nor did we know what it was like, nor what was stored in it, nor by what people it was populated, nor in which part of it we were located."

But above all, the treasurer worried that they didn't have enough provisions for a march inland. This last point was crucial, because Cabeza de Vaca did not share Narváez's optimism about the lands they had seen during their reconnaissance tour. Far from showing signs of being able to support a traveling army, he said, it was "poor land and uninhabited."

What Cabeza de Vaca proposed as an alternative to Narváez's plan is not clear. In his memoir he says he told Narváez he thought they should load everything back on the ships "and go seek a port and a land better for settling." In the other surviving narrative of the expedition— the so-called Joint Report of the Survivors, which, it should be remembered, Cabeza de Vaca also helped to write—he argued that the ships should be left where they were at Boca Ciega. "And, this done, the governor and those under his command then could go inland, and they would have a place, a marked spot, where they could return to find the people whenever they wished."

In the ensuing debate, no one disputed Cabeza de Vaca's dire summary of the current situation. But the idea of getting back on board the ships, which had been nothing but trouble for the enterprise thus far, was not a popular notion. "To embark was to tempt God," the head priest, Juan Suárez, said.

And as for leaving the fleet in the shallow bay where they currently were, that was out of the question because it wasn't adequately protected or deep. You couldn't even call it a port, said Narváez. Furthermore, there was no food supply at Boca Ciega to support the crew who would have to remain with the ships. No one needed to be reminded of the calamitous outcome of the recent Ayllón expedition to the Carolinas, which had attempted to settle in a place with no food to eat and no Indians to force to work.

The cleric Suárez spoke at some length. He reiterated the facts of the geography as far as they knew them: there was the salt water of the Gulf lying to their west, and there was the salt water of the great bay they had discovered laying a day's march to the east. They knew from seeing it that the bay extended far inland, an observation that corroborated Miruelo's assertion that the bay he knew of extended inland twelve leagues. (A rutter, or pilot's guide, from the same period described a bay in that vicinity as being "large, ten leagues long and five leagues wide at the mouth.") Finally, they could be reasonably certain the opening wasn't to the south of where they currently were because Miruelo would have found it and met the reconnaissance team on the bay or have come back and informed the other ships.

If they stayed near the coast and headed north, Suárez said confidently, they would have to come across the mouth of the bay. "They could not miss it," he promised.

Cabeza de Vaca was still unconvinced. Hadn't they already sailed along the coast to the north of their present position for two days prior to their arrival at the shallow bay? They hadn't seen the opening then, so how could they be so certain they would find it now? It was stormy then, Suarez would have replied, stormy enough that a ship had been lost and they had stayed offshore. In land as flat as Florida, even a large opening would be easy to miss.

But to Cabeza de Vaca, the fact that Miruelo had not yet reappeared was all the more reason not to split the company and send both parts to who knows where. The ships should stay in the shallow bay precisely because they "were waiting for the brigantine and the larger ship which were supposed to be coming with provisions from Havana," he insisted.

Cabeza de Vaca lost the argument. When Narváez asked that the opinions of the other officers present be recorded, Alonso Enríquez, the purser, said he agreed with his commanding officer. The inspector, Alonso de Solís, also sided with Narváez. Only the notary, Alaniz, agreed with the treasurer that it would be wiser to leave the ships somewhere certain before setting off into the continent with the majority of the expedition. Having duly consulted his officers, Narváez announced that he would carry out his plan.

At this point Cabeza de Vaca made a request that soured his relations with Narváez for the remainder of the expedition. Not satisfied by having his positions heard and recorded, but outvoted and overruled,

Cabeza de Vaca attempted to pull rank as the king's treasurer. "I, having seen his resolution, requested on behalf of Your Majesty that he not leave the ships without their being in port and secure, and thus I asked that my request be certified by the notary we had there with us," Cabeza de Vaca recalled.

It was Narváez's turn to be appalled. In accordance with his contract with the emperor, he had consulted with the other royal officials as required, he had listened to their opinions, he had won over the majority of them by the force of his arguments. Cabeza de Vaca had no right, he said, to make such a request in the name of the king, and he flatly refused to allow Alaniz to even prepare the document. Instead, he ordered the notary to prepare a document certifying that there was not enough food in the current location to support a colony. Nor was there an adequate port to protect the ships. Because of these certified factors, he told Alaniz to write, the king's governor had decided to move the colony to another location. Alaniz complied, though neither he nor the document ever made it back to Spain.

Narváez was disgusted with what he considered the namby-pamby concerns of Cabeza de Vaca, and he didn't want him around making any more absurd requests if he could avoid it. It was he—Narváez and his friends—after all, who had conquered Cuba and Jamaica and Hispaniola, and they hadn't done it by sticking around harbors worrying about ships. It was outrageous that this glorified butler, who had done nothing in the Indies but manage to lose a couple of ships in a hurricane, in a harbor, was presuming to know better than he did how to settle and pacify La Florida. As for not knowing what lay ahead, what did Cabeza de Vaca imagine exploring to be?

Since Cabeza de Vaca was so concerned for the vessels and apparently so afraid of going inland, Narváez told him, he should take command of the ninety men and ten women who were going to stay with the ships. Go find your safe harbor, he said, while I and these brave men and horses with me will go and conquer Apalachee. He made this suggestion, Cabeza de Vaca remembered pointedly, "in the presence of those who were there."

Now Cabeza de Vaca was publicly insulted, and he refused the offered position. Narváez repeated the suggestion, and again Cabeza de Vaca refused. Narváez didn't have the authority to force the royal treasurer to stay with the ships, so there was nothing to be done but adjourn the meeting and ready the troops for the coming march to Apalachee. Rations were issued; a paltry two pounds of cassava bread and a half pound of salt pork per man. This was, at best, a few days food, but the land party could at least console themselves that there were even slimmer rations for those who were to proceed with the ships.

As the preparations for departure continued through the morning and into the afternoon, Narváez fumed at Cabeza de Vaca's insolence and worried about proceeding inland with a divided leadership. He sent an aide across the camp to where the treasurer was packing his own entourage with a message. This time he didn't impugn Cabeza de Vaca's courage, but said he couldn't entrust the job to anyone else. The fleet was supposed to establish a base of operations when they reached the port, so he needed someone with authority for the position. "He was beseeching me to take charge of it," Cabeza de Vaca recalled. But again, he refused the offer.

Finally, Narváez came in person and all but begged Cabeza de Vaca to take command of the ships. It was a matter of reputation and honor, Cabeza de Vaca explained. "I responded that I refused to take that responsibility because I was certain and knew that he would not see the ships again nor the ships him," he remembered telling Narváez. But he would still rather accompany a doomed land party than "give occasion that it be said, as I had opposed the overland expedition, that

I remained out of fear, for which my honor would be under attack." In sum, he announced grandiosely, "I preferred risking my life to placing my honor in jeopardy."

Narváez couldn't argue. Honor was serious business among Spaniards of the period, as it often is with fighting men. It wasn't something that could be earned, however; it came with birth. As the historian J. H. Elliot has written, honor was "an attribute of nobility, the exclusive preserve of the high-born." Honor could be lost, however, and Cabeza de Vaca and Narváez both knew it. As Cortés had said in his final speech to his troops before he confronted Narváez in Cempoallan, "[I]t is better to die worthily than to live dishonored." In the end, although Narváez asked several other members of the expedition to go speak with the treasurer and try to convince him otherwise, Cabeza de Vaca would not consent to take command of the ships.

The treasurer wasn't the only member of the party with premonitions about the coming march inland. At some point during the day of preparations, the woman who had spent much of the past year making pessimistic prognostications took Narváez aside and told him not to go inland. No one was going to come out alive, she told Narváez. Or at best, a few might come out, but only through the miraculous actions of God.

For sixteenth-century Castilians, such predictions were not blather to be taken lightly. Like most Europeans of the period, the conquistadors had no trouble mixing large doses of secular superstition in with the "revealed miracles" of their Christianity. As Simon Schama has pointed out, even to such scientific geniuses as Kepler and Newton "astrology meant as much as astronomy." Christopher Columbus, meanwhile, was famously "stargazy," having filled the margins of his copy of Plutarch with notes about "auguries, portents, and occasionally more recondite forms of divinations like Numa's conjuration of demons."

With their long heritage of religious miscellany, Spaniards were particularly good at picking and choosing whatever wisdom suited them from a wide range of sources. "A free mixture of community traditions, superstitious folklore and imprecise dogmatic beliefs," is how one historian described the religion of the average sixteenth-century Spaniard; "part pagan," wrote another, "believing in portents and omens no less than in the mysteries of the Church."

Narváez had consulted with the soothsaying woman at other times during the expedition, but at this point he was not in a mood to be dissuaded from marching to what he saw as his true destiny in Apalachee and beyond. After conquering Mexico, Cortés had taken as his personal symbol a man standing beside the wheel of fortune ready to nail it in place with a legend that read "I shall hammer in the nail when I see that there is nothing more to possess." Whether Narváez saw the image after his release from Cortés's prison cannot be said, but the alternate prophesy that he now described to the naysaying woman was taken straight from the real experiences of his old nemesis.

Anybody who went with him was going to have to "fight and conquer many and very strange peoples and lands," Narváez assured her. "In conquering them, many would die, but those who remained would be of good fortune and would end up very rich according to the information he had about the wealth that there was in that land."

Historians have tended to side with the fortune-teller, describing Narváez's decision to split his forces and separate the majority of them from the fleet as a turning point from which there was no possible outcome other than disaster. Samuel Eliot Morison, an admiral as well as an historian, called the decision "fatuous," and deemed Narváez "the most incompetent of all who sailed for Spain in this era." Cyclone Covey, an early translator of Cabeza de Vaca's narrative, called the decision a "stupid" one that "sealed the doom of his expedition," and added that Narváez himself was "a grasping bungler." Robert Weddle called him "aggressive and brutal, as well as impulsive and stupid." And Cleve Hallenbeck branded Narváez "a man of little ability, judgment, or foresight . . . the tragic experiences of Narváez's predecessors in Florida, Juan Ponce de León, Francisco de Garay, and Lucas Vásquez de Ayllón, had taught him nothing."

But Narváez wasn't looking to the example of Ayllón, who did divide his ships from his men with disastrous results. Or of Ponce de León or Garay. Like most of his other decisions, good or bad, he made this one based on what had worked for him before in Cuba, where he had ranged overland with an army less than half the size of his current one. He had discovered gold; he had gotten rich! He also drew on what had not worked for him more recently in Mexico, where his troops didn't quite mutiny but weren't quite loyal either. Now here they were, only a week on the ground in La Florida, and his treasurer was fomenting discord and demanding notarized documents undermining his authority.

Most of all, though, Narváez was thinking about the Jack of Hearts, Cortés, who when faced with wavering resolve among his own rank and file ran his ships aground on the shores of Mexico. "Thinking that if I left the ships there they would make off with them and leave me practically alone, I found a means under the pretense that the ships were no longer navigable to pile them up on the shore," Cortés wrote in a letter to the emperor that was published in 1522 and that Narváez certainly read. "On this all abandoned any hope of leaving the land and I set out relieved from the suspicion that once my back was turned I should be deserted by the men whom I had left behind in the town."

Elsewhere Cortés explained that without the fleet his troops "had nothing to rely on, apart from their own hands, and the assurance that they would conquer and win the land, or die in the attempt."

What had worked in Mexico for Cortés would work again in La Florida for Narváez, and the sooner the ships were gone the sooner he and his army would, like Hannibal, be across the Rubicon. Then the only direction available to the three hundred people who had tied their fates to his would be onward with him to glory and wealth.

As for the righteous and timid Cabeza de Vaca's unwillingness to stay with the ships, there was nothing more to be done. Honor was honor. Narváez gave command of the fleet to a judge named Caravallo and made ready to march north.

8

Across the Withlacoochee

On that same afternoon, which was either Friday the 1st of May, 1528, or Saturday the 2nd, the ships slipped back out of the opening on the falling tide. On shore, a long, vaguely organized line of men and animals disappeared into the forest. The vanguard included some of the forty horsemen and all of the chained-up native "guides" captured during the previous week. The back was presumably protected by a rear guard of horsemen as well. But in between, little about the three hundred members of Narváez's army to conquer North America resembled an organized fighting force. There were no uniforms; each man chose his own style of armor, and bought and owned it outright. Clothing, too, was a matter of personal selection and varied depending on the wealth and prestige of the conquistador. The fashion of the day was for doublets of linen or cotton that were tight-fitting around the chest. They wore their sense of style on their sleeves, which were adorned with rolls at the shoulders or, as the Gentleman of Elvas said of his comrades in De Soto's army, "many plaits and slashes." Puffy pants ended at mid-thigh or knee, below which they wore stockings. The richest among them, including Cabeza de Vaca and Narváez, wore silk from Grenada, and velvet. "They loved color," the historian Charles Hudson has said of the conquistadors, "green, blue, black, and especially red."

Within the column snaking its way north through the forest from Boca Ciega Bay, people organized themselves largely based on the identity of their primary patron or master. Compared with the North American expeditions of De Soto and Coronado that followed in his wake, Narváez's was a relatively down-at-the-heel army. Still, the richer members of the expedition had their own personal entourages of slaves and free servants who marched together in small clumps. Some of the wealthier caballeros also brought with them poorer cousins and others who were allied with them in an informal, manorial way. "Criados," they were called.

Cabeza de Vaca had his own special entourage. In addition to his personal equipment, the treasurer was required to transport a special chest or chests. In the last paragraph before the traditional signature "I, The King," his commission read: "I command you that all the gold, pearls and those things inferior, coming to your possession as our fifths of excise and dues, as well as in all other ways, be placed in a chest with three different keys, one to be kept by you, and the others by our Comptroller and Factor of said land, in order that no gold be taken thence except by hands of the three, avoiding frauds thereby and the irregularities that might otherwise occur."

The king's coffers were still as empty as everyone else's on the expedition, but the day was yet another beginning point and the mood was guardedly optimistic among most of the company. It wasn't as heady as the day they had sailed from Sanlúcar de Barrameda, now already a year in the past; everyone knew that a faction led by Cabeza de Vaca believed they were following a madman to their doom. Still, those who had joined the expedition of their own free will hadn't come this far to rot on ships. They came to test their Christian arms and will against the naked savages, and so far there had not been a European casualty in battle. Their rations might be low, but within two days, Narváez promised, they would be in the beginning of the corn-growing country that the reconnaissance team had reached. And from there, it would be onward to the golden temples of Apalachee.

But there was no corn after two days of marching. No corn after three days of marching, nor five, nor seven. In order to be certain of finding the expected opening to Tampa Bay, Narváez kept the army as near to Florida's Gulf Coast as practical. This made for particularly toil-some going, mushy and damp. "Obstructed by woods and swamps," De Soto's men said of the region a dozen years later, "the land round about was greatly encumbered and choked with a vast and lofty forest." By the second week, however, the wide swamps along the coast north of Tampa Bay had forced the army inland on to the drier, sandier terrain of the Weeki Wachee dune field and the Chassahowitzka coastal strip. This was better for the horses, which were useless to the point of being liabilities in the swamps. It was easier on the foot soldier's feet as well. But the forested dunes were no better for their stomachs. Each person's pound of bread by now was gone, their half pound of bacon a memory.

Meanwhile another whole week went by with no sign of natives, no sign of corn, and no game that they were good enough hunters to shoot. Just trees and more trees, some of which they were reduced to eating: the only food they found in this maddening shady place were the hearts of young palmettos, which they chopped open with the swords they had expected to be using against cannibal kings, dog-faced monsters, and beautiful one-breasted Amazons.

Nights brought no relief. People collapsed in clumps wherever they were when the light ran out, or wherever they found a good patch of palmetto to chop open and devour. Guards were posted, but no one really slept soundly. Even though Cabeza de Vaca recalled that "during this entire time we did not find a single Indian, nor did we see a single house or village," they could never be certain they were safe. As a contemporary remembered of the campaign in Mexico: "We were all accustomed to sleep ready shod, with our arms on us and our horses bitted and saddled, and with all our arms ready for use." But the morning light always brought nothing but the trees. By this point they would have welcomed a fight. Even hostile Indians would have food.

Going hungry wasn't a new experience to Narváez, particularly if he originally came to the New World on the second voyage of Columbus, as some suggest. Scarcity and starvation were common facts of life during the initial conquest of Hispaniola, and he probably reminded his followers that no gains had come in the New World without hardship. The head priest, Fray Juan Suárez, could speak as well of his own harrowing journey across the mountains and deserts of Mexico.

But for the majority, including the treasurer, it was an unexpected trial. "We were most certainly new to these hardships," Cabeza de Vaca wrote later, "beyond the fatigue we suffered, we came very worn out from hunger." Hunger made some men quick to anger: where were these so-called guides they had captured taking them? It made others sullen and quiet. But no one needed reminding that there were no ships in the harbor behind. Just as Narváez planned, there was now only the golden city, lying somewhere ahead of them.

"Apalachee," the survivors later recalled, "was what they most wanted in the world."

By the end of two weeks in the Florida jungle any change was welcome, and at last on the fifteenth day there was a perceptible lightening of the sky in the canopy ahead. Maybe it was finally the bay, some thought, and the ships would be waiting. But when the vanguard finally broke through to the water's edge it was only a winding tea-colored river. The Withlacoochee meanders out of the Great Green Swamp of central Florida before making its way about a hundred circuitous miles to the Gulf of Mexico near the present Floridian villages of Cracker-town and Yankeetown. For most of its length and most of the year the Withlacoochee is a slow stream, but where and when Narváez and his army reached it, the current was too strong and deep to wade. As was usual with Spanish expeditions of the period, most of the men didn't know how to swim.

The porters and slaves were put to work chopping trees into lengths that could be lashed together into rafts. It was slow work, made slower by their exhausted and famished state. Swarms of mosquitoes devoured the sweating laborers, who at last managed to cobble together a few logs and begin ferrying people across. It took the better part of the afternoon, but Cabeza de Vaca remembered that by day's end, "with very great difficulty," the entire company was on the north bank of the river—at which point, two hundred well fed, but unhappy, Indians marched out of the woods.

At least, the Indians looked unhappy. Narváez, flanked by armed men, approached the leader and began the usual theater of hand signs and single words; pantomimes of eating to show the desire for food, samples of corn and gold held out to show what they were looking for. Beads, bells, and iron chisels were offered for trade. "Apalachee," they said hopefully, and pointed north. "Apalachen, Palachen." The enslaved guides from Tampa Bay were brought forward. But whatever Narváez did or said to the river people, it didn't work to his satisfaction, and he ordered an attack.

"They gestured to us in such a way that we had to turn on them," said Cabeza de Vaca blandly. As usual, there's maddeningly little detail given in the surviving narratives about casualties on either side. All they say, in fact, is that a half-dozen Indians were quickly captured and added to the chain gang.

Who these people were is hard to say. The river marked the transition between the various chiefdoms of the Safety Harbor culture and a territory dominated by other peoples, about whom far less is known. The fact that they appeared and shook their longbows at the expedition as soon as it crossed the Withlacoochee suggests they were defending that boundary. They may have been part of a culture known to archeologists today as the Alachua, who migrated into the lands between the Withlacoochee and Suwannee Rivers around 600 A.D. They came from somewhere to the north, possibly in Georgia, pushing out a previous culture. Unlike the Safety Harbor peoples, they generally didn't build mounds, but they did pile up sprawling shell middens, including at least one that covers an area larger than twelve football fields.

More importantly for the hungry foreigners, they grew corn. When the six new captives guided the company to their village a half league away, the Spaniards were overjoyed to see it was surrounded by cornfields: "great quantities of maize, ready to be harvested." Like the English pilgrims in Cape Cod a century later, Cabeza de Vaca says they all "gave infinite thanks to our Lord for having aided us in so great a need," but no thanks that anyone remembered to the local women who had cleared the fields and planted them. Then they helped themselves. For three days, the army did little or nothing but stay around the village devouring corn and resting sore muscles.

Whether they recovered enough strength to rape and pillage is not said, but reports from other expeditions of the period suggest it was not a fortunate thing to be a young woman in the village where a Spanish army encamped. Nothing in Narváez's past suggests he possessed a more conscientious attitude than Cortés in Mexico, whose men complained and argued over the division of "good-looking Indian women." Or than De Soto, whose secretary noted that the women and girls who "were not old nor the most ugly" were enslaved in order "to make use of them for their lewdness and lust," and baptized "more for their carnal intercourse than to instruct them in the faith." If they had any sense, the Alachua villagers probably fled as soon as Narváez and his army arrived.

Cabeza de Vaca spent many of his spare moments wondering about the ships, and by now he wasn't alone in his obsession. The starvation march of the previous weeks had focused the thinking of some of the other officers, who now began to lean toward the treasurer's view that they would be wise to find the port and the ships sooner rather than later. By now Miruelo might even be back from Cuba with two ships full of supplies, they mused. The Indians told them that the ocean wasn't far away.

But when Cabeza de Vaca, Solís, and several others approached Narváez to suggest he send a scouting party to the coast, he was less interested in the ships than ever. After fifteen days' march without running into the expected opening to the bay, he had decided that it didn't exist after all, or that they had missed it altogether. He was also convinced that they were much farther inland than the Indians were suggesting. "He replied to us that we should not trouble ourselves with talking about that," Cabeza de Vaca recalled, "because it was very far from there."

True to form, though, Cabeza de Vaca kept talking about it. In fact, he says he "begged" Narváez repeatedly to reconsider, and at last the one-eyed governor succumbed. The following morning, therefore, Cabeza de Vaca took Captain Alonso del Castillo and his company of forty and headed west, following the winding river downstream. They were on foot because Narváez wouldn't permit them to take horses on a quest he felt was useless at best and dangerous at worst. But they made good time, and by noon the water at their feet tasted brackish. They had reached the estuary, proving that at least they had been right and Narváez wrong about their distance from the sea.

But there was no view to the open Gulf of Mexico, only countless dishonest passes between swaying sawgrass hummocks that appeared to go on all the way to the horizon. Every step along the muddy shore sent millions of tiny crabs in clicking masses up into the grass in front of those in the lead, like a retreating wave of crustaceans that flowed back onto the shore behind the last of them to pass. There were countless birds working the shallows, and sprays of mullet in great schools out in the estuary, flickering up out of the water to escape larger fish below. But there were no ships on the horizon. Only grass and more grass.

At some point Cabeza de Vaca and his men removed their boots in order to wade out and look for the open sea. They slogged on this way for five or six more miles, the water never above their knees. In places the bottom was firm packed mud, which made for easy going. Elsewhere, though, they hobbled across vast beds of oysters, "from which we received many cuts on our feet and that were the cause of much difficulty for us."

Finally, after several hours of this they reached a place where the Withlacoochee River cut a deep channel through the flats in front of them, across which they couldn't pass. On the other side of the deep water, to the south, it looked as if there might be some higher ground, but there was no way for them to get there. No way either to continue along the side of the channel they were on.

The forty barefoot conquistadors stood there, five miles out into the middle of an estuary, looking at the endless undulating saw grass, the wheeling birds, wondering what to do next. The sun by now was on its way down in the direction they wished to travel but could not: on its golden way down over Mexico. There was no sign of a port, no sign of the ships. No sign of hope or help. They turned around.

When they got back to the camp, Cabeza de Vaca convinced Narváez to send another exploratory party down the other side of the river. That Narváez didn't resist this new request suggests that the discovery that they were close to the sea had altered his attitude somewhat. Here they were, after all, in a village that supported two hundred warriors and had a large supply of corn. If, in fact, he could find a serviceable harbor only a half day's march away, it might be possible to establish a temporary base here for their assault on Apalachee. Yes, he would send another party, and this one could take horses.

Because of their wounded feet, neither Cabeza de Vaca nor Alonso del Castillo went on the second mission. Instead the new party was lead by a captain named Valenzuela, who was in Narváez's inner circle and who, for what it's worth, had the same last name as Narváez's wife. He recrossed the Withlacoochee at the same place the army had come in the opposite direction a half a week previously and, with fifty foot soldiers and six men on horseback, followed the sinuous stream down its southern bank. As Cabeza de Vaca had suspected, the land on this side of the river was drier, and Valenzuela and his men were able to progress all the way to the open gulf. For a day or more they studied the long, horizontal boundary between water and sky, but there were no verticals breaking the grey-blue view, no masts.

The hope that they might spot the three ships under the command of Caravallo was not entirely fanciful. After all, when the expedition divided into land and sea factions roughly three weeks previously, these vessels had left the shallow bay of the landing site with orders to head north along the Florida coast. From what Cabeza de Vaca was able to learn many years later, the ships did do just that, but as with everything regarding the fleet from the moment it left the coast of Cuba, the language is ambiguous when it comes to distances and locations. "The ships set sail and continued their voyage, and they found no port ahead, and they turned back," is all Cabeza de Vaca says.

How far north did they go before turning around? It stands to reason that they went at least the fifteen leagues within which the pilots had predicted the mouth of the bay would be found. They also presumably made an effort to get further north than the expedition's initial sighting of Florida two days before entering Boca Ciega Bay. In other words, they very well may have sailed past the mouth of the Withlacoochee River, both on their way up the coast, and again when they were heading back south. But they didn't do it during the two days that Valenzuela and his company spent exploring the coast, and like Cabeza de Vaca a few days before, Valenzuela returned to the main camp disappointed. There was no bay or port deep enough to permit ships to anchor, he told Narváez, but only broad expanses of knee-deep water. They had seen a half-dozen canoes crossing from one side of the bay to the other, full of Indians who "wore many plumes." And that was all.

The ships by then were most likely already back in Tampa Bay enjoying the provisions Miruelo had brought back from Cuba and wondering what had become of Narváez and his army. Cabeza de Vaca learned later that after giving up the search for the bay to the north and turning south, the three ships had at last found the long-sought harbor "five leagues below where we had disembarked . . . and it was the same one that we had discovered, where we found the crates from Castile."*

Whether Miruelo was already waiting for the fleet when it arrived in Tampa Bay or arrived there a few days after the ships is not important. It typically took vessels of the time about four days to make the crossing between Havana and Tampa, so he had plenty of time to have made the round-trip while Caravallo and the other ships were still traveling north. What was important to the men and women on the rest of the fleet was that he had successfully collected the ship that was supposed to join them in Havana and had brought it back to Tampa Bay with him. And that both vessels were loaded with fresh supplies.

Narváez's fleet was intact again and reasonably well provisioned. But where in the world was the land party? While Caravallo and Miruelo debated how next to deploy the ships, a hundred miles to the north Narváez ordered his men to break camp and push on to Apalachee.

* It is this description, placing the original "small bay" five leagues north of the mouth of Tampa Bay, that makes Boca Ciega the most likely landing place.

9

The Sound of Flutes

Dulchanchellin applied his paint and sharpened his exquisitely long fingernails. For a week or more he had received regular reports from his spies of a loud and mysterious group of bearded men and strange animals pushing their way toward his land from the Potano villages to the south. They were now only five days' travel away, and the time had come to confront them, to find out who they were and what they wanted in Timucua territory.

The ochre and other pigments were really just accents to highlight the magnificent canvas that was his body; if descriptions of other Timucua-speakers pertain to those of the Suwannee Valley culture, to which he likely belonged, most of Dulchanchellin's skin was covered with elaborate and beautiful tattoos, which were pricked in with thorns and porcupine quills. "The forepart of their bodies and arms they also paint with

A Timucua lord preparing to lead his followers into battle. Engraving (after an original by Jaques Le Moyne) from De Bry's Americae, *part II, 1594.*

pretty devices in azure, red, and black, so well and properly, that the best painters of Europe could not improve on it," said a sixteenth-century French explorer who encountered the Timucua a little north and east of where Narváez was. Another Frenchman, René de Laudonnière, who attempted to establish a colony in Florida in 1564, said of both men and women "the most part of them have their bodies, arms, and thighs painted with very fair devices, the painting whereof can never be taken away, because the same is pricked into the flesh."

The long nails were practical as well as ornamental. "They let their nails grow long both on fingers and toes, cutting or scraping the former away, however, at the sides with a certain shell, so as to leave them very sharp," said an illustrator who went along with the Laudonnière expedition. "And when they take one of the enemy they sink their nails deep in his forehead, and tear down the skin, so as to wound and blind him."

When Dulchanchellin was ready, he draped a painted deerskin over his shoulders and summoned his bearers and a company of his fighting men. They were armed and decorated like their leader, but their intent wasn't hostile. In fact, Dulchanchellin wanted to be certain not to surprise the strangers, perhaps causing them to react hastily, so he also summoned his court musicians.

By the time Narváez and his army heard the wailing sound of Dulchanchellin's flutes wafting through the forest, they were once again in a state of near exhaustion and starvation. They had left the village by the Withlacoochee River in late May, slightly rested by their stay and partially rejuvenated by the corn they had appropriated. For a while they made good progress north through terrain they described as "flat land with hard sand and many, although sparse, pine groves, with the pine trees somewhat far apart." This was easier ground to travel than the denser forests they had come through, but as usual it was broken up with the multitude of swamps and sloughs in that part of Florida. "Many large and small lagoons," is how Cabeza de Vaca later remembered them, "some very difficult to traverse."

Worse than the occasional hard going, however, was the return of empty stomachs. The plentiful corn of the town near the Withlacoochee had proved once again to be more of an anomaly than a harbinger of well-fed days to come. Occasionally in those weeks after leaving the Withlacoochee, they passed through deserted villages where they found and devoured small amounts of grain. These most likely belonged to a people known as the Potano, whose main population centers were to the east of the route taken by Narváez and company. Survivors of the De Soto expedition mentioned Potano villages with names like Ytaraholata, Utinamocharra, Malapaz, and Cholupaha, but very little is known of the Potano, other than that they usually decorated their pottery with the imprints of corncobs.

But there was never enough corn in the Potano villages to satisfy three hundred appetites, and more often than not the army marched for days on end—sometimes as many as five—without seeing any sign of either Indians or corn. They saw plenty of deer in the woods, but they were never able to shoot any and finally stopped wasting their crossbow points trying; they were not hunters. In "extreme need of supplies" is how the survivors later described the situation.

On top of it all, there were the merciless clouds of biting flies and mosquitoes that descended on both the people and animals whenever they neared the swamps. The Narváez sources, obsessed as they were with hunger and disease, don't describe the torment, but the English naturalist William Bartram, who visited Florida in the 1770s, remembered traveling "almost from sunrise to his setting, amidst a flying host of these persecuting spirits, who formed a vast cloud around our caravan so thick as to obscure every distant object; but our van always bore the brunt of the conflict; the head, neck, and shoulders of the leading horses were continually in a gore of blood: some of these flies were near as large as humble bees."

It was now the middle of June, and many in Narváez's army were beginning to weaken noticeably. Others, with their immune systems depleted by malnutrition and exhaustion, began to suffer from chills and fevers, the first symptoms of a mysterious illness that became gradually more apparent with each passing week. And even the healthiest among them had festering sores on their backs "from carrying their weapons on their shoulders," sores that wouldn't heal and couldn't be helped.

So when, on June 17th, they heard music in the woods, they

didn't know whether to be alarmed at the prospect of a battle in their condition or cheered by the prospect of at least finding people from whom they might get some food. "Flutes" is Cabeza de Vaca's term, but other descriptions and illustrations suggest the breath was blown through the instrument rather than across an opening as in a modern flute. In 1564, the French Huguenot artist Jaques Le Moyne de Morgues met a Timucua lord who was escorted by "twenty pipers who were playing some primitive thing discordantly and raggedly, merely blowing the pipes as hard as they could. These pipes are no more than extremely thick reeds with two holes, an upper one where they blow and a lower one where the breath comes out, as with the pipes or tubes of organs."

Bartram, who otherwise found Native American music "irresistibly moving, attractive, and exquisitely pleasing," was also unimpressed with the wind players he heard. They have "a kind of flute made of a joint of reed or the tibia of the deer's leg," he wrote. "On this instrument they perform badly, and at best it is rather a hideous melancholy discord, than harmony. It is only young fellows who amuse themselves on this howling instrument."

Melodious or howling, the flutes announced a diplomatic rather than military approach. "Messengers from Uçachile, a great cacique, went and came, playing on a flute for ceremony," remembered one survivor of the De Soto expedition. "Every day they came out to the road, playing upon flutes, a token among them that they come in peace," said another. Similarly, when Dulchanchellin and his large honor guard emerged into view, it was immediately apparent to Narváez and his officers that no attack was imminent.

Nonetheless, it was an impressive sight. The retinue Le Moyne described included "seven or eight hundred splendid-looking men, strong, hardy, athletic and highly trained as runners, who were carrying their weapons in the way they usually do when about to go to war." The

Timucua were larger than the Europeans and, as mentioned, painted and tattooed in a manner that a later visitor described as "hiero-glyphics: commonly the sun, moon, and planets occupy the breast; zones or belts, or beautiful fanciful scrolls wind round the trunk of the body, thighs, arms, and legs, dividing the body into many fields or tablets, which are ornamented or filled up with innumerable figures, as representations of animals or battle with their enemy, or some creature of the chase—and a thousand other fancies."

Some wore intricate feather-work: Le Moyne in 1564 saw "many pieces of a stuff made of feathers, and most skillfully ornamented with rushes of different colors." He also said "all the men and women have the ends of their ears pierced, and pass through them small oblong fish-bladders, which when inflated shine like pearls, and which, being dyed red, look like a light-colored carbuncle." They wore their hair very long, but trussed it up on their head in a complicated bun secured with "a lace made of herbs." Feathers and arrows are mentioned by later sources as being tucked into the knot.

From his perch on the shoulders of his bearers, Dulchanchellin surveyed the collection of strangers. They had unusual clothing and skin of various colors, and he may have wondered if it was natural or applied the way he and his people painted themselves red. A few were positively black, most were lighter with hairy faces, while the porters had skin more like his own before it was tattooed. They were all gaunt and dirty but looked formidable nonetheless. Those on the backs of animals were particularly impressive, sitting almost as tall as he was on his litter. He instructed his bearers to take him over to the one-eyed one who appeared to be the leader.

Dulchanchellin and Narváez met for an hour, and through the usual theater of pantomimes and attempted pronunciations of the few local place names they had picked up, Narváez thought he got the

Timucua leader to understand that they were on their way to Apalachee. Even better, "It seemed to us that he was an enemy of the people of Apalachen, and that he would go to help us against them."

In his memoir, Cabeza de Vaca stressed that it was only by hand-signs and gestures that the Spaniards came to believe Dulchanchellin was an enemy of the Apalachee, but the conclusion is supported by the experience of the De Soto expedition eleven years later. The previously mentioned chief, Uçachile, was similarly hostile toward his northern neighbors. The archeological record, as well, indicates a strong cultural division between the people of the Suwannee River and the Apalachee to the north.

Narváez was elated by the prospect of an alliance. He knew Cortés had only toppled Montezuma's great empire with the aid of allies gathered during the march inland to Tenochtitlan. They were "numberless" by Cortés's own estimate, "more than one hundred and fifty thousand men." Narváez had even seen some of these local warriors used against himself in the disaster at Cempoallan. But now, here at a strategic point on his own march toward his own land of plenty, a "great lord" had come out and announced that he also was an enemy of Apalachee. With the right gifts, this Dulchanchellin could become Narváez's own version of Cortés's Totonic ally, his own "fat cacique." He ordered the trinkets brought out: "beads and bells and other items."

The beads were of the turquoise colored Nueva Cadiz style, which were square in cross section, or of the blue and red faceted chevron style, which were rounder. The bells were what modern archeologists call Clarksdale hawk-bells, because they were sometimes used by the Spanish on the feet of hunting birds and because the first specimen was found in a presumed De Soto archeological site in Clarksdale, Mississippi. They were small brass globes, about an inch in diameter, that resembled sleigh bells and were often attached to the tackle of the Spanish horses, which may have added to their allure among the Indians. As for the "other items" mentioned, small iron chisels and scissors have turned up in archeological sites from the period. There were other goods that didn't survive to become a part of the record: Ayllón brought bright-red caps and kerchiefs to the Atlantic coast among his trade items a few years before, along with linen shirts, and combs.

By the end of the parley, Narváez was confident that he had closed the deal. Dulchanchellin, too, was in a generous mood, and grandly removed his painted deerskin cloak and presented it to the foreign cacique. Then, after motioning to Narváez and his army that they should follow him, he ordered his bearers to carry him home. The hungry army followed along dutifully.

Late in the day they arrived at the banks of the Suwannee River, which rises in southeast Georgia and wanders for 250 miles across northern Florida to a swampy ending in the Gulf of Mexico. The Timucua had no trouble crossing, having come over it in order to meet Narváez and his army. But the Spaniards, with their heavy gear and inability to swim, were at a loss. The river was too wide to throw down a bridge of logs, and the current was too swift for the sort of makeshift rafts they had constructed to cross the Withlacoochee a few weeks before. This time, therefore, the slaves and laboring class were put to work felling an ancient tree and transforming it into an immense dugout.

The hidalgos and caballeros among the company were prevented by their code of honor from working on the boat construction, and most of them sat in the shade napping or watching the progress and discussing the implications of Dulchanchellin's visit. There wasn't much to say, just small talk about how it would be good to have full bellies again once they got to the village. Talk turned to horses, as it always did with hidalgos, and to bragging. Finally, Juan Velázquez got bored enough, big-headed enough, hungry enough, or just plain stupid enough, and in a grand gesture of chivalric bravery, he charged into the water on his horse, where he was immediately swept out of his saddle by the current.

Either Velázquez was not a swimmer or he was wearing his armor. He hung desperately onto his reins while the river carried him and his horse downstream. On shore, everyone ran along the banks, yelling encouragement, wondering how to help. In the end, though, the horse could not save the man but the man could, and did, drown the beast. Dulchanchellin's people found the bodies of both and told the Spaniards where to go to collect them.

It was a sobering event. Velázquez was a native of Cuellar, and almost certainly a nephew or cousin of Narváez's old patron, the governor of Cuba, and possibly an in-law of Narváez himself. But more than his rank and connections, and the senseless nature of the accident, his drowning was startling. Despite all the hardship and hunger, other than the sixty who disappeared in the hurricane in Cuba nearly a year before and those on the ship that wrecked off the coast of Florida, no one on the expedition had perished. "His death gave us much grief," remembered Cabeza de Vaca.

They gave him a Christian burial there beside the Suwannee, and then ate his horse. It was a bittersweet feast, to be sure, but the animal "fed many that night."

The following morning they crossed the river and set off along the path through the forest to Dulchanchellin's village, which was another day and a half away. Having made the decision to be hospitable to the strangers, Dulchanchellin immediately sent provisions over to them when they arrived and set up camp just outside of his town. In addition to maize, the Timucua raised beans, squash, pump-kins, and tobacco, which they stored in granaries constructed of stones and earth, and thatched with palm fronds. They also harvested acorns and hickory nuts from the surrounding forests and were superb hunters. Having eaten nothing for two days but 1/300 of a horse per person, Narváez's army was overjoyed at the bounty.

But in a way that was becoming depressingly familiar, the alliance between Dulchanchellin and Narváez evaporated almost as soon as it was formed. That same night, when a few of Narváez's men went down to the watering hole, the twang of a bowstring broke the silence and an arrow whizzed through the group. It either missed its Spanish target entirely or glanced off his cuirass, for "God willed that they not wound him," but the good will was shattered.

No reasons for the sniper attack are given. It may have been unauthorized action by one of Dulchanchellin's young warriors, signify-ing disunity over his policy of accommodation. It could have been in revenge for some abuse by the Christians toward their hosts; during the conquest of Cuba, Las Casas had urged Narváez to segregate his troops from the Indians in order to prevent undesirable and pro-vocative violence. Finally, it may have been an intentional probe or provocation, though that seems least likely given the lateness of the hour and the apparent lack of preparations for combat among the rest of Dulchanchellin's people.

It's notable that the attack at the water hole came so soon after the accidental death of Velázquez and his horse: in Mexico, Cortés was extremely careful to hide the corpses of the first horses killed, fearing the demystification of the Spaniards and the animals in the eyes of the Indians. But there's nothing to suggest the natives of North America ever harbored the idea that the invaders were anything other than

ordinary mortals, albeit bearing high-tech weapons. Narváez's predecessors, Ponce de León, Francisco de Cordóba, and Lucas Vasquez de
Ayllón, had been attacked outright almost as soon as they landed. And
when De Soto explicitly tried to convince a great king who lived on
the Mississippi that he and his fellow Spaniards were deities, he
received the following reply: "As to what you say of your being the son
of the Sun, if you will cause him to dry up the great river, I will believe
you: As to the rest it is not my custom to visit any one, but rather all of
whom I have ever heard, have come to visit me, to serve and obey me,
and pay me tribute, either voluntarily or by force." De Soto was no
Moses, or at least the Mississippi was no Nile, and Old Man River kept
on rolling along, even after De Soto's own corpse was sunk in the river
to hide his death from the Indians.

The men from the watering hole rushed back to tell Narváez and
his officers of the attack, but as it was growing dark and there was no
sign of warlike activity in the town, he decided to wait until morning to
take up the matter with Dulchanchellin. But at first light, there were
no Timucua to be found, "because all of them had fled." Once more,
therefore, after taking time to collect what food they could find in the
abandoned town, the expedition set out along the road to Apalachee
with neither allies nor willing guides. They were not alone for long,
however. By mid-morning the rear guard noticed that "Indians who
came prepared for war" were following them.

Narváez ordered his captive guides to call the pursuers closer, but the
overtures were ignored. He sent a company back to engage them, but
the Timucua fell away, always staying just out of range or disappearing
into the forest on either side of the path. Then, as soon as the column
began marching forward, they reappeared behind it.

It was a tiresome game, and after several attempts to engage the gadflies directly, Narváez laid a trap. The main column clumped forward as noisily as possible, the rear guard charged backward once again. But this time, when the harassing Timucua were driven out of sight, a small company of horsemen hid themselves on either side of the road. Then came the tense minutes, with the mounted ambushers stroking the necks of their horses, willing them to silence as first Narváez's rear guard passed noisily by and then, as hoped, came Dulchanchellin's fighters. Silent, silent, and then, all at once, charging, snorting, yelling "Santiago."

As Cortés had instructed his horsemen to do, and as they had practiced at home with squashes and pillows, Narváez's cavalry aimed their long steel-tipped lances into the necks or faces of any painted body that wasn't quick enough to get off the open road and into the cover of the forest. Aim lower and you risked getting your lance stuck in a writhing torso that could pull you off your horse. In the end, an unknown number of Timucua were killed, and three or four were captured alive. "And we took these Indians as guides from that point onward." The harassment from the rear stopped.

"They led us through terrain that was very difficult to traverse and wonderful to see," said Cabeza de Vaca in a lovely and dramatic section of his memoir.

There are great woods there and marvelously tall trees; and there were so many fallen trees on the ground that they barred our way, so thoroughly that we could not get through them except by going a long way around them, and with great difficulty; and of those that had not fallen, many were split from top to bottom from the lightning that strikes in that part of the world, where there are constantly great storms and tempests.

We marched with these difficulties until the day after the feast of Saint John, when we came in sight of Apalachee without the knowledge of the Indians of that land; we offered many thanks to God when we saw that we were so close to it, believing that what we had been told about that land was true."

The promised land of Apalachee at last lay before them. It was the 25th of June, 1528, nearly two and a half months since the day they had first come ashore. It had been a hard and disappointing slog, but they had only lost one man and one horse, which was good. Those who knew Mexico could tell immediately that Apalachee was no great capital like Tenochtitlan, fit to remind them of the imaginary cities of their chivalric novels. But half-starved and exhausted, and without any allies, they were in no condition to topple an empire anyway.

"On finding ourselves where we desired to be, and where they told us there were so many foodstuffs and so much gold," said Cabeza de Vaca, "it seemed to us that a great portion of our hardship and weariness had been lifted from us."

10

In the Land of the Apalachee

His men may have been happy to see Apalachee at last, but Narváez was dismayed by the appearance of the place. It was nothing but forty scrawny houses, built low to the ground out of thatch. It was so small, in fact, that he didn't even bother to go in himself but sent Cabeza de Vaca and Alonso de Solís in to secure the place with a company of only fifty foot soldiers and nine cavaliers. "The Spaniards attacked it daringly," said the survivor's report, "but they found no resistance. There were no men, they were all away, so they took the women and children."

Someone escaped unnoticed, however, and ran to tell the Apalachee men of the invasion. While Cabeza de Vaca and his troops were wandering around the town wondering where all the promised gold was, they were suddenly attacked by the townsmen who rushed in and let loose a hail of arrows. Solís's horse was immediately hit and killed, but none of the Spaniards were seriously injured, and the defenders were driven out without being able to rescue their families. "In the end they fled and left us alone," said Cabeza de Vaca, who sent word back to Narváez that all was clear to bring the rest of the army into town.

The initial absence of the men of Apalachee confirms Cabeza de Vaca's observation that the army had arrived in the region without being detected. Throughout most of the American Midwest and Southeast, territories were centered on rivers, with native nations controlling the good growing lands on both sides of the stream. In Florida, however, the spring-fed rivers typically don't generate fertile floodplains, and rivers tended to be borders between peoples. The Withlacoochee had marked a transition between Safety Harbor and (presumed) Alachua peoples, and the Suwannee was similarly a border between the Alachua and Dulchanchellin's Timucua. And at some point after leaving the Timucua, the army crossed the Aucilla River into Apalachee territory.

From the Aucilla, Apalachee land extended west to the Ochlocknee River and north to the neighborhood of the modern border with Georgia. In the south it ended at the Gulf of Mexico in the corner of the Panhandle. Nowhere in the territory, however, were there any peaks of the great spine of mountains that now bear the Apalachee's name. French cartographers who had seen neither the geography nor the Indians named the Appalachian Mountains on the rumor that the Apalachee Indians possessed gold and the theory that gold came from mountains.

But there was no gold in Apalachee. No silver. No precious stones or pearls.

The only good news was there was plenty of food: "a great quantity of maize that was ready to be harvested, as well as much more that they had dried and stored," said Cabeza de Vaca. The towns and villages through which Narváez and his men had passed during the march up from Tampa Bay were influenced by the corn culture of the great river valleys to the north, but Apalachee was the real thing. It was, in other words, a full-blown, highly stratified, corn-fed Mississippian nation.

The storming of the village in Apalachee was the first contact between Europeans and the Mississippian cultures that had flourished for centuries in the great river valleys of North America. At places like the Toltec Mounds and Baytown in Arkansas, or Moundville in Alabama, or Spiro in Oklahoma, and most of all near the confluence of the Missouri and Mississippi rivers at Cahokia, Mississippians built cities of earthen mounds with buildings on top and levees surrounding them. Their architectural energy had peaked before Columbus's first voyage, but the nations were still in the fullness of their power when Narváez and his army arrived. And though the battle between Cabeza de Vaca and the Apalachee defenders was lopsided in favor of the intruders, it was an anomaly. Starting with the Apalachee, various Mississippian people eroded and destroyed the grandiose dreams of conquest not just of Narváez, but also of the even larger armies of De Soto and Coronado that followed in his wake.

Only after centuries of plagues and pandemics had reduced populations to a point where Mississippian cultures disintegrated into smaller, less stratified forms of organization did the French and English heirs to Spanish imperial ambitions defeat them. So diminished were Mississippian societies by that time that the northern Europeans were incredulous that the ancestors of the Indians they encountered in the eighteenth and nineteenth centuries could have built the abandoned mound cities. Nature, or the Mexicans, must have done it, some argued. Others thought only the Danes could have achieved it, or

A 20-inch-high pre-Columbian copper breastplate recovered from an Apalachee archeological site at Lake Jackson, Florida. (Courtesy of the Florida Division of Historical Resources)

perhaps the Tartars. Even Martians were suggested. Some said the Spanish themselves built the mounds, and that their accounts of powerful kings and queens carried in litters by adoring and occasionally uppity vassals were vastly overstated.

But outsiders didn't build the Mississippian cultures. They were built by the river-valley Indians on corn (maize) and population growth that began around 750 A.D. and replaced the "late woodland" culture that preceded it. Whether more corn led to more people, or more people led to increased reliance on agriculture is not clear; the bow and arrow, which appeared only a few hundred years before corn, may have spurred larger populations until the game gave out. Climate change has been suggested as a factor, as has the invention of baby food. But whatever the cause, by the eighth century A.D., Mississippian populations were growing rapidly and archeologists know they were eating more corn because their remains have the corn-eater's telltale rotten teeth.

Most communities grew at least three varieties of maize, which ripened at different times in the season. As late as 1753, a French missionary in Louisiana wrote that "it is useless for me to enter here in detail all the different ways in which maize may be treated," and then went on to discuss breads, porridges, smoked dishes, hominy, gruels, and other preparations. Mississippians invented new styles of cookware to accommodate their corn diet including *cazuela* bowls for stews and flat ceramic griddles for cooking pancakes in bear grease. Served with the corn were all manner of fish, game, nuts, berries, wild salads, as well as cultivated squash and beans. But whether the women captured and held captive by Narváez in Apalachee cared to prepare all these delicacies for the occupying army is another matter.

After two days, the Apalachee men returned in peace and politely asked that their families be released to them, which Narváez ordered his men to do. This unexpectedly generous gesture on the part of Narváez reflected an awareness of the relatively weakened state of his army. But whatever goodwill was engendered by the release of the women and children was undermined by his decision to hold the male chief of the town as a hostage.

Like the decision to separate from the ships, critics of Narváez, beginning with Cabeza de Vaca, identify this as a crucial failure of judgment. It was an action, remembered the treasurer, "which was the cause of [the Apalachee] being greatly offended." Once again, however, Narváez's strategy deserves to be viewed in context. Holding a cacique hostage was a standard strategy among the conquistadors. It may even have been a familiar tactic to the Mississippian Indians themselves, whose own warfare, says anthropologist David Dye, "was based on organized squadrons that sacked civic centers and captured ruling elites." As usual, Narváez needed to look no further than Cortés and Montezuma for an example of regime change through decapitation. But also as usual, what had worked for Cortés (at least temporarily) was a disaster for Narváez.

Part of the problem was that Apalachee society wasn't as bureaucratically sophisticated as Montezuma's Mexico, so controlling a single leader didn't assure the cooperation of the rest of the nation. A bigger part of Narváez's problem was that he didn't actually have the paramount chief of the Apalachee in his possession; he had the mayor of a small border town.

Narváez and his officers believed throughout their stay in Apalachee that they were in the leading village of the province, but they were wrong. This became apparent to historians as soon as the survivors of the De Soto expedition returned with descriptions of the far larger Apalachee town called Iniahico, or Anhayca Apalache, in which they spent the winter of 1539–40. That town was described by some as having 250 "large and good houses," including a royal compound for the principal chief of the country. Another De Soto survivor said that in order to get to Anhayca they traveled through a "very populous" land that included "many open districts like villages," and that when they got there all five hundred members of the army found lodging in the suburbs of the main town. Debate about the location of De Soto's winter camp ended when an archeologist who was looking for something else entirely found it under downtown Tallahassee in 1987.

By contrast, the village of forty huts that Narváez's army occupied was not very deep into Apalachee territory; only a day's travel or less past the Aucilla River. This explains the disappearance of the men of the village for two days after their women and children were taken hostage; they went to get their orders. Apalachee and other Mississippian cultures were not the egalitarian noble savage variety popular in the American imagination. Everyone was ranked according to their kinship to a semi-mythical ancestor, and a person's rank determined whether he or she had political power, owned certain prestige possessions like jewelry, got to eat certain foods, or participated in religious activities. It wasn't quite a caste system; there were elaborate rules regarding marriage that were specifically designed to stir the economic pot. But everyone knew their place: as one student of the culture wrote, "large-scale corporate labor and social inequality are often considered hallmarks of Mississippian chiefdoms."

What all this meant for the men of the village of forty huts, who returned home to find their families taken hostage, was that consultations with their social superiors were in order. There were several tiers of political authority in Apalachee society, some of them hereditary offices with titles like the *chacal*, the *inija*, and the *inija principal*. Above the local government were regional governors, and at the top was the paramount chief. Over the centuries in Apalachee, certain families had consolidated power, until they constituted almost a royal family. When Spanish missionaries came to Apalachee in 1608, for instance, the caciques of the two main Apalachee towns, at opposite ends of the territory, were brothers.

Runners went immediately from the occupied village northwest to Anhayca-Apalache with the news of the invasion and a request for assistance and instruction. Others headed along the Aucilla River to Ivitachuco, the second most important Apalachee town, which was far closer. Some Mississippian cultures had a separate war chief and peace chief, and Ivitachuco may have been the head peace town. Anhayca was the head war town.

With three hundred armed aliens occupying a border town, the war council held sway and Narváez's hostage, whoever he was, was deemed expendable. As soon as the women and children were safely away, two hundred Apalachee defenders stormed into the town with burning arrows flying. "They attacked us with so much skill and swiftness that they successfully set fire to the houses in which we were lodged," remembered Cabeza de Vaca. The Spanish stumbled out of the smoky houses, coughing and gasping, but it was too late to do much other than watch the attackers sprinting away across the cornfields to the swamps beyond. "We could not do them any harm except to one whom we killed."

The following day, another army of two hundred Apalachee attacked the village from the other side. They were not the same group as the day before, having come "from another area and from other towns and peoples." Apalachee warriors a century later were described as "painted all over with red ochre and with their heads full of multicolored feathers," and those that attacked Narváez and his army were probably similarly attired. The Spaniards were better prepared this time, but once again, after a brief melee in which one insurgent was killed, the Indians just evaporated into the surrounding swamps and woods.

The Apalachee never again chose to confront the Spanish occupiers head-on in a large-scale pitched battle. To some this suggests there wasn't enough central authority in Apalachee to coordinate an all-out effort to drive out the strangers. But a better explanation is that it had become obvious to the Apalachee that the techniques they used in their raiding parties across the river were not working against this large army of aliens with their metal clothing and snorting beasts. Two consecutive attacks from opposite sides of town had failed to drive the occupiers out. The cost, meanwhile, had been high: several of their own young men were dead, and neither account mentions any Spanish casualties. If Apalachee resistance had simply evaporated after the two frontal assaults, the argument that they lacked the political cohesion to resist might stick. But the Apalachee resistance didn't go away. It just changed its strategy. It went guerilla.

Archers harassed Narváez's people any time they were in small groups or away from their stronghold in the burned-out village center. "The Indians were in the marshes and the thicknesses of the wooded areas and from there they would shoot their arrows at all who passed," the survivors remembered. Later, against De Soto's army, Apalachee strategy was the same: "They now engaged us in daily skirmishes."

The new tactic played to the Apalachee's strengths. Like their Timucua neighbors, they were fabulous archers, unlike any the Spaniards had seen before in either Europe or the New World. Their bows, according to Cabeza de Vaca, were as thick in the middle as a large man's arm and were eleven or twelve hand-spans' long. One De Soto survivor said the bows were "perfect," and another account added that they were as tall as the archer. When the Spanish soldiers tried to pull the twisted deerskin string of a confiscated Apalachee bow, they couldn't get it back as far as their faces before their arms started shaking and their strength and aim failed. The Apalachee themselves, however, could easily pull and hold the bowstring well behind their ears.

The earliest European accounts of Floridians consistently describe the Native Americans as larger and stronger than themselves. Typical is Cabeza de Vaca's comment that the Floridians he encountered "are of such large build and go about naked, from a distance they appear to be giants. They are a people wonderfully well built, very lean and of great strength and agility." As usual, it's an assessment echoed by the De Soto troops of a decade later, one of whom said simply, "These Indians of Apalachee are gigantic."

Apalachee arrows were "made of certain canes, like reeds, very heavy, and so stiff that one of them, when sharpened, will pass through a target. Some are pointed with the bone of a fish, sharp and like a chisel; others with some stone like a point of diamond: of such the greater number, when they strike upon armor, break at the place the parts are put together; those of cane split, and will enter a shirt of mail, doing more injury than when armed." This propensity for cane arrows to split and enter the holes in chain mail caused some of De Soto's men to abandon the chain armor in favor of Mexican-style cotton protection.

The accuracy and power of the Floridians' arrows astounded the Europeans. The sixteenth-century historian Garcilaso the Inca, with typical hyperbole, tells of arrows driven entirely through horses: "entering the chest, the arrow had passed through the center of the heart, the stomach and the intestines, and finally had stopped in the bowels." He also describes tests the Spaniards set up in which native prisoners shot arrows through two or even three layers of armor, or entirely through massive oak trunks.

Cabeza de Vaca is more believable when he says he saw an arrow driven six inches or so into "the base of a poplar tree," though he, too, says others saw arrows split oak trees the size of men's thighs. Other witnesses added that "the thickness which the arrows pierced is unbelievable unless seen." The public in Spain got their chance to see for themselves the power of Floridian archers a few decades later, when Timucua marksmen were sent across the Atlantic in 1567 as curiosities and consistently outperformed the best European archers in exhibitions.

Their facility with their weapons came from lifetimes spent hunting game, but they knew how to hunt men, too. Border warfare was endemic, and despite persistent rumors that the Europeans introduced the practice to America, the collection of enemy scalps was already an important status marker before the Spaniards arrived. The tool of choice was a sharp reed, and among the Apalachee, a single scalp entitled a young man to enter the *tascaia* or entry-level warrior class. Three scalps resulted in a promotion to *noroco*; ten scalps, with at least three of them taken from enemies who were themselves decorated warriors, and a man became a *nicoguadca*, or great warrior.

When they were not at war, the Apalachee maintained their fighting trim through rough games. They were, in fact, a singularly sports-crazed people. Both men and women played lacrosse, the semi-universal sport of Native America. Various versions of soccer were also popular in the Southeast. They played a game common among Mississippian cultures called *chunkey*, in which spears were thrown at a rolling disk or ball. But the sport that meant the most to the Apalachee was only played in Florida and southern Georgia. It was called simply "the ball game" and it was a combination of hacky-sack, rugby, soccer, and basketball, with a generous helping of extreme fighting.

The object of the game was for teams of forty or fifty to move a small leather ball down the field by whatever means hands and feet would allow and then kick it against a tall goalpost. If the post was hit, a team scored one point, but if the ball could be sunk into the eagle's nest at the top of the pole, two points were scored. Matches began with a respected elder tossing out the first ball and went on for hours or even days with no time-outs but plenty of injuries until one team scored eleven points. When games got too close, hooliganism was likely to break out among the fans; at five ball games in a row that were held at a Spanish mission near Tallahassee in the 1600s, "not one," said a certain Friar Paiva, "concluded without becoming a live war."

Apalachee sports madness alarmed generations of missionaries like Paiva, who came a century after Narváez. "The ballpost of the devil," Paiva called it, and instituted a commission to look into the sport. In addition to the violence and the "non-Christian overtones" of the pregame ceremonies, Paiva didn't like the way the stars of the game were overpaid and got away with sexual indiscretions for which the hoi polloi would be punished. "No matter what it was, the chiefs and leading men overlooked it all and covered it up . . . fearful that if they punished him he would move to another village."

On the nights before game day, in particular, there was a general permission to "touch and fondle, etc. anywhatsoever woman that was present, whether married or single, because if she did not consent, they considered it certain that all the games that were played on that pole, they would be destined to lose. For which reason the leading men went about solicitous, begging them not to defend themselves." Paiva was especially unhappy when absolutely everyone in town dropped everything they were doing to go watch the game, leaving him alone in his church with no one but the altar boy and the sexton.

Narváez and his army were in Apalachee for nearly a month at the height of the ball game season, but they never heard or saw any evidence of it. This isn't really surprising. The game functioned explicitly as a surrogate for war, and probably wasn't played during times of actual conflict, when young men could better distinguish themselves by ambushing careless Europeans.

Ironically, one of the first of Narváez's army to be killed by the Apalachee was himself a Native American. Don Pedro, the Mexican prince who had witnessed his own country's fall to the Spaniards and was now hoping to help conquer another, took a fatal arrow while going to get a drink. Several others who were with him were also wounded, but when they looked up to try to return fire, there was no one to be seen.

The Indians shot anywhere from three to six arrows in the time it took to load and aim either a harquebus or a crossbow. But even when the Spanish thought they were prepared, they couldn't seem to strike a blow in response to the snipers: "The Indians are exceedingly ready with their weapons, and so warlike and nimble, that they have no fear of footmen; for if these charge them they flee, and when they turn their backs they are presently upon them," said a De Soto survivor. "They avoid nothing more easily than the flight of an arrow. They never remain quiet, but are continually running, traversing from place to place, so that neither crossbow nor harquebus can be aimed at them."

For twenty-five days Narváez kept his army in the village, always under the threat of attack by the insurgents. "The Indians made war on us continually," remembered Cabeza de Vaca, "wounding the people and the horses when we were at the places where we went to get water, and doing this from the lagoons and so safely that we could do them no harm, because they shot arrows at us while being submerged in them."

Three times during the period, small sorties of Spaniards went out on horseback to look for richer prospects. Three times they returned with nothing to report but land that was "very thinly populated and hard to march in because of the difficult trails and woods and lakes that were there."

By the third week of July 1528, Narváez and his officers had had enough of the village of forty huts. Morale was at its lowest point yet; they had marched across Florida and captured Apalachee on the premise that there was gold to be had and civilization to spread. Now here they were, hunkered down in a burned-out town in the middle of nowhere, getting shot at by ungrateful and unrepentant naked giants every time they turned their backs for a moment or two. The Apalachee "were beginning to wound their people," the survivors later recalled. It was a quagmire, and everyone smelled disaster.

Some of the men with horses began to murmur among themselves. Despite taking the precaution of sending his ships away, Narváez was losing control of his army. His body, too, now began to fail him. He was racked with chills and fevers. Like many of his men, he was sick and getting sicker.

With their two months of immersion language skills, the Spaniards interrogated their captive Apalachee cacique and their Timucua prisoners. In every direction around them, they were told, the people were even poorer than they were in the village of forty huts. In every direction but one, that is. Toward the sea, they learned, in a town called Aute, lived friends of the Apalachee who, the Indians said, "had a great deal of maize and they had frijoles and squash, and that because of being so close to the sea they obtained fish."

The people of Aute, which was technically within the Apalachee sphere of influence, couldn't have been very good friends of the cacique of the village of forty huts, the historian Paul Hoffman has suggested: "How else to explain directing the Spaniards to them?"

One possible reason was that you couldn't get to Aute without crossing a vast swamp.

11

Chest-High in Hell

There would be no gold, no gangs of new slaves, no harems of compliant women, and no flocks of new converts to the true faith. As the army made ready to leave the village of forty huts—gathering what food remained and loading it onto the backs of their porters and slaves—there was no denying the obvious. There was no new Mexico in La Florida, and they were in retreat. No one even hoped for riches in this new place they were headed, this Aute. They hoped for beans and fish. A few of the most optimistic, or wishful, among them talked of a harbor and the ships. Most didn't talk at all.

The Apalachee, meanwhile, bided their time. For the previous month, Narváez's men couldn't go to relieve themselves without fearing at attack. But the warfare seemed to stop the moment the army marched out of the village. Even when they sloshed through potentially dangerous lagoons and passes, there was no sign of trouble. They marched all day and made camp, Cabeza de Vaca remembered, "without seeing a single Indian."

The second day also started out well, with no sign of the resistance. The road toward Aute was wet, often up to the Spaniards' ankles or calves. Then the path disappeared entirely into what looked to be a large swamp. They paused, debated, but the guides in their iron collars insisted it was the right road. Up to their ankles they walked. Up to their knees, thighs, waists. They were wading now through tangles of fallen trees on a path that only the guides could see at all. Still, though, there was no sign of trouble.

When they were up to their chests in water in the middle of a massive blowdown of trees and roots, the arrows suddenly rained in. Panicked horses screeched and reared as points of bone and stone buried deeply into exposed flanks and necks. The enraged men stumbled forward, looking in vain to either side for a view of the attackers. Once in a while, remembered Cabeza de Vaca, he saw an archer up on a fallen log pulling his string back to his ear and letting fly. But the attackers only stayed in sight long enough to shoot one or two arrows and then vanished again into the oozy maze of trunks. "They can shoot arrows at two hundred paces with such great skill that they never miss their target," he said. "They wounded many of our men and horses."

Swords, lances, horses, artillery—the prize weapons of the empire— were all but useless in the situation. The harquebusiers might have managed to get off one shot if their powder was dry and loaded before they entered the swamp, but reloading was out of the question. Only the crossbows were able to offer any resistance, and a few patient crossbowmen did manage to wait until they had a good look and sent a bolt into the trees. But after only one shot, a crossbow was nearly useless as reloading required connecting a block and tackle to the line and then

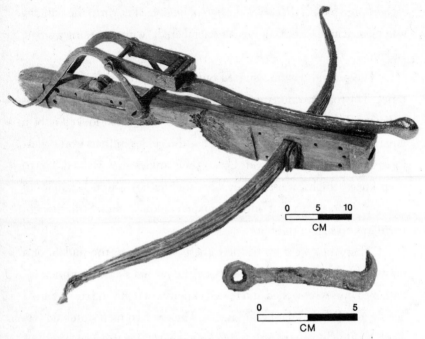

Crossbow recovered from a 1554 Spanish shipwreck off the coast of Texas.
(*From* Nautical Archaeology of Padre Island, *courtesy of the Texas Historical Commission*)

bending over and cranking on a pair of handles, an operation that was almost impossible in water up to one's armpits. In a similar swamp battle, De Soto's soldiers remembered being "harassed more by their own rage than by the weapons of their opponents."

Their padded cotton coats, intended to stop the reed arrows, were soaked and leaden. Their metal armor was almost deadly should one fall over. For once, the porters, slaves, and others with less in the way of protective armor were better off than their heavily dressed masters; they ducked as low as they could in the water and plodded on. The only thing that prevented Narváez's entire army from being bogged down and massacred altogether was that the floor of the swamp was sandy enough to give good footing. Finally, the vanguard began to notice water getting shallower. Then it was at their knees; they were near the end.

A phalanx of Apalachee was waiting for them. "It did us no good to get out of it," Cabeza de Vaca recalled. Progress stalled. In frustration as much as anything else, Narváez ordered an all-out assault. Even the horsemen were told to get off their animals and charge the Indians on foot. It was a desperate, roaring push. As always, though, the Apalachee strategy was to fall away and the conquistadors managed at last to drive the Indians far enough back so that they themselves had time to get fully out of the water and along the road toward Aute. At least they hoped it was toward Aute; during the battle, their captive guide had been liberated by his countrymen. And they hoped, too, that the road would remain drier.

But it didn't. A few miles ahead it disappeared into another swamp. This fen was even bigger than the last one, a mile and a half long. At the water's edge the vanguard stopped and stared in disbelief, wondering what sins they had committed to deserve this. There was nothing to do, though, but say a prayer and wade in. Once again they found themselves up to their chests in water, wondering when the attack would come. But thankfully it didn't come, a turn of events that Cabeza de Vaca attributed only to the Apalachee having used up their ammunition in the morning's fight.

In camp that evening both Spaniards and Indians attended to their wounds. Many Florida Indians carried an herb that they called *chitubexatica*, which was supposed to speed the healing of all kinds of injuries. Aside from that, very little is known of Apalachee medicine other than that in the Spanish mission period of the 1600s, it was the last of their traditional practices they were willing to give up, which was understandable given the state of Spanish medicine at the time.

In Narváez's camp, they began by trying to extract any arrowheads that hadn't been removed immediately at the battle scene. This wasn't always easily done; after a similar battle, a De Soto survivor remembered putting "one knee on the chest of [a wounded soldier] and another on his forehead while trying in vain with both hands to extract the arrow nailed through his eye." Open wounds were sometimes seared with hot oil, and scabs were similarly anointed with cooler salves that were concocted on the spot from available materials. After the big battle at Mabila, De Soto's men "occupied themselves in opening the bodies of dead Indians and taking out the fat to use as unguents and oils for treating wounds." Likewise Cortés's men "bound up the hurts of the wounded with cloths, for we had nothing else, and doctored the horses by searing their wounds with the fat from the body of a dead Indian which we cut up to get out the fat."

There were other techniques as well, none of them particularly scientific. De Soto had with him a medic named Sanjurge, who healed wounds "with oil, dirty wool and incantations." When his dirty wool and oils were lost in a fire he gave up curing for a while, until he discovered that an unraveled Indian blanket and some pork lard would work almost as well. In the 1600s a Spanish missionary on the Texas coast reported that a colleague treated the wounded with "tepid wine, which is, they say, an excellent cure for stabs in the head." In Narváez's camp, however, the wine was long gone. And if the new wounds weren't bad enough, the old fever was gaining ground among the men.

Most of the injuries were apparently not immediately fatal. Indeed, for all the disease and warfare since the army arrived in Apalachee territory, the number of casualties mentioned in the primary sources remained suspiciously low. The three deaths described by Cabeza de Vaca were all persons of high status, suggesting that selective memory was at play. More to the point, when numbers of survivors are mentioned later in the accounts, people and horses have disappeared without explanation.

The morning after the great swamp fight brought no relief. The wounded and the merely weary in Narváez's would-be civilizing army rose and shouldered their loads and began to march again through the interminably soggy ground to . . . where? It didn't much matter anymore, just forward, toward the sea along a path that periodically disappeared under water and had to be found again without the aid of guides. Day after day for nearly two weeks they trudged, never knowing when the next attack might begin. Not all the fens were as solid underfoot as the site of the swamp attack; some of the worst had no standing water, just open grass that looked good until you sunk up to your knees and looked reflexively around hoping not to see an ochre-colored archer in the distance looking back at you. Sometimes, though, you did: Cabeza de Vaca was wounded in one such skirmish. A few Apalachee were killed. Narváez, now wracked with chills, traveled at the rear of the column. And so it went. But progress was steady, if progress is defined simply as forward motion.

Aute wasn't a single town, but rather a collection of villages on the Wakulla River, due south of Tallahassee in what is now the St. Marks National Wildlife Refuge. Archeological digs there have turned up early European trade goods like iron scissors and brass beads, and one burial site "discovered" in the 1930s even contained the telltale chevron beads and Clarksdale bells of the Narváez and De Soto expeditions. No one knows how many times such strange and precious trinkets might have been passed along among the Indians before someone was finally buried with them, so the location of the cemetery is only a general indicator of Spanish presence. Still, the early sixteenth-century artifacts from the St. Marks cemetery have been called "the best evidence for the Narváez expedition."

Beads and bells aside, there's no hint in the written accounts of peaceful trading between the people of Aute and the wounded and feverish army that limped toward town in the summer of 1528. The defenders knew of the impending disaster long before Narváez and company came within sight of their little clearing along the banks of the river, with its collection of houses and gardens, and crops of corn, squash, and tobacco coming along nicely in the languid July heat. Someone had come down from the village of forty huts to give them the news, and the men of the town went out along the road to help harass the strangers in the morass. The women and children, meanwhile, set about to harvest whatever they could, to pack it up, and take it away to a safe place.

When the ragged army was only a few miles outside the town, the defenders of Aute made a last attempt to delay its arrival with an attack on the rear guard. The first sign of trouble were the shouts and cries of a young boy who was the servant or slave of a Spanish officer named Avellaneda. He had lagged too far behind the column and was attacked by snipers. Hearing his cries, Avellaneda turned from somewhere a bit further up in the column and charged back on his horse. But it was too late to help the boy and then, suddenly, he too was hit. "The Indians struck him with an arrow at the edge of his breastplate, and the wound was such that almost the entire arrow passed through his neck, and later he died there," remembered Cabeza de Vaca.

While this was going on, the women of Aute were gathering what last belongings they cared to carry with them into exile. Rather than leave the invaders with shelter, they set fire to their houses. Rather than leave them with food, they set fire to the fields. When the Spaniards slumped in the next day, bearing the body of Avellaneda and carrying others who were wounded, Aute was nothing but a smoldering ruin. All that remained were a few maize, bean, and pumpkin fields that had failed to burn.

In addition to wounds, hunger, and fatigue, the mysterious illness was spreading rapidly. It wasn't smallpox, which they would have recognized, as almost everyone in Spain at that time had either battled the disease themselves or seen it in their families. What's more, smallpox would have appeared earlier if they were carrying it with them from Cuba. Largely on the basis of Cabeza de Vaca's odd observation regarding midsummer Florida that "in that region it is very cold," those who have tried to guess the malady have tended toward various fevers like malaria or typhoid. Whatever it was, many in the army were already sick and "each day more were falling ill."

One of the sickest was Narváez. In a reversal of the usual dynamic between himself and Cabeza de Vaca, on the third day in the burned-out village Narváez called the treasurer to his bedside and "beseeched" him to go look for the sea. He left immediately, taking with him captains Dorantes and Castillo, the head priest, Suárez, and fifty foot soldiers. They followed the Wakulla down to its confluence with the St. Marks River and from there down to Apalachee Bay. By late afternoon they had reached salt water.

Salt water, yes, but as always in this cursed place, there was nothing but shallows and mudflats. No port, no ocean, and of course, no ships. There were, however, oysters: great beds of shellfish that were virtually exposed at low tide, ready for the picking and roasting, breaking and slurping. It was a bonanza of protein, and they sat around their beach fires gorging themselves. It "pleased the men very much and we gave many thanks to God for having brought us there," recalled Cabeza de Vaca.

But oysters turned out to be the only positive aspect of the mission. When Cabeza de Vaca took a smaller party of twenty men to reconnoiter the nearby coast in search of the open Gulf, they returned after two days with the same old bad news: nothing but shallow bays penetrating deep into the mainland, and sawgrass prairies stretching away to the horizon. There was nothing more to do but return to Aute and report to Narváez that the real coast was still far away and not easy to get to on foot or horseback.

The news back at Aute was no better. While the exploring party was away, the Indians took advantage of the split forces of the Spaniards and staged a large nighttime attack. As usual with these lightning raids, casualties were not high on either side, just a few moments of mayhem followed by a quick retreat. Even if one assumes more fatalities among the foot soldiers, slaves, and other less exalted members of the expedition than is reported, Narváez's army was still relatively intact. They were sick and wounded, to be sure, and hungry. Yet despite their condition, they had repelled a nighttime attack by the local resistance. But everyone wondered how long it could last.

In light of the negative nature of Cabeza de Vaca's report, Narváez's decision the following day to march by the same route to the same shallow bay is telling. The place had nothing other than oysters to recommend it, but they were out of options and even a bad place was better than where they were. They couldn't defend themselves indefinitely from nightly attacks, and even if they could hold Aute, why do it? There was no gold. There were no converts. There was no port. There was no point.

As hellish as all the previous marches of the past five months had been, this one was qualitatively different. The horses no longer carried the best and brightest—or at least richest—of the hidalgo warriors. They carried the sick, and there weren't enough of them for the job.

Other feverish conquerors straggled along as best they could or were carried on makeshift litters. Everyone who could bear anything at all hauled corn taken from the fields of Aute, though almost unbelievably, some of the prouder hidalgos still refused to engage in anything that smacked of common labor.

No one doubted anymore that they were in retreat from nowhere to nowhere. "Each one can imagine for himself what could happen in a land so strange and so poor and so lacking in every single thing that it seemed impossible either to be in it or to escape from it," said Cabeza de Vaca.

The few in the company who were able to imagine an escape, did so only for themselves. With their warhorses turned into ambulances, and their commander turned into an invalid, a cabal of caballeros whispered along the road to Aute. The idea was simple and obvious; those who still had horses and health would abandon everyone else and ride off "to find relief for themselves." Cabeza de Vaca didn't name any names, but he said the conspiracy included the majority of the remaining horsemen, of whom there had been forty-two at the outset of the expedition.

Some translators interpret Cabeza de Vaca's narrative to suggest that the conspiracy got so far that the participants "began to steal away" or "began to leave secretly," but it doesn't appear that any actually deserted. Before the plan progressed that far, someone confessed. Narváez by now was "altogether powerless, without strength or the means to impose authority," and it fell to Cabeza de Vaca to prevent the dissolution of the company. He called the conspirators before him and the other senior officers and publicly shamed them for "abandoning their captain and those who were sick and without strength." Most of all, though, he told them that by leaving without permission, the deserters would be disobeying the commands of their king in Spain and thus "removing themselves" from his service.

Whether fealty to the king in fact changed the minds of the con-spirators, or whether Cabeza de Vaca chose to stress it in his memoir because he hoped to impress the king himself is impossible to say. But the renegades "agreed to remain, affirming that what would be the fate of one would be the fate of all without any one abandoning the others."

Narváez's response to the incident is particularly interesting given his otherwise autocratic reputation. Unlike Cortés, who hung one deserter and chopped off the toes of another, Narváez ordered no pun-ishments of any kind. Instead he called everyone to him and asked each individually for an opinion about what the army's options might be. Whether this was part of a deal with the conspirators is unsaid, and the "everyone" should certainly not be assumed to include all the slaves and porters. Still, it was an uncharacteristically democratic appeal that shows Narváez now knew what everyone in his army knew, which was that they were stranded in the middle of a soggy nowhere and neither he nor anyone else had a plan.

The only idea that kept coming up was to build boats in which to sail away. But as soon as someone suggested it, someone else pointed out why it was impossible. There was a carpenter among the company, a Portuguese man named Álvaro Fernández, but he had no tools with which to saw rough timber. He had no hardware with which to join it together. They had no oakum with which to caulk their seams. No fiber from which to twist ropes.

Two days went by, with everyone "searching and thinking of how to save the lives of these people and how to get out of there." The mys-terious disease, meanwhile, showed no signs of abating. The third of the men who were already sick were now "gravely ill," remembered Cabeza de Vaca, and the number was "increasing by the hour." Every-one in camp by the bay suspected they would catch it eventually.

"Conversation ceased," he said of those days beside the oyster beds, and everyone retreated to their own thoughts and memories for the rest of the day. And to their prayers. Everyone took to wondering, in other words, why in God's name they had followed Narváez into such a mess.

12

Into the Gulf . . . Again

The attack in the middle of the swamp left the army wounded. The mysterious disease spreading through the ranks left them weak. The aborted attempt by the horsemen to desert left them bitter and mistrustful. But none of this, when it came down to it, was as bad as the view from the beach of unbroken shallows and sawgrass islands. No ship would ever be able to find them here, even if they managed to get an immense cross into the highest tree.

"We held it to be certain," said Cabeza de Vaca, "that nothing could follow but death."

At last, after three days of this, somebody had an idea. Who it was is not clear, but he wasn't one of the elite horsemen, for he knew too much about metalwork and blacksmithing to be an hidalgo. He asked for a chance to speak with Narváez and told the sickly governor of La Florida that he thought it was possible to build a makeshift forge, with which they could melt down their war hardware and make the necessary tools and nails needed for boat building. It was an audacious scheme, but no one had a better idea. No one, in fact, had any other idea.

When eyewitness accounts are limited and ambiguous, as they are in the case of the Narváez expedition, every pronoun becomes potential grist for later speculation by historians and other storytellers. It's worth noticing, therefore, that Cabeza de Vaca doesn't say "the governor" or "Narváez" ordered the new plan to be put into effect, as he consistently did earlier in the narrative. This time, it's "We said he should set to the task" and "We agreed to make the nails and saws and axes and other tools of which there was such great necessity from the stirrups and spurs and crossbows and other iron objects that we had."

This governing "we" also decided that all the horses and healthy men would make periodic raids back up to Aute in order to gather food during the boat-building period. The first of these sorties set off immediately and collected several hundred bushels of maize. Naturally there was resistance from the villagers when the horsemen thundered into town, lances sharpened, saddle baskets empty. But despite regular "fights and skirmishes," in four raids over the next two months the Spanish stole more than 640 bushels of corn. It was an amount "sufficient for them to eat while they remained there and even to take some with them."

For protein, the governing "we" made a radical decision to slowly kill and eat the horses. No one needed reminding that their grand mission of conquest was over, but this willful killing of horses—repeated once every three days—symbolized the collapse of the old order they had hoped to bring with them and impose on Florida. In Spain, even the king himself could not sequester a hidalgo's mount. They named the place the Bay of Horses in honor of the sacrificed animals.

The vaunted hidalgo pride was severely wounded by having to slaughter the horses, but it was not altogether gone. Some members of the company, with nothing left of their status but pride, clung to their old pretensions and prerogatives with even greater fervor than before and refused to lift a finger in menial labor. To encourage greater participation, only the sick and those who worked were given horse meat, which changed a few proud minds, though not, it seems, that of the honor-obsessed Cabeza de Vaca. In a summary of his hardships, he said, "I could never eat of them."

Construction began on August 4th, almost exactly three months after separating from the fleet in Boca Ciega Bay. One team built the forge, fashioning a bellows out of deerskins and hollowed-out logs. Others cut and hauled firewood into piles and cooked it at a low smolder under leaves and dirt to make the charcoal that would be needed when the time came to fire up the contraption. Horseshoes, slave chains, stirrups, spurs, crossbows—all the available iron was piled up. Among the first tools made were saws to cut the ax-felled trees into lumber.

Just the appearance of a strategy, no matter how long a shot it was, galvanized the energy of the two hundred or so members of the army who were still marginally healthy. A Greek soldier with the mellifluous name Teodoro Doroteo solved the problem of caulking by collecting pitch from the surrounding pine trees. Others shredded mountains of palmetto leaves for use as oakum to be jammed between the boards before sealing. A ropewalk was rigged up and teams twisted palmetto fiber together with horsehair taken from the manes and tails of the slaughtered animals. The resulting ropes were a bit stiff, but serviceable. Shirts were requisitioned and sewn into sails. One company searched up and down the coast for rocks to use as ballast, but found none. Another team collected oysters in the nearby bays to supplement the horse meat.

Some translators describe the boats that took shape that August as "rafts," though a raft typically wouldn't be caulked or ballasted as the accounts say these were. Others have called them barges, though in modern usage a barge would have no sail. Most translators, therefore, interpret Cabeza de Vaca's word, *barcas*, as simply "boats," which in any case they were. They were flat-bottomed, or nearly so, if only to facilitate getting out of the knee-deep bay where they were built. And though they had sails, oars and oarlocks were also included. In the end, five boats were built, each between thirty and forty feet long. In both size and function, they were ungainly and rustic versions of the shallow-draft, open-decked, forty-foot-long brigantines with which the men were already familiar.

Progress was fast. The disease had moved into a killing phase, taking someone almost every day, which tended to focus the attention of the healthy on the preciousness of time. There was also continued resistance from the local Indians, who never attacked the camp outright but chose their targets at moments of lapsed security. Twice, groups gathering shellfish in the shallows of the estuary were attacked within full view of the main camp, and in both cases help was unable to get to them before "they were riddled with arrows." Ten died this way.

Between the nearly daily funerals for the victims of disease and attack, Narváez's men sawed and hauled, caulked and tarred, twisted and sewed. "We worked so eagerly beginning on the fourth day of August," said Cabeza de Vaca, "that by the twentieth of September five boats were finished." With a great cheer they rolled the hulls on logs into the water, where they leaked alarmingly. But as the wood swelled up, and the caulkers attacked the worst spots with more palmetto oakum and pine tar, the seepage eventually slowed. Masts and rigging were added, and what ballast there was was packed into the bottoms.

Two days after the boats were finished, Narváez ordered the last horse killed. With the previously slaughtered animals, the butchers had hung the severed quarters from tree limbs and carefully flayed the hides off of the legs whole, two men pulling the skin down to the hoof inside out while a third occasionally worked at any recalcitrant sinews with a sharp dagger. The resulting skins were then dried in the sun, turned back hair-side out, and tied off at the ends. Filled with fresh water and stowed in the bottoms of the boats, they would hopefully hold enough for the upcoming voyage. This final horse, killed and eaten on the 22nd, however, was butchered more conventionally. There was no time to cure the skin. The day had come to embark.

The remaining maize from their raids on Aute was carried out to the boats in baskets; rations would be tight, but there was enough to keep them from starving for at least a few weeks. What was left of their clothing after the sails were made was also stowed, along with their stock of trade goods. Swords, helmets, and any other metal gear that had escaped the forge were carried out. Finally, the men themselves climbed in according to divisions that had been previously worked out by Narváez. In the boat under his own command were forty-nine people, including himself. The same number went in two other boats, one under the joint command of the head priest, Suárez, and the comptroller, Enríquez, and the other under two captains named Téllez and Peñalosa. The fourth boat, under the command of captains Castillo and Dorantes, carried fifty men. Cabeza de Vaca and Alonso del Solís took command of the final boat, with forty-nine other passengers. In total, 242 people pushed off the shore of the Bay of Horses, somewhere in the Florida Panhandle. Nearly sixty people—or twenty percent of the army—had perished since they had left Boca Ciega nearly half a year before.

Other than the horse skulls and makeshift mangers that De Soto's army later found at the Bay of Horses, Narváez's great army of conquest left little behind in Florida besides the bodies of its victims and those of its own dead. There were a few beads and bells that circulated for a while in the native economy before being buried or lost. Some have suggested Narváez and company brought diseases that resulted in massive epidemics after they were gone, but their brief and hostile encounters with the Indians were not the type that typically transmit pathogens, and De Soto's men, a dozen years later, did not find the Apalachee diminished.

In the longer run of North American history, it's immaterial if Narváez brought the diseases or if they arrived with later expeditions. Disease and death did eventually come to the Indians of Florida with De Soto, or Menéndez and the missionaries of St. Augustine, or some Arawak refugee up from Cuba, or the French, or the English, or the Dutch, or the captive Africans, or all of the above.

In the case of the Apalachee, it wasn't disease that finally did them in, though successive waves of epidemics weakened them immeasurably. A century after driving Narváez and his army from their shores, they had become Catholic farmers, exporting grain to Cuba and elsewhere. But their population dwindled, and in 1704 a series of raids by Creek Indians in the employ of the English colonists from the north killed, enslaved, or forced into exile the entire remaining population of people still calling themselves Apalachee.

Some were shipped to Barbados to mill sugar, some to Carolina to harvest tobacco, and many went to New England, New York, and Pennsylvania to clear forests and build stone walls. Hundreds, or thousands, of Apalachee simply integrated themselves into neighboring territories, though the English and Creeks hunted them out of Timucua lands once they got there. Many were killed outright, and by 1714 wild buffalo were roaming in the old fields where they had never been seen before. There was not a person who publicly called him- or herself Apalachee in the entire region that had once been theirs.

For Dulchanchellin's Timucua peoples the outcome was less dramatic but not much different. There were epidemics in 1613, 1617, 1649, 1659, and 1672. The mercenary Creeks got there too, again supplying the English slave market. The official "last" Timucua, a man named Juan Alonzo Cabale, died in Cuba in 1767.

The Tocobaga and their Safety Harbor culture dissipated into oblivion during the first half of the 1700s. Not without a trace, however. In the Cove of the Withlacoochee, not far from where Narváez and his army crossed that river, is a place called the Tatham Mound that was "undiscovered" until 1984. It was used by Safety Harbor peoples for burials as early as 800 A.D. and as late as shortly after the arrival of Europeans. The telltale beads from the early sixteenth century have turned up there, along with some metal items including a plate of Spanish armor. Also in the mound was a severed left arm, and a truncated shoulder blade that a forensic expert called "typical of a downward blow from behind with a sword."

Finally, in the upper layer of the mound, archeologists found the bones of more than seventy people who died of some unidentified disease within a relatively short span not long after the arrival of the Spanish in Florida. Their pallbearers had scraped away the top layer of the mound and built up its sides with more sand in order to make the top large enough to accommodate the dead. They placed various ceramic vessels with holes carefully punched out of them on the clean sand, and laid out the deceased in neat rows. Bodies and bones from a nearby charnel house were also brought to the mound and spread

"Rites observed at the funeral of a chief . . ." Stylized engraving of a Floridian burial *(after an original by Le Moyne) from De Bry's* Americae, *part II, 1594.*

among the disease victims. The whole was then covered with a final layer of clean sand.

At the summit, the mourners performed an elaborate cleansing ceremony. They brewed and drank a bitter, holly tea called "the black drink" out of special shell cups, twenty of which they then placed in a straight north-south line across the center of the mound. At the very top of the mound a single shell teacup was put inside a specially made ceramic pot, and further down archers ceremonially shot dozens of arrows into a small area of the mound's eastern wall. Then, when the cleansing was over, the survivors walked away and never returned to the Tatham Mound.

Leaves and humus built up over the cups left on the surface. No human visited the site for more than two hundred years, until the 1830s when Oceola, the leader of a Seminole band pushed down from the north by the American military, set up a camp nearby. By that time, the Safety Harbor people as a separate culture were long gone, and according to the dean of Florida archeologists, Jerald Milanich, "The only descendants of the original inhabitants of Florida who maintained their ethnic identity . . . was a group of Apalachee who had fled west, ending up in Louisiana on the Red River. They numbered forty-five individuals in 1825."

West, as it turned out, was also the direction in which Narváez and his men hoped to flee in their makeshift boats in September of 1528.

13

Father of Waters

If you draped a hand over the side of one of those boats, your fingers hit water before your wrists reached the gunnels. No one expected the ungainly craft to ride high, given the roughness of their tools and the greenness of their lumber. But one thin *xeme*, the old Spanish term for the distance between the tip of a person's thumb and the end of the forefinger, was troublesome. They had seen too many storms in the Gulf of Mexico to think a few inches of freeboard was going to get them far in open water. But for the time being it didn't much matter; there was no open water.

Everywhere was waist deep or less, and everywhere the coast was impossible to read. Over and over again the lead boat saw a break in the grass and made for it, only to find when they got there that instead of an outlet to the gulf proper, it was another inlet to nowhere. Part of the difficulty was they weren't even certain which direction would bring them most efficiently to the open gulf. They knew that the Gulf Coast of North America formed an arc, with Florida on the east and Mexico on the west, but where they were on that curve, or how sharply it turned at the Panhandle, they had no idea. Should they head generally west or south to find that open water? No one knew. The professional sailors had long ago been left with the fleet back in Boca Ciega, so they traveled, Cabeza de Vaca said, "without any one of us who went having any knowledge of the art of navigation."

The fear of facing the open gulf in overloaded boats, real as it was, was more than offset by their hope of being rescued at sea. This wasn't an entirely unfounded fantasy. Other times during the early decades of the Spanish invasion of the New World, ships had rescued ill-fated conquistadors against daunting odds. Twenty years before, in 1508, Narváez himself had saved the remnants of Alonso de Hojeda's failed colony of Urabá. Facing starvation on the coast of South America, this mutinous group sailed for Hispaniola and wrecked instead on the coast of Cuba. Half of them died there before one Spaniard and several native paddlers canoed a hundred miles of open Caribbean to Jamaica, where they convinced Narváez to go look for the survivors.

So there was hope. Narváez's wife, who had spent years trying to pry him loose from Cortés's prison, was at that moment sending rescue ships up and down the Florida coast looking for her husband's lost army, and would continue to do so for more than a year. The ships of Narváez's own fleet, too, were looking for the land party, though not everyone on board was sanguine about the chances of success. The prime mover was the ever-pessimistic clairvoyant, who immediately after the departure of the land party told the other women on board that they would never see their husbands again. They should cut their losses, she said, and "look to see whom they might marry, because she planned to do it." According to Cabeza de Vaca, who learned about it years later from people who had been on the ships, "she and the rest of the women married and lived with the men who remained on the ships."

He didn't comment on whether he or any of the others baking in the labyrinthine sloughs of the Florida Panhandle were reminiscing about their wives as their lifeboats wandered in circles in the shallows. The healthy among them rowed despondently, or got out and waded to raise the boat off the mud when necessary. Once in a while their sails filled with slight puff, but not often enough, and not to any sustained effect when they constantly had to change course to follow serpentine channels. Meanwhile the sick, including Narváez himself, hunched side by side in the midday sun, shivering and sweating and waiting for something to change. But nothing did change as the days went by in five boats "so crowded that we could not even move."

Whenever there was a choice of directions, they opted for a westward course. Not everyone necessarily agreed with this policy, arguing instead for making their way south along the Florida coast back toward Tampa Bay and Cuba, rather than west for Pánuco. Any ships looking for them would surely be coming from that direction.

But discussion of heading back the way they came always ended with the question of what they would do if they did not in fact find any ships between where they were and the tip of La Florida. They knew that when Columbus was marooned on Jamaica in 1503, Diego Méndez paddled a dugout from there to Hispaniola, and that Hojeda's man paddled from Cuba to Jamaica. But the prospect of attempting to cross to Cuba with only one *xeme* of freeboard was not appealing even to desperate men. Furthermore, the Calusas living at the tip of Florida already had a rough reputation, having killed Ponce de León and attacked several other expeditions. By going west, at least if they didn't run into ships, they would eventually get to the Spanish outposts of Mexico without having to leave sight of land.

But no one really knew how long "eventually" might turn out to be. According to the best estimates of the time, the distance from the tip of Florida to Pánuco was supposed to be something over three hundred leagues—a thousand miles, give or take. By their own estimation they had already traveled two hundred and eighty leagues, or something over seven hundred miles, from their initial landing place, so they had reason to believe they must be getting close to the settlement at Pánuco. But that estimation of their progress was so wildly exaggerated that it's hard to even make sense of today. The truth was that they were still a thousand untracked miles away from the Spanish settlements on the Gulf coast of Mexico. A thousand miles, that is, if you don't count the miles spent wandering and weaving up and down nameless creeks and inlets looking for open water.

After a week lost in the shallows, the boats approached an island "near the shore." As usual, the exact location is unknowable, but the prime suspects are the string of barrier strands that create Apalalachicola Bay: Dog Island, St. George Island, St. Vincent Island. Cabeza de Vaca's boat was ahead of the others at the time, and he saw five canoes paddling out toward them from the direction of the island. As soon as the Indians figured out how many Spaniards there really were, however, they turned and fled back toward shore. Cabeza de Vaca ordered his men to pull hard on the oars in order to try and catch up, but by the time they got to the island the Indians had disappeared inland.

They had made the mistake of leaving their empty canoes on the beach, however, and Cabeza de Vaca decided they looked useful enough to steal. With the canoes in tow, he and his crew continued down the coast to where the other four Spanish boats were by now beached in front of an abandoned village.

Little is known about the original Indians of the western Panhandle other than a few tidbits of information from the 1600s, when Christianized Apalachee were occasionally sent over to the region from the Florida missions, armed with Spanish guns to solidify some wobbly conversions among peoples known as the Pensacolas, the Chacatos, and Chines. Also in that century, reconnaissance teams from Mexico found bark houses, feather headdresses, and "a fire burning, over which was a very tasteless stew of buffalo entrails in a crudely shaped earthen pan, and the flesh of the same animal roasted, or rather singed in some places and raw in others." There was no buffalo stew when Narváez and his men came ashore, but there was a good supply of "mullet and dried roe," which the locals had caught with nets and in weirs.

With their newly requisitioned canoes now loaded with confiscated fish, the fleet continued down the coast to the end of the island. There they crossed over to the mainland, which they hadn't laid eyes on since setting out from the Bay of Horses a week before. Even more thrilling, though, were glimpses of the blue gulf waters through the pass. At last they were at the coast; or, depending on how you looked at it, *at least* they were at the coast. It was the feast day of St. Michael, the 29th of September, and they named the passage between the island and the mainland St. Michael's Strait in his honor.

As good as it was to see open water again, the sight of waves and whitecaps drove home the reality that their low-riding boats were not remotely seaworthy. They were able to remedy the problem somewhat by breaking apart the five stolen canoes, which produced enough lumber to build up the sides of their own craft by about two spans of a hand. What they couldn't fix, however, were their water bottles. The horsehides were rotting and leaking, stinking and ultimately "of no use whatsoever." As a result, in the following days, the failure of their fresh water supply became a much graver threat than the waves of salt water.

Thirst was new, and painful. Just about the only good thing about the Florida peninsula had been that there was usually no shortage of fresh water; more often there was too much of it. Now, with their fish and corn, there was enough to eat, but the men almost couldn't get anything down due to dehydration. Just when they had at last found the open gulf, progress westward slowed to a crawl, as they were forced to spend whole days poking up into small bays and inlets in search of fresh water.

They must have found some here and there during the next month skirting the low, lush coast of Alabama: a stressed, sun-baked body won't survive a week without a drink, and neither eyewitness report mentions any casualties during that time. Cabeza de Vaca remembered a few small fishing villages, inhabited by Indians he described as "poor and wretched." And at least once they were shadowed for a while by a canoe, but its occupants paid no attention to their entreaties. They found enough to stay alive, in other words, but they were always on the brink of losing their weakest members.

The brink finally caught up with them on a small island they had come across, where they went ashore hoping to find a spring or stream. Those with energy wandered around in desultory groups. Those with nothing left sprawled on the beach or just slumped in their boats, waiting for news of water. No one watched the sky, however. By the time someone finally noticed a storm brewing, it was too late to collect the scattered troops and get everyone back on board before the seas kicked up into whitecaps that made a crossing to the mainland out of the question. For five days the wind blew in a rainless gale that prevented them from sailing. Tongues cracked. Lips cracked. Eyes glazed. Heads pounded. Reason fled. The island turned out to be bone dry.

When a half-dozen men died "very quickly" after attempting to drink salt water, the others' assessment of the risk of taking to the boats began to change. They pushed the craft out into the gray and white sea and clambered aboard but regretted the decision almost immediately. Despite the raised sides, water poured in over the gunnels, soaking the parched rowers in water they dared not drink. More than once some-one yelled that they were sinking, and it did seem as though all five boats were about to go down. The nearly dead men, crammed side by side in row after row, prayed and pulled on their oars with some last reserve of energy, or bent to bail what little they could with their cupped hands or whatever else they still had that might hold water just long enough to lift it over the edge. At some point during that day, Cabeza de Vaca said, every single one of them thought that the end had at last come.

But somehow, each time, the end didn't come after all. They pulled and bailed and pulled some more, and by late afternoon they were near the mainland. That was only a small consolation, however, as there was nowhere to put ashore and no way the boats would make it through the night at sea. The sun dropped relentlessly toward the frothy grey horizon.

In the twilight, the five boats finally rounded a point, in the lee of which the sea lay down. A flotilla of canoes raced out to greet them, paddled by "large people and well proportioned" who, the Spaniards were very happy to see, did not carry bows and arrows. The communi-cation that followed was rather one way: "The Indians who came in them spoke to us," said Cabeza de Vaca, "and without wanting to wait for us, turned back."

No one in either group had any idea what the other was talking about, but the Indians didn't appear overtly hostile, and Narváez ordered the boats to follow the canoes. Even if the Indians were warn-ing the strangers to stay away, it would have done no good. Where there were people, there was water, and the shabby fleet rowed along trying in vain to keep up with the swift canoes ahead. In a few miles they arrived at a seaside village of tidy houses made of woven reeds lashed over wood frames.

Some in the company were still "very sick," but Narváez himself had regained enough strength to go ashore and greet the leadership of the village. The head man wore a resplendent muskrat coat and seemed quite friendly. He took Narváez into his own house and offered him dried fish and fresh water. Narváez, in return, gave him "beads, rattles, and some corn they had on board."

The villagers liked the beads, but they were thrilled to see the corn. They ate it immediately and asked for more, suggesting they weren't themselves farmers. Narváez ordered it given to them, confirming that after more than a month in the boats, the army was not starving. It was corn well spent, Narváez thought, if it would buy his army a bit of peace in the village where they could drink the water and regain their strength.

And it seemed to do just that. That night Narváez was a guest in the chief's own residence, and Cabeza de Vaca and the other officers were lodged nearby. The rest of the army bedded down on the beach, or in less important houses of their hosts. Everyone was exhausted, glad to be full of fish, glad to be on land, and most of all glad to not be thirsty. They slept soundly until sometime after midnight, when their new friends tried to smash their heads in with rocks.

Three of the sickest conquistadors, who were lying on the beach, were killed instantly. The cries from the beach woke Narváez and Cabeza de Vaca, but not before Narváez was wounded in the face with a rock. He too would have been killed if Cabeza de Vaca and several others hadn't charged into the house and grabbed the formerly friendly village leader before he could finish the job. They managed to hold him for a moment, but like Narváez, he escaped when his own warriors rushed to his defense. He left behind his fur coat, however, which the Spaniards confiscated.

In a state of confusion the army retreated to the beach to regroup. For safety, it was decided that Narváez and the other wounded should spend the night aboard the boats anchored offshore while fifty of the fittest fighters remained on the beach to stand guard. Two more times during the night the townspeople attacked, hurling rocks and spears, wounding a few more Spaniards and driving the group closer to the beach.

In the dark, after the second assault, Cabeza de Vaca and Dorantes discussed their options. They couldn't continue losing ground all night, that was obvious, or by dawn they would be fighting up to their waists in salt water. Nor were they prepared to retreat to the boats with their wounded compatriots; the wind was still howling around the point. As they had done on the road to Apalachee, therefore, Dorantes and a group of seventeen crept forward during the lull between attacks and hid themselves in the reeds off to one side. Minutes of silent waiting stretched on, until they began to think that perhaps the violence was over for the night.

But it wasn't. The third wave of attackers did come down to the beach to harass the strangers, and as Dorantes hoped, they went right past the ambushers. Suddenly this time there were roaring men with steel swords slashing away behind the rock-throwing villagers, calling out the names of Christian saints while severing limbs and laying open bellies. "Many of the Indians were quite cut up," the survivors later remembered. Caught for a while in a pincer, the villagers at last retreated, though not without inflicting their own damage. Every member of the Spanish party that stayed on shore during the night was injured in some way. Cabeza de Vaca, who like Narváez was wounded in the face, thought the only reason more Spaniards weren't dead was that the Indians had very few arrows.

In the light of morning, Narváez and his officers assessed the situation. The village was now abandoned by its owners, and the Spaniards would have been happy to leave the place as well were it not for the storm still raging. The wind had come around to the north now, turning bitterly cold. It was the beginning of November, and their shirts had long since been made into sails. Those who weren't sick with the fever were wounded, and everyone was still recovering from dehydration. Another attack might come at any time, but the conquerors were in no condition to move.

Having seen enough of the Spanish knives, the villagers never reappeared. In their town, Narváez's men chopped up thirty canoes for firewood, for materials to make crude shelters, and for some measure of revenge. They rested, and tended as best they could to the new batch of wounds. Mostly, though, they watched the weather, waiting for the wind to drop enough to get back in the boats and push on west.

When they did shove off a few days later, their fresh water situation was slightly improved by the addition of a few earthen jugs and bottles from the village. Nevertheless, after less than a week's travel, they were again forced to pull into an estuary to look for fresh water. Once more, they encountered canoeists. Other than the usual inconclusive debates among historians over the location—was it Mobile? Were they the Choctaws?—what's interesting about the encounter was the decision of the Greek boat caulker, Doroteo Teodoro, and an unnamed African to go ashore with the canoeists.

A chorus of voices from their comrades told them they were crazy fools to go, that they had lost their minds from thirst and fatigue and should rest and reconsider. Narváez, in particular, "tried very hard to prevent [Doroteo Teodoro] from going," but his authority had waned to the point where he was no longer able to assert his will over the individual members of the expedition. Teodoro said goodbye and climbed over the edge of the boat into the canoe. "And so he left," said Cabeza de Vaca, "and he took a black man with him." Whether this man was Teodoro's slave, as most assume, or just someone of the same mind-set was left unsaid.

There are many stories of Europeans and Africans "going native" in the early decades of the Spanish conquest. Most were survivors of ruined expeditions or shipwrecks, like the two Spanish women, "naked as Eve," that Narváez himself had come across during the conquest of Cuba. Or Gerónimo de Aguilar and Gonzalo Guerrero, who wrecked on the coast of the Yucatan eight years before Cortés arrived there. Aguilar, whose mother at home in Spain had taken to howling "this is the flesh of my son" whenever she saw meat of any kind, was happy to be rescued. But Guerrero had a local family and declined the opportunity, going so far as to advise his in-laws to waste no time in attacking the Spaniards.

De Soto's army, in particular, shed members as it passed through what is now the southeastern United States. In one notably multiracial incident, a survivor remembered "a comrade deserted who was named Rodriguez, a native of Peñafiel (Spain), and also a shrewd young Indian slave from Cuba, who belonged to a gentleman called Villegas, and a very shrewd slave of Don Carlos, a native of Barbary (North Africa), and Gómez, a very shrewd black man." This Gómez was apparently shrewdest of all, for he lived with the great queen of the region, Cofitachequi, "and it was very certain that they held communication as husband and wife." Another De Soto deserter went native to avoid paying his poker bill. Using homemade cards, he bet his horse and lost it. He bet his clothes and lost them. He bet his favorite slave and then thought better of parting with the pretty teenager. "In fear of being made to pay for gaming debts in the person of an Indian girl, his concubine, he took her away with him," recalled the Gentleman of Elvas.

Teodoro and the unnamed man who got out of Narváez's boats and climbed into the canoes may not have intended to go native. When they agreed to go ashore, two people from the canoes came aboard the Spanish boats as collateral for their return. But hours passed, Narváez's men dozing side by side in their galley seats, and the canoe didn't reappear from the passes through the reeds into which it had disappeared. Finally, after dark, some canoes approached, but neither Teodoro nor his companion was aboard. Nor was there the promised water on board, though the Indians had brought back the empty vessels that Doroteo had taken ashore to fill, as if to accentuate the fact that they hadn't delivered on their (perceived) promise of water. Most alarming of all, the two hostages in the Spanish boats almost succeeded in jumping overboard and had to be tied up. "They left us very perplexed," confessed Cabeza de Vaca.

In the morning, canoes approached from several directions at once, appearing out of unseen passages. Some carried lords or caciques of the village, people with long, flowing hair and furs like the one the Spanish had taken the previous week. When they came within hailing distance they urged the strangers to follow them through the marshy inlets back to their village. There they could retrieve Teodoro and the other man, they seemed to promise. They could trade for furs, food, and whatever else they wanted.

But Narváez and his men were in no mood to trust friendly overtures from unknown Indians, particularly after someone yelled out that other canoes were circling around to block the exit from the estuary. Narváez had seen enough of swamp warfare, and he hastily ordered a retreat toward the sea. The Greek and the African had made their

choice to go ashore; they would have to live or die with its consequences.

Twenty canoes followed them out of the grassy lagoon, pelting
them with stones thrown from slings and hurling a few spears their way
as well. They wanted their hostages back, but since they didn't bring
Teodoro and the black, Narváez didn't release the Indians, who had
been tied up ever since their failed escape attempt the night before. In
the end, the wind picked up, filling the tattered sails of the five boats
and convincing those in the canoes to turn back to shore. Everyone
was "saddened at having lost those two Christians," but there was
nothing to do but sail away.

The last clues on the fate of Doroteo Teodoro and his African
companion come from the De Soto sources. Traveling along a river—
perhaps the Alabama—a dozen years later, De Soto's men "had news of
how the boats of Narváez had arrived in need of water, and that here
among these Indians remained a Christian who was called Don
Teodoro, and a black man with him." That source doesn't say how long
the two remained among them, but another De Soto survivor says it
wasn't happily ever after: "In that town Piachi it was found out that
they had killed Don Teodoro, and a black man."

How many weeks went by on those boats after they left the estuary is hard to say, though progress west was at last steadier. During the
shortening autumn days, the five awkward craft spread out a bit along
the coast of Alabama and Mississippi. Men mumbled to themselves in
varying states of dissolution, or prayed continuously, or stared silently
out at the steel-grey waters, scanning the horizon for masts of ships that
never appeared. Evenings, they tried their best to gather the fleet back
together, usually to anchor somewhere near water, though sometimes,
if the moon was out and the wind favorable, they sailed on through
the night.

At one such dusk Cabeza de Vaca's boat was traveling in front and rounded a point to find an immense river pouring into the gulf. He ordered his men to stop, as the lead boat always did when a decision needed to be made. The anchor—nothing more than a bundle of rocks tied to the end of their palmetto rope—splashed overboard, and Cabeza de Vaca stood and waved to the other boats in the distance behind. But Narváez had found something interesting of his own and refused to come to where they were. There's an aggrieved tone in Cabeza de Vaca's telling, hinting of the ever-present tension between the two men, and portending as well the even greater friction to come. He could wave all he wanted, but Narváez clearly wasn't coming. So Cabeza de Vaca finally ordered his own boat to backtrack to where the other four were anchored in a bay full of islands, where the river that he had found was seeping over in one of its minor mouths.

"And there we came together, and from the sea we drank fresh water," Cabeza de Vaca remembered.

The men were revived by the drink and tired of eating their meager rations of raw corn while shivering side by side in their seats. They begged to go ashore and build a fire. But as there was no firewood on the little islands of the bay, someone from Cabeza de Vaca's boat suggested they continue up the coast to the river, where there was sure to be driftwood. It wasn't far away, they promised, as they set off toward the point, with Cabeza de Vaca probably thinking to himself that if Narváez had only come when he waved they would all be sitting around a warm fire by now instead of rowing.

But when the ragged navy rounded the headland, what they found on the other side was far more of a river than they had bargained for. It was unlike any they had seen before in Europe or the New World. This would be no evening row upstream to collect a little firewood with which to toast their suppers. Instead, the mile-wide current of the

Mississippi, draining the vast heart of the continent they had set out to conquer nearly two years before, caught them up and spit them far out to sea like bits of bad food. There, a wicked north wind picked up the work and pushed them out some more.

In the falling darkness they ate their raw corn and watched America disappear.

14

Castaways

They struggled to stay near the land with all that remained of their strength. The flat-bottomed boats were poorly equipped to tack up against the wind, so the basted-together shirts were hauled down and stowed, and the half-dead men just pulled away on the oars like galley slaves; worthless arms and spent backs straining against the wind and current.

But it was no use; the land didn't get closer. When they were a little more than a mile out from shore and Narváez ordered the anchors thrown over, it was already too late. The men in the bow played out all 150 feet of the homemade hawsers without finding bottom. "We could not determine whether the current was the reason," recalled Cabeza de Vaca. Another day and another night went by and still they couldn't make the land, though by the end of the second day their rock anchors at last struck sand.

They could make the beach by nightfall if they pulled hard, but what they saw on shore wasn't good. All along the coast the locals had lit fires, on which they had piled some seaweed or other rotten fuel, sending up immense columns of smoke. The meaning was unambiguous; they were being watched. They would have to go ashore eventually— their water supply was again gone—but if they had to die fighting, they might as well do it by daylight. Bobbing there, just behind the line of the surf, they hunkered down in their crowded seats, or leaned back against each other as best they could for yet another night on board.

They were as used to life on the boats as was possible under the circumstances. Nearly forty days had now passed since they set out from the Bay of Horses—the length of a usual crossing from Spain to the New World, the length of time they had spent in the storm-tossed gulf on their way from Cuba to Florida. With the exception of eight or nine unhappy nights on the dry island and in the various hostile villages, all had been spent cheek by jowl in the boats. All things considered, the unlikely craft had served them very well.

Nights were cool now, as it was early November, but everyone slept well. Well enough that when the north wind once again picked up, no one noticed the anchors dragging. In the dark, the boats drifted away from shore, undoing all of the previous day's efforts and then some. They drifted unevenly and in varying directions, so that when the sun finally woke Narváez's army, neither land nor their fellow travelers were anywhere to be seen.

The sight of that unbroken boundary between sky and water in every direction severed some of the men's last shreds of will. For most of them, however, it was just one more numbing moment in an endless line of disappointments. Unlike earlier setbacks, this one left nothing to discuss in terms of options. Those who could row simply put their calloused hands once more to their waterlogged oars. With the sun rising to their left, they pulled toward the north, wondering how far apart five boats could drift in only one night.

Sometime after midday, someone in Narváez's boat cried out that he saw a speck in the distance. A little later, off to the other side, another appeared. By late afternoon Narváez was able to call across the water to Cabeza de Vaca's boat. What should they do under the circumstances? he asked the treasurer.

Cabeza de Vaca didn't think long before hollering back that he thought Narváez should not allow the group to fragment any further than the wind and currents of the gulf had already done. Specifically, he thought they should make every effort to join with the third boat visible in the distance. It was essentially the same position he had taken when Narváez wanted to divide the force at Tampa Bay: stick together, for honor and duty. "In no way should he leave it," Cabeza de Vaca recalled saying.

But once again, there was another opinion. This time it was Captain Pantoja, who had been with Cabeza de Vaca during the hurricane and was now a passenger of Narváez's boat. In his opinion they couldn't risk waiting for the third boat: if they were unable to reach land that day, he said, they "would not do so in six more, and in that length of time death by starvation would be inevitable."

Narváez thought about the wind. It was still out of the north, meaning that every moment they tarried they drifted further from shore. He looked at Pantoja, and at Cabeza de Vaca, and the half-dead crews of their two boats. The third boat was far away in the wrong direction, further offshore. It was so far away that he still couldn't even tell which boat it was. He made up his mind.

Looking back at Cabeza de Vaca, Narváez ordered him to urge his own boat crew to pick up their oars and row hard for shore, "because only by the strength of their arms could land be taken." Pantoja was right, he said. They couldn't risk waiting for the third boat. It was too far out to sea. Leave them. Row! He ordered his own men to put their backs into it.

Cabeza de Vaca followed orders, and for a while the two boats traveled along together. But after an hour or so, Narváez's boat began to pull away. The account written jointly by the survivors says Narváez's boat was "lighter and could move faster, as it was less burdened," but in Cabeza de Vaca's personal memoir, the reason is more sinister: "Since the governor carried the healthiest and most robust men among us, in no way were we able to follow or keep up with him."

Cabeza de Vaca's narrative is considered a masterpiece of colonial literature, and as such, volumes of essays have deconstructed it, reconstructed it, unpacked it, and interrogated it for its value as an historical account, as a source on precontact Indians, and as a window into the Spanish imperial idea. The critique began in Cabeza de Vaca's own time with Oviedo, who decided the "joint report" of the survivors was the more reliable source, and culminates for the time being in Adorno and Pautz's massive translation and commentary. But packed or unpacked, what can be said unequivocally is that Cabeza de Vaca knew his story was his best asset, and he knew how to tell it well. In his preamble to the king, he asked that his tale serve in lieu of more traditional spoils like gold or territory, "because this alone is what a man who came away naked could carry out with him."

In the two boats off the coast of Louisiana, all of Cabeza de Vaca's foreshadowed tensions between himself and Narváez came at last to an irreconcilable head. In Florida, Cabeza de Vaca had convinced the mutinous horsemen to stay loyal to Narváez, "to remain, affirming that what would be the fate of one would be the fate of all without any one abandoning the others." But here, using the same argument, he couldn't convince Narváez himself to wait an hour for a boatload of his straggling followers. And that act of betrayal was just an appetizer.

After five more miles of hard rowing, when his men simply could not keep pace with Narváez's stronger crew, Cabeza de Vaca called out. The sun was low in the sky, he pointed out. Night was coming. Shouldn't they tie the two boats together so that they might not separate during the night? he asked. But Narváez looked back at the men in the other boat, at Cabeza de Vaca standing there waiting to catch a tossed line. A moment passed in silence. Then he ordered his man not to throw the rope and not to catch it if Cabeza de Vaca tried to throw one.

It was all any of them would be able to do to get themselves ashore that night, Narváez said by way of explanation. It wasn't much of an explanation, and Cabeza de Vaca was dumbfounded. In one last effort to respect the old code of behavior, he asked what was it that Narváez was commanding him to do.

"It [is] no longer time for one man to rule another," he remembered Narváez telling him. "Each one should do whatever seemed best to him in order to save his own life, [and] that he intended so to do it. And saying this he veered away."

Narváez had abdicated. At its heart, Cabeza de Vaca's memoir of the expedition traces a relentless descent from the expected order of things. In the beginning, the Holy Roman Emperor makes official appointments and paper contracts with privateer warriors. A tempest stirs the pot in Cuba, relocating the expedition from its original destination, but not upending the established hierarchy of legal proceedings. In Florida, all the king's men hold formal consultations in the presence of a scribe, where there is dissension, but orders are nonetheless given and followed. The *requirimiento* is read to the Indians, though none of them hear it. In the Panhandle, amid signs of dissolution, Narváez submits to a sort of informal democracy in which he asks "everyone" their opinion. And finally now, having been hurled out to sea by the enormous power of the Mississippi, the king's governor has announced to the king's treasurer that there is no king and no empire in lifeboats, there is only survival. It is every conquistador for himself.

All order was gone, and from this point forward in Cabeza de Vaca's story, there is nowhere to go but into absurdity. "Some very novel things may be read in it," Cabeza de Vaca said of his memoir, "very difficult for some to believe." The novel things—miracles and abominations, some of which are indeed very difficult to believe—all take place after Narváez's declaration of independence.

Cabeza de Vaca never saw Narváez again. He tried for a while longer to encourage his rowers to keep up with the other boat, but with each stroke the distance between them grew until eventually Narváez's boat disappeared over the horizon and Cabeza de Vaca told his own men to rest at their oars.

Whether Narváez got to shore that same night, as he hoped, is unknown. But his relatively strong rowers eventually made a landfall near Galveston, Texas, and resumed working their way west. As they had done before the Mississippi, they hugged the beach, always with an eye out for signs of fresh water or food, but not seeing much of either. What they did see one day off in the distance on the beach, was a long, dark line. It was so small at first that it wasn't clear if it was people or just another blurry illusion thrown up by the sameness of the sand. When they pulled close, however, they saw that it was the survivors from the priests' boat, which had capsized and been lost a few dozen miles back, between the mouths of the Brazos and the San Bernard rivers. They were making their way weakly forward, nearly dead from hunger and thirst, jealous of seagulls but unable to catch even the occasional crab. They ate seaweed, which bloated the bellies of some.

Narváez ordered his boat to land, and off-loaded most of his own passengers "so that they might walk along the shore so the boat would be lighter, and because they were weary of the sea and had nothing to eat." But he himself stayed on board with a skeleton crew of rowers. They traveled like that for another few weeks, with the boat just enough offshore to be out of the gray November surf but close enough to come in and help ferry the walkers across the various inlets and tidal sloughs that periodically open in that long barrier beach. On the evening after everyone had been ferried in this way across the large opening between the Matagorda Peninsula and Matagorda Island, roughly halfway between Galveston and Corpus Christi, he stayed in the boat as usual.

Narváez had taken to sleeping apart from the main company, with only Campo, his personal page, and a pilot named Antón Pérez on the boat with him. It's tempting to speculate what, if anything, might have been in his mind as he lay down to sleep that evening with nothing left to show for his army and his empire but one leaky scow and seventy-some starving and beaten men on a godforsaken sandbar. Did he hear his own disembodied voice telling him to carry on, as many who survive against all odds report hearing at critical moments? Did he think of food? Or fresh water? There were neither on board.

Whatever recovery he had enjoyed from the illness in the Florida Panhandle was long since undone by hardship and relapse. The Narváez who had gone to arrest Cortés was "very muscular," with a booming if ineffectual presence, but the Narváez who stayed in his boat while his men slept along the shore was "very thin and ill and full of leprosy." This was no worse—and no better—than most of his men, but

that evening he took the precaution of designating a successor, announcing that should anything happen to him, Pantoja was to take over.

His old friend Gonzalo Fernández Oviedo y Valdés, writing several decades later, wondered if Narváez ever thought of some of the
conversations they had had back in Spain before anything had a
chance to go wrong. "I believe Pánfilo must have remembered more
than once the advice I gave him in Toledo," Oviedo commented. He
had told Narváez to stay home, to be thankful, to enjoy his wife and his
Cuban wealth.

Did Narváez think of María de Valenzuela and their children as
he lay in the boat that night? Or of Cortés in his gold-drenched
Tenochtitlan? Or of Governor Velázquez of Cuba, dead in his grave?
Did he recall his old chaplain, Las Casas, telling him to go to hell after
that first great massacre in Cuba? Were there stars over Texas that
night? Did he see them? Did he feel the anchor slipping once again,
and did he care? Did he pull the anchor up?

The next morning, when the men on the beach woke up, the boat
was gone. "A very strong wind arose and took them out to sea and they
were never heard of again," say the narratives.

"The sea swallowed them."

15

The Isle of Bad Fortune

Narváez was dead, along with his dream of a North American empire. But some 250 of the men and boys who had followed him to La Florida were still alive, spread out in various states of desperation along the coast of Texas.

While still at sea a few weeks before, when Cabeza de Vaca concluded that his own crew of rowers could not keep up with Narváez's and ordered them to rest at their oars, they had waited for the third boat, which they could still see far behind them. It was the one commanded by Captains Téllez and Peñalosa, and after discussing Narváez's shocking assertion that it was henceforth every boat for itself, the two crews decided to try to stay close together.

Given the moral reprobation heaped on Narváez for abandoning his subordinates by writers beginning in his own time and continuing to the present day, it's interesting to note that Pantoja's predictions of doom for any boat that tarried at sea came very close to coming true. For five days the boats of Cabeza de Vaca and Téllez and Peñalosa struggled against the winds and currents, losing strength and unable to get ashore. What's more, despite their best efforts to hang together, they were once again separated by a night storm, this time permanently. Between the cold from the repeated drenching by November waves and the lack of drinking water, many of the passengers slipped into a senseless stupor. Late on the fifth day after parting from Narváez, there were only five people in Cabeza de Vaca's boat who could still row. The rest, he remembered, "were fallen on top of one another in it, so close to death that few were conscious."

By dark of that same day, there were only two left who were strong enough to operate the tiller: Cabeza de Vaca and the helmsman. They were now entirely reliant on their makeshift sails to move them toward shore. A few more cold hours passed, and even the unnamed helmsman asked Cabeza de Vaca to take over from him. He was certain that he was about to die any moment, he explained apologetically, and then lay down and closed his eyes. For hours in the dark after that, Cabeza de Vaca leaned against the tiller, the only conscious being in a boat full of bodies.

But the helmsman didn't perish. When Cabeza de Vaca checked at midnight, "to see if he was dead," he found him revived enough to take another watch. Fatigued now himself, Cabeza de Vaca tried to sleep, but found he couldn't. He lay there, listening to the sea, thinking his own morbid thoughts. "Certainly, at that hour I would have willingly chosen to die rather than to see so many people before me in that condition," he remembered.

In the darkest hour, right before the dawn, the sound of the sea changed. In his semiconscious state, it took a while for Cabeza de Vaca to comprehend what he was hearing. But suddenly, it clicked, and both he and the helmsman realized almost simultaneously that they were listening to the thunder of waves crashing on a beach. In the blackness they groped for the anchor, found it, and threw the line over the stern. Only a few dozen feet paid out before the bundle of rocks hit bottom. The waves were louder now, nearer.

As anxious to be ashore as they both were, neither was desperate enough to want to land the ungainly boat in the dark. They prayed the anchor would hold, checked it constantly, listened—is the wind coming up? And though the waves always did sound as if they were getting louder, they managed to keep behind the surf line until the eastern sky lightened.

The jolt of the great wave that pitched the forty-foot boat up onto the beach shocked most, but not all, of the near-dead passengers out of their lethargy. As soon as the long, low beach appeared like a line of white against a grey background, Cabeza de Vaca had taken an oar, and with the helmsman at the tiller, the two pointed the bow toward shore. Their hope for a smooth surf in to the beach didn't quite work out, however. Just as they approached the shore an immense set of waves roared in. The last one lifted the stern precariously high, leaving the man at the back looking down at the boat below him and leaning with all his pathetic weight against the tiller in an effort to keep the clunky thing from broadsiding and broaching. In the benches, men who hadn't moved in half a day or more began to come to as the cold November brine poured over them.

For once, the worst didn't happen and the boat stayed reasonably straight. The wave heaved them up onto the sand about as far, Cabeza de Vaca thought, as a horseshoe pitch. There, the semirevived passengers tumbled out into the surf, "half walking, half crawling" their way to slightly higher ground at the back of the beach. There were more than a few, however, who didn't revive and had to be hauled out of the boat by the others.

According to Cabeza de Vaca, the date was November 6, 1528, but the elapsed time since leaving Apalachee suggests it was more like the second half of that month. At any rate it was bitterly cold. Someone cobbled together a fire. Someone else found some water, and the men crowded around, slurping up what they could, attempting to fill the few jars they still had. Rations had been strictly adhered to at sea, and there was still a little corn in the boat, which they began to toast and eat. With the heat and the food, and the adrenaline, strength temporarily flowed back into many limbs. Just the change of being on land was tonic to some.

One who was particularly revived was Lope de Oviedo (not to be confused with the historian of the same surname). From the top of the dunes he and Cabeza de Vaca looked over the pancake-flat land they had worked so hard to get to. There wasn't much to see, just an expanse of tough grasses stretching away indefinitely, cut through here and there with glinting water. But in the distance in a few places they could see higher hummocks of trees. They weren't much more than low mounds breaking the line of the horizon, but Cabeza de Vaca thought if Oviedo could make his way to the closest one and climb a tree, he might be able to get a wider view.

It was a copse of oak trees, great thousand-year-old behemoths with spreading branches that sagged all the way to the ground so that even a weakened man like Oviedo could virtually walk right up one to get a view of the surroundings. From the treetop he could tell immediately that they were on an island, most likely either Galveston or its neighbor to the west, the Oyster Bay Peninsula, which at that time may have been disconnected from the coast. More exciting to Oviedo though were the ruts and trails he'd followed through the underbrush to get through the trees. They could only have been made by cattle, he thought, and where there were cattle there must also be Europeans. He rushed back to tell Cabeza de Vaca.

This was titillating news, but by no means conclusive, and Cabeza de Vaca told him to go back and take a closer look for a road that might lead somewhere. Oviedo took the widest path he could find, but found neither cattle nor Europeans. He came instead to a deserted Indian village, from which he stole a few things including some dried fish and "a small dog." Or at least he thought the village was deserted: by the time he got back to the beach with his loot, two hundred armed Indians were following him.

They weren't in hot pursuit, or even showing signs of animosity, which was a good thing since there was nothing that the cold, wet, would-be conquerors of North America could do but hope for mercy. One or two Spaniards stood on wobbly legs and attempted to look ready to put up a defense, but most just slouched where they were and peered up like wounded skunks, waiting to see what would happen to them next.

"It was out of the question for us to think that anyone could defend himself," Cabeza de Vaca recalled, "since it was difficult to find even six who could raise themselves from the ground."

All that was left in the great arsenal of conquest were a few cheap manufactured trinkets. Cabeza de Vaca dug into the gear for the usual "beads and bells," which he and Solís then carried solicitously up the beach and presented to the assembled archers. By now they had seated themselves on a nearby bank of grass where they could see both the boat wreck and its victims, and be seen by them. They were large men, nearly naked, with pierced nipples and ears through which they had pushed inch-thick reeds of varying lengths. "Our fear made them seem like giants," Cabeza de Vaca remembered.

The baubles did their work. The bells in particular were of interest; in addition to the usual assortment of shell beads and pottery shards, archeologists on the Texas coast have found tiny bells called "tinklers" that the precontact coastal Indians manufactured from small olive-shaped shells using coyote teeth for clappers. Solís and Cabeza de Vaca presented the gifts like penitents seeking salvation, and after a moment's consideration, the giants accepted their offerings. As a sign of friendship, each took an arrow from his quiver and presented it to Cabeza de Vaca. Tomorrow morning, their hand gestures seemed to suggest, they would bring the hungry foreigners food.

At dawn, as promised, a contingent arrived with fish for the castaways to eat. The leeward shore of Galveston Island is laced with inlets, bays, and tidal streams that in fall and early winter are choked with spawning black drum, redfish, sea trout, croaker, and sea catfish. The islanders caught them in great numbers in weirs and traps, and were experts as well at shooting fish with arrows from their dugout canoes. They also brought roots to eat, dug with great effort from immense stands of cattail.

The locals returned the next day as well, bringing with them not only more food but also the women and children of the village, that they too might see the strangers who had washed up. The adult women wore Spanish moss, and the young, Cabeza de Vaca noticed, "cover[ed] themselves with deerskins." It was another good day of trading, "and thus they went home rich in the bells and beads that we gave them," he said.

For virtually the first time in the history of the expedition, good relations with the local Indians did not immediately deteriorate. For a week, the islanders brought supplies of cattail roots and dried fish to the castaways on the beach. There was plenty of driftwood for fires, and slowly, with sleep and warmth, strength crept back into Cabeza de Vaca

and his crew. It was as good a situation as they had had since leaving Boca Ciega Bay, but who knew how long it could last? Days were
notably short now, and the beach was not a place to spend the oncom-
ing winter, counting on the continued hospitality of strangers.

One morning after the Indians had delivered some breakfast and
then gone on their way, Cabeza de Vaca gave the order to relaunch the
boat. The waves by now had half-buried the hull in the sand, so they
stripped off their clothes to keep them dry while they worked to free it.
It took the better part of the morning on their knees scooping away at
the sand with bare hands, sticks, and shells just to dig it out. Eventually,
though, they got the hull loose and righted it. Everything they still possessed was put back aboard, and they stood naked, at the water's edge,
waiting for Cabeza de Vaca's signal to shove off.

It was exhausting, he recalled later, "because we were in such a
condition that other much less strenuous tasks would have sufficed to
place us in difficulty." Men groaned, shouted, heaved. And slowly,
slowly, the gawky craft inched toward the surf. Once the bow was floating in the water, those at the front clambered on board and took up the
oars. Others continued to shout and push from behind, climbing in
only as the boat made its way into deep enough water to support their
weight without grounding. All who could lift an oar now pulled with
all they could.

But they didn't make it.

Cabeza de Vaca figured they were "at a distance of two crossbow
shots out to sea" when the first big wave washed over them. This is
a tricky distance to translate: tests done in the 1940s with reproduc-
tions of period weapons have shown that sixteenth-century crossbows
could fire a bolt nearly four hundred yards, but that the practical range
for aiming was more like fifty to seventy-five yards. Given that the first
wave struck while some of the men were still outside the boat pushing,

and that waves large enough to break eight hundred yards offshore would have convinced even desperate men to wait for calmer seas, the boat was most likely a hundred yards from the beach when trouble began.

The wave was so suddenly cold and powerful against their naked bodies as it poured over the bow that almost everybody simply let go of the oars. Out of control now, the boat lurched immediately broadside, and the next wave simply rolled it over. Most of the men jumped or tumbled free and managed to thrash their way back to the beach, but three, including Cabeza de Vaca's fellow commander, Solís, held onto the swamped boat. When it rolled they were trapped underneath, and when it sank they drowned.

These are the first three deaths that are specifically accounted for out of the forty-nine persons who began the voyage in Cabeza de Vaca's boat. There were surely others, however. Some of the five who had died of thirst off the coast of Alabama; some who gave out during the days at sea when Cabeza de Vaca says everyone but himself and the pilot were unconscious. But several dozen—maybe even forty—members of his original complement were still alive and managed to wade ashore. "The sea, with a single thrust, threw all the others, who were in the waves and half drowned, onto the coast," he recalled. From this point in the story onward, however, the numbers dwindle, often without explanation.

Everything was lost, including the clothes they had carefully taken off and stowed in the boats to keep dry. They had long ago given up their hope of conquering great lands and spreading news of the One True God to the heathens. They had eaten their beloved horses, fled from the Apalachee Indians, and been deserted by their governor. But the Spaniards among them were still, up to that moment, in some measure conquistadors; they had their steel swords even if they were too weak to wield them. They had a boat and a place to go. Some still had their helmets and their beads and bells to trade. They had porters and slaves. They had clothes.

But now, whether slave or conquistador, hidalgo or commoner, they were alike: forty naked, drenched human bodies, shivering uncontrollably in a cold north wind on a Texas beach in late fall coming onto early winter. Even to themselves, now fairly used to seeing each other in states of near starvation, they looked beyond hope. The ribs of every one of them were visible, remembered Cabeza de Vaca. Some wept openly. Others gave up, sat with their arms wrapped around their knees, blue lips and skin, waiting for death. A few who were not ready to face eternal judgment, however, fanned the embers in the campfires. And when "God granted" that a flame was found, they piled on driftwood from as far as they could drag it until they had built several roaring bonfires.

Nakedness wasn't just a practical issue. It was also a symbolic turning point, after which the Spaniards could no longer differentiate themselves from those whom they had come to conquer. As the historian Felipe Fernández-Armesto has pointed out, "clothes were the standard by which a people's level of civilization was judged in Medieval Latin Christendom." The Spanish obsession with clothing was so deep that Cervantes later parodied it: when all else has failed, Don Quixote decides the only way to prove that his love for Dulcinea has driven him truly out of his mind is to get naked. "For the love of God, my master," his trusty sidekick Sancho begs, "let me not see your Grace stripped, for I'd feel so sorry that I'd never stop weeping. . . . If your Grace wants me to witness some of your insane actions, please perform them with your clothes on and be brief about it and to the point."

Ironically, their nakedness doubtless saved more than a few from drowning. But once back on shore they looked at each other's shivering flesh and were confronted with the awful possibility that what they had always believed was Spanish cultural and moral superiority over the rest of the world was, in the end, just material superiority. Their "civilization" of tools, trinkets, and clothing had washed away. They named the island Malhado, or "bad fortune," and began to pray.

"And thus we were beseeching our Lord for mercy and the pardon of our sins, shedding many tears, each one having pity not only for himself but for all the others whom they saw in the same state," said Cabeza de Vaca.

Out of fear that the islanders might try to prevent their escape, the Spaniards hadn't told their hosts of their plans to relaunch the boat and leave. At sunset, therefore, as they had done every day, the Malhado islanders came back to the beach with food. But after one look at the situation they turned and began to leave, lest whatever bad thing had happened to their new friends might somehow happen to them. Only after Cabeza de Vaca chased them down and explained the situation—the boat had turned over, three men had drowned, the two bodies lying there not far from the huddled mass of naked sufferers were in fact dead—did the islanders come close. When they fully understood what had happened, they sat down with the men and began to cry.

The Indians of Malhado Island turned out to be fantastic weepers. They positively howled for more than half an hour and carried on "so sincerely that they could be heard a great distance away." Some of the Narváez survivors later figured out that these people always cried long and hard for the dead, and often for the living as well. But under the current circumstances, their sympathy was less comforting than it might have been, for it just rubbed in to the Spaniards how far they had fallen. In the imperial mind, you had to be pretty badly off indeed if even the Indians were feeling sorry for you.

"To see that these men, so lacking in reason and so crude in the manner of brutes, grieved so much for us increased in me and in others

of our company even more the magnitude of our suffering and the estimation of our misfortune," remembered Cabeza de Vaca. The curious
tone of surprise at the thought that Indians might be capable of empa-
thy is even clearer in the survivors' joint account of their ordeal: "They
began to cry with the Christians *as if* they sorrowed over the happening" (italics added).

It's a telling moment, in which the would-be conquerors are at
last forced to look their would-be victims in the eye. Here begin the
"novel things" Cabeza de Vaca had predicted for his readers: the weak
are now strong and sympathetic, and the strong are now pathetic and
meek. Spanish imperial reality, as more than one literary scholar has
noted, is hereafter inverted in Cabeza de Vaca's memoir.

Who these Malhado islanders were is not a simple thing to
deduce. Unlike the Apalachee and Safety Harbor peoples that the
expedition had encountered in Florida, the coastal Indians of Texas
were seasonally migratory hunter-gatherers who left little or nothing in
the way of architectural remains. What's more, after the Narváez survivors passed through, no European is known to have interacted with
the coastal Texans until the hapless French explorer La Salle briefly
arrived in Matagorda Bay nearly a century and a half later.

By that time, waves of disease and displacement were emanating
into the region from the Spanish to the south and west, and to a lesser
extent from the French and English to the east and north. Native life
was in flux, with collapsing local populations and immigrant groups
like the Apache, Comanche, and others pushing in from the European
frontiers. The result was an impenetrable tangle of ethnic identities:
there are more than a thousand "tribes" mentioned in the documentary
sources for the region. The first twenty-three of those are in Cabeza de
Vaca's narrative, including the Hans and Capoques he said lived on
Malhado Island.

The safest approach to their identity would be to leave it there without attempting to elaborate. That said, the Hans and Capoques were probably related either to people later known as the Akokisa or to those now referred to by archeologists as the Karankawa. Or both: the Hans and Capoques spoke different languages, and Galveston Island was near a transition zone between Akokisa and Karankawa. Whoever they were, in the wake of the boat wreck Cabeza de Vaca thought they represented his company's only hope for survival through the upcoming winter. When the weeping subsided, therefore, he suggested to his men that they try to convince the Indians to take them home with them to their village.

It was another inversion of expectations: instead of bringing civilization to grateful heathens, the leader of the conquerors now begged to be given the privilege to learn to live like the locals. Not everyone in his company agreed with the plan, however. A faction among the naked and shivering were downright terrified by the prospect of moving into an Indian village. The main dissenters were those who had previously been to Mexico, either with Cortés or with Narváez, and were certain that once in the heathen's lair they would become human sacrifices to some devilish idols. They remembered Cempoallan, where every day, according to Bernal Díaz's recollections, there were "sacrificed before us three, four, or five Indians whose hearts were offered to the idols and their blood plastered on the walls, and the feet, arms, and legs of the victims were cut off and eaten, just as in our country we eat beef brought from the butchers." Or they remembered the rack at Tenochtitlan that supposedly held 136,000 skulls.

"We should not even speak of it," they said of Cabeza de Vaca's plan.

But he was now in sole command of this particular remnant of the expedition, and he overrode their concerns. Not that he thought their fears unjustified; he later confessed that he, too, worried they would be killed in the village. But there was no other choice, he told his fellow sufferers. Staying on the beach for the coming winter with no tools, no boat, and no clothes was certain to kill them all, probably sooner rather than later. He cut off discussion, turned again to the islanders, and begged as best he could with hand gestures and signs for them to take in and care for him and his motley crew.

Even though they had been feeding the castaways now for a week or more, this was a lot to ask. The appearance of two hundred warriors on the day the Spaniards first landed suggests the nearby village or villages supported a population of at least four or five hundred persons. But unlike the corn-growing cultures to the east, the Texas coastal peoples were not likely to have on hand the sort of surplus necessary to support the sudden addition of forty starving and sick individuals. Nonetheless, the islanders "took great pleasure" in the prospect of aiding the strangers and told the castaways to wait there on the beach for them to return. They then collected huge loads of driftwood from the beach and hurried off in the direction of their town.

This was strange and worrisome: the firewood was something new. Throughout the rest of that cold day, the forty naked conquistadors huddled by their fires and wondered about the arrangements. Why couldn't they have simply gone to the village immediately? What was all the wood for? Those among them who were opposed to the plan from the beginning grumbled aloud that it could not be good. The fires were for roasting men, they thought.

At dusk, the islanders returned and announced it was time to leave. A few of Cabeza de Vaca's men had revived a bit, but most were still so weakened from exposure that they were incapable of walking far or fast. The islanders urged them on, and when that failed they simply picked them up and carried them. Into the darkening night the survivors were hustled along on strong shoulders, and after a short while the warmth from the fire on the beach was only a memory. The cold and uncontrollable shivering set in anew. But just when the castaways began to fade they arrived at a roaring fire of driftwood that had been built not for roasting, but for reviving.

"Fearing that on the road some one of us might fall unconscious or die, they made provision for four or five very great bonfires placed at intervals, and at each one they warmed us," recalled Cabeza de Vaca. "And when they saw that we had regained some strength and warmth, they carried us to the next one, so rapidly that they almost did not let our feet touch the ground."

Finally the village itself appeared out of the dark, and the survivors were deposited in a shelter that had been specially prepared for them. It was almost certainly constructed in the traditional Karankawa way: a frame of long willow poles, sharpened and driven into the ground at both ends, and covered with mats and skins. Often, only the windward side of the frame was covered leaving one side open to the air. At the back would be platforms to sleep on, as well as more skins and mats. But the only detail Cabeza de Vaca remembered was that there were "many fires" in the house, around which he and his comrades heaped themselves in their desperate attempts to get warm, to get rest, and in many cases simply to stay alive another day.

With their patients attended to, the rescuers began to make music. All through the night the Malhado islanders sang and danced in the village center. Cabeza de Vaca and the others had no way of knowing the significance, religious or otherwise, of the goings on, but it didn't sound overtly mournful or solemn. It sounded rather like a "great celebration."

In their convalescents' hut, the half-dead foreigners listened and wondered. "There was neither rejoicing nor sleep," said Cabeza de Vaca, "as we were awaiting the moment when they would sacrifice us."

Only in the morning, when their hosts arrived with a healthy breakfast of roots and fish did the terror begin to subside.

16

Figueroa's Attempt

Something caught Cabeza de Vaca's eye. Breakfast was over, and most of his men were dozing in the shelter the Indians had made for them. Others who were strong enough sat by the fires, listlessly watching themselves being watched by curious children of the village. Only a few, including Cabeza de Vaca, had the strength and will to be up and about, taking stock of their new home and the people who lived there.

It may have been a pair of scissors or an iron chisel that he saw hanging around the neck of one of the islanders. Or it could have been a scrap of fabric. But it was clearly something made by Europeans. This in itself wasn't really noteworthy, since up until the loss of their boat, he himself had been trading bells and beads in exchange for food. What sparked Cabeza de Vaca's interest in this particular trinket was that he was certain it had not been among the trade goods he or the men in his boat had supplied. He approached the wearer.

The castaways believed themselves to be quite close to the Spanish settlement at Pánuco by now, so part of him dared to hope that the islander would somehow signal that he traded for the item in a town of Spaniards. But Pánuco was in fact still hundreds of miles away, and the answer he got after the usual round of pointing and gesturing was that another boatload of strangers like himself had come ashore a few miles back to the east. This wasn't as good as hearing they were almost to Mexico, but it was still very good news, and he immediately sent two of his healthiest men to go with some local guides to investigate.

The day before Cabeza de Vaca's boat had originally washed ashore, the boat under the command of captains Castillo and Dorantes had successfully beached five miles up the same coast. They, too, had been met by friendly Malhado islanders who were happy to trade with them. And as it turned out they, too, had recently learned of the existence of other castaways on the island and were at that moment on their own way to investigate.

Just as the Malhado islanders had been shocked when they first came down to the beach and found Cabeza de Vaca and his men naked and shivering, Castillo and Dorantes were astonished to see their fellow expeditionaries looking like beaten animals. It actually frightened them, because the nudity and vulnerability of their fellow conquistadors exposed just how close they themselves were to such absolute desperation; their own clothes were ragged, but they somewhat hid the exposed ribs and wasted muscles. Had they only known how badly off Cabeza de Vaca and his men were, Dorantes and Castillo said, they would have brought the few remaining clothes from their boat.

That boat was still intact, though not in very good shape. Nevertheless, Cabeza de Vaca, Dorantes, and Castillo decided that repairing it seemed their best hope. But with two boatloads of survivors and only one boat, a decision had to be made. They could do as Narváez had done before he was blown out to sea, putting the sickest on board and traveling in tandem with walkers along the coast. But the sick may have been too sick and too many for such a strategy: in Cabeza de Vaca's party especially, even the strong were barely sturdy enough to walk. With winter upon them, the idea was rejected.

Three times before, Cabeza de Vaca had self-righteously opposed attempts to divide the company, but now he had come to the same conclusion that his former commander had: the strong could wait for the weak only at their peril. "All together we agreed to repair their raft, to go forward in it those of us who had the strength and will to do so," he now said. Those without the requisite strength or will would have to "remain there until they recovered to the point where they could go along the coast as they were able."

Cabeza de Vaca doesn't explicitly say that he himself would be in the boat party, but the pronouns imply it. The plan only fell apart when the boat wouldn't float. The wood was worm-eaten and waterlogged, and there were "other defects" as well. After a day of hard digging they loosened it from the sand and eased it back into the water, but it wouldn't hold anyone up. When it sank altogether, they resigned themselves to spending the winter on Malhado.

Around the fire that evening they weighed their options. It was obvious that despite the hospitality of the islanders, for many in the company spring would be too late: an hidalgo named Tavera had died that very day from exposure and starvation. As usual, there was no consensus about how far they had already come and how far it still must be to Pánuco, but everyone agreed that they ought to at least try to get word of their location out. If even a small group of the strongest among them could manage to get to the Spanish outposts, they could send a ship back for the others. It was a terribly long shot, but it was worth a try.

Other than general robustness, the primary criterion for selection for the mission was an ability to swim. The islanders could be convinced to ferry them to the mainland in their dugout canoes, but after that the idea was to move quickly, which meant not spending time looking for fords or boats to get across any rivers or inlets. Only five fit the bill: a hidalgo named Figueroa would lead the attempt, accompanied by the Portuguese carpenter Álvaro Fernández, "Estudillo, a native of Zafra," and someone named Méndez. The fifth person was an Indian from an island called "Avia." This Avia may have been Malhado itself, as it certainly would have behooved the party to take a local guide if they could convince one to go. He could just as well have been from Cuba or another Caribbean island, in which case he was almost certainly a slave.

They set out immediately with high hopes, but little or nothing in the way of supplies. There was, as it turned out, plenty of water to cross. Immediately west of Galveston are a succession of four rivers in the course of thirty miles that required them to wade or swim. They passed Oyster Creek, the Brazos River, the San Bernard, and Caney Creek. Along this stretch they also passed the wreckage of the friar's boat but saw no sign of its passengers, who had themselves already walked west.

Eventually they trudged out onto the Matagorda Peninsula, where only a few weeks before, the survivors of Narváez's boat had joined up with those of the friars'. It's an endless, featureless, howling barrier beach in winter, and within days of their departure from Malhado the weather, already cold, took a turn for the worse. Gulf coast winters are not severe, but fast-moving polar cold fronts called "blue northers" frequently drop the temperature rapidly below freezing. All through January and most of February of 1529, the five ragged

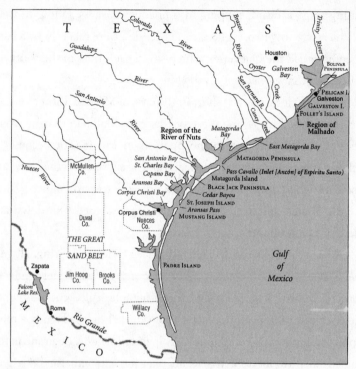

Detail of the Texas coast in the vicinity of Malhado island. (Courtesy of the University of Nebraska Press)

swimmers tucked their heads down, closed their eyes as nearly shut as they could, and willed themselves forward through the wind and sand. There was nowhere to sleep but in the lee of a log, nothing to eat but a little seaweed. A hundred and twenty miles they plodded on, across the sand, to the mile-wide Pass Cavallo, across whose currents they could not have swum even if they weren't nearly dead from exposure.

Somehow, though, they managed to get to the other side, either by finding a canoe, or with help from local Karankawa Indians. But not long after crossing the pass, either to the mainland or more likely across the opening to Matagorda Island, members of the team began to lie down and die. Estudillo, Fernández, and the "native of Avia" all succumbed, refusing to go forward, slipping into unconsciousness, failing to wake up. The remaining two, Figueroa and Méndez, were taken in by a band of people called the Quevenes, which saved their lives in the short run though not, as it turned out, in the long run.

Even the long run was short in the case of Méndez. Either because he had promised his fellow survivors back on Malhado that he would not give up until he got to the Spanish in Mexico, or because he couldn't stand the thought of remaining a captive, at the very first opportunity he started out down the sand again toward Pánuco. When his new masters discovered his absence, they chased him down and killed him on the spot.

After that, Figueroa decided to bide his time until spring. He may have lost even more courage after meeting up with Hernando de Esquivel, a captive of a nearby band of people called the Mariames. The encounter was not by chance; when those holding Figueroa mentioned to him that there was another Spaniard nearby, he immediately finagled an introduction. It was an exciting moment for both men because Esquivel had been on the friar's boat when the makeshift fleet was scattered off the coast of Louisiana and, with that crew, had reunited with Narváez's boat along the Matagorda Peninsula. Up until this meeting between Figueroa and Esquivel, no one from either party had any idea what had become of any of their fellow expeditionaries, though they held out hope that someone had gotten through to Pánuco and was sending back help.

But when they met, Esquivel had a grizzly tale to tell. It wasn't far from where they currently were, he told Figueroa, that Narváez had drifted off to his presumed death at sea leaving eighty or so members of his former army stranded on the beach. As Narváez had directed, Pantoja immediately took charge and for a few weeks led the company reasonably well on its ragged march along the barrier islands. But as the days spread to weeks, and November stretched into December, a dangerous level of dissension began to percolate among the company. The friars, who even in the Florida Panhandle had believed Pánuco was always just around the next bend, now became convinced that they must have passed it while at sea. They were marching in the wrong direction, they began to say to the rank and file, and many believed them, including Esquivel himself.

This kind of confusion and second-guessing in a company of desperate men was beyond Pantoja's ability to manage. He became increasingly authoritarian in his efforts to keep the band moving, and by the time they got to the end of San Jose Island and the Aransas Pass, near the very bottom corner of Texas, he was downright abusive. As members of the company began to die of hunger and cold, said Esquivel, an officer named Sotomayor cracked. In a fit of rage he "gave Pantoja such a blow that it killed him." It was a sobering moment, the hollow men sitting listlessly by while one of their putative leaders murdered another, but no one was really sorry to see the end of Pantoja, and no one had the energy to intervene.

Whether Sotomayor took over command after the murder is somewhat moot as there were fewer and fewer decisions to make. When they had first arrived at the wooded tip of San Jose Island, there was a group of Karankawa living there, probably those called the Quevenes. But as soon as these people became aware of the hoard of starving strangers trudging down the beach toward them, they sensibly packed their houses and other belongings into their canoes and paddled away across the pass. The presence of the Indians may have given the Spaniards initial confidence that a living could be gleaned there: fresh water and firewood could be found nearby, as well as a few crabs and shellfish. But even the Karankawa rarely tried to survive out on those wind-blown barrier islands through the winter.

There was, in fact, only one major decision made during those months at the bitter end of San Jose Island, and no one cared to take credit for it. At some point, the living began to eat the dead, cutting the flesh into strips and drying it in what sun there was, or in the smoke of their fires. From eighty survivors, the party dwindled inexorably to forty and then to twenty, and to ten. Finally only Sotomayor and Esquivel were left alive, and for the last few weeks, they camped there among the bones of their comrades, watching each other's health dwindle, wondering the same thing. "And the last one to die was Soto-mayor, and Esquivel made jerky of him, and eating of him, he maintained himself until the first of March."

That was the day one of the Indians who had abandoned the place the previous winter came back across the opening in his canoe to see if the strangers were dead yet. Finding only Esquivel there among the remnants of his former comrades, the man took him into custody. Whether he did this out of sympathy, horror, or simply to get a new slave is not revealed, but Esquivel was still in his possession when Figueroa came and met with him.

Between them, Esquivel and Figueroa could now account for four of the five boats that had set out from the Florida Panhandle: two on Malhado and two at Matagorda. Of the fate of the fifth and final boat, which had not been seen or heard of since it separated from Cabeza de Vaca's boat at sea, they could only speculate. They hoped beyond hope that it had gotten through to the settlements, but in fact it, too, had already long since come ashore. As its forty-five crew members stumbled and crawled up onto the beach on Mustang or Pedro Island, in the bottom corner of Texas, they were quickly slaughtered by a group of Indians called the Camones, who took their meager possessions and traded them with other Indians up the coast.

When Esquivel finished telling his story of cannibalism and captivity, Figueroa tried to convince him to flee. Now that it was spring, he argued, together they had a good chance of making it west and south down the coast toward Pánuco. But Esquivel refused, not because he was afraid to leave, but because the priests had convinced him that they had already passed Pánuco in the boats and that it now lay to their east. Figueroa couldn't believe what he was hearing, but he didn't get a chance to press his case. While the two Spaniards were arguing geography, his keepers decided it was time to go and took him back to their village somewhere else along the coast.

He was still living there some months later when once again he learned that there were other strangers like him in the vicinity. Again he was taken to visit, this time across the inlet to the tip of Matagorda Island. But though he was overjoyed to discover that a dozen of his former campmates had made the trek up the beach from Malhado Island under the leadership of Castillo and Dorantes, once again the general news was not good. In fact, the story Castillo and Dorantes had to tell of what they had endured during the long winter on Malhado was almost as harrowing as Esquivel's report on the fate of the two crews under Pantoja.

17

The News from Malhado

When it was their turn to tell what they knew, Castillo and Dorantes told Figueroa that back on Malhado, and back at the beginning of that terrible winter, the dying had begun less than a week after he and the other swimmers had set off down the beach to look for help. The spate of winter storms sapped what strength was left in the castaways who remained behind, and most of them succumbed to disease and exposure before the year was out. By early 1529, fewer than twenty remained alive out of the eighty who had landed on the island. The weather was so harsh that even the Malhado islanders were unable to collect the cattail roots they were accustomed to gathering, and the fish they usually speared and netted were gone from the winding shallows on the bay side of the island.

For most of the castaways the cause of death wasn't starvation so much as exposure, but there were five notable exceptions and their reaction to the hunger nearly caused the execution of the rest of the company. They were part of a group of six men who didn't live in the village proper, but camped instead out on the coast not far from where the boats had come ashore. They may have been among those who were most terrified at the prospect of living among the Indians, or they may have been posted on the beach to keep an eye out for ships. For all anyone on Malhado knew at that point, the five swimmers had gotten through to Pánuco and sent someone back to look for the others.

As they waited in vain, death came in small doses. One by one the cold and hunger defeated them and with or without discussion, they too began to eat the bodies of their comrades. "They ate one another until only one remained," said Cabeza de Vaca, "who because he was alone, had no one to eat him."

It's not clear how the cannibalism was discovered by the Indians of Malhado Island, that is, whether the sixth man survived to tell the tale or whether the chain of events was deduced from the sight of one man's uneaten body and five men's picked bones. But either way, the Indians were disgusted and furious when they found that the Europeans had eaten each other, and it immediately created a crisis atmosphere for the other survivors on the island. Cabeza de Vaca says the news "produced such a scandal among them that without a doubt, if at the start they had seen it, they would have killed them, and all of us would have been in grave danger."

It was another reversal of the expected order of things in imperial Spain. Along with sodomy and human sacrifice, cannibalism was one of the standard justifications for enslaving Indians and taking their possessions, and stopping such culinary and sexual evildoing was believed to be one of the reasons God had made Spain so powerful. Yet here on Malhado, it was the Christians who devoured each other, and the heathens who were outraged.

Ironically, the coastal Indians have traditionally been portrayed in Texas histories as voracious man-eaters. The reputation originated with a 1719 account by Simars de Bellisle, who lived for two years in the vicinity of Galveston. He described a raid in which the Indians captured an enemy who was up in a tree collecting nuts: "One of them cut his head off and another one cut the arms off while they skinned him at the same time," he reported. "Several of them ate the yellow fat, which was still raw, and finally they devoured him completely."

Spanish missionaries picked up where Bellisle left off, publicizing hearsay accounts of knife- and shell-wielding Karankawa dancers circling a victim tied to a post. "When they see fit they go up to the patient, cut off a piece of his flesh, pass it over the fire and dripping with blood, they eat it in sight of the victim, accompanying this by horrible gestures and incomparable voices," wrote a certain Friar Morfi, who later admitted he never saw it himself.

The reputation for cannibalism among the Karankawa became so entrenched in local lore that current scholars generally begin their discussions by describing them in such terms as the "most maligned and misunderstood Native American peoples who once inhabited Texas." The accepted wisdom today is that some "ritualized" eating of human remains probably took place, but that Friar Morfi was a fabricator, and Bellisle was either a fabricator, an exaggerator, or simply didn't recognize the ritualistic nature of the repast he witnessed.

The only cannibalism the Narváez survivors saw was a little ceremonial sipping of pulverized shaman's bones mixed with water, a practice that modern anthropologists believe was intended to deny the dead the opportunity for an afterlife. In a final bizarre twist on the conquistadors' Christian worldview, the men on the beach who no doubt prayed fervently for their own eternal souls before eating human flesh brought on the wrath of the Indians precisely because they were consuming the potential afterlife of their brethren.

The cannibalism crisis on Malhado only passed because the perpetrators were all dead. But the survivors' troubles with the islanders weren't over. Every day during January and February of 1529 the eighteen expeditionaries who were still alive woke up to the sound of weeping. A deadly stomach illness had broken out, killing many of the islanders. Malhado tradition demanded that grieving parents mourn for a full year, covering themselves in ashes and rising before dawn to keen. What's more, relatives of the deceased were not permitted to seek their own food for three months, but relied on their neighbors to feed them. That January, however, there were simply too many mourners and not enough neighbors. "In most of the houses there was very great hunger in the effort to keep their custom and ceremony," Cabeza de Vaca recalled.

Eventually the bereaved decided they knew the origin of the troubles. The strangers had brought this death to the island, they argued to their leaders, and only if the last of them were killed would the sickness abate. There was an informal trial of sorts, a debate among the Malhado leadership that was swinging toward execution, until one of the headmen asked his neighbors to explain why, if the Spanish were powerful enough to bring such a disease to Malhado, they themselves were dying even more rapidly than the Indians? He pointed out that the castaways' own leader, Cabeza de Vaca, was at death's door.

They were allowed to live, but when spring came and the majority of the castaways wanted to move on, the islanders were happy to see them go. By that point the Narváez survivors had been distributed in small groups to various island villages and then further dispersed when

"*Carancahueses*," *by Lino Sanchez y Tapia. This is the only known image of the Karankawa Indians made by an artist who actually saw them in person. (Courtesy of the Gilcrease Museum, Omaha)*

the villages broke up into smaller family units to go to winter camps in the myriad bays and inlets of the mainland.

These moves were part of the regular annual migration cycle for the coastal peoples, but didn't result in an overwhelming improvement in conditions. For three months they subsisted on nothing but oysters and other shellfish collected from vast beds that became exposed at low tide, washed down with brackish water. This kept the humans only slightly better fed than the clouds of mosquitoes that descended every evening, driving everyone into lean-tos clogged with the thick smoke of smudge-fires, built not for warmth but to keep the insects at bay.

By the time the oyster season wound down in early spring, most of the survivors were ready to push on at all costs toward the Spanish settlements on the coast of Mexico. The islanders were returning in dribs and drabs from the oyster camps to the villages of Malhado for the summer season of fishing and root eating, and from them Dorantes and Castillo learned that only fifteen of their company had survived the winter. Two were cousins of Dorantes, Pedro de Valdivieso and Diego Dorantes. Diego de Huelva was also already back on Malhado and anxious to make the attempt, as were five others known only as Benítez, Gutiérrez, Chaves, Tostado, and Estrada. On another island nearby was the Moroccan, Esteban, along with a priest remembered only as "the Asturian" because he came from that region of Spain. They were brought over to Malhado to join the attempt.

The scribe, Alaniz, was alive and on Malhado, but he was too ill to consider traveling. The same was true of Lope de Oviedo, who had been the healthiest member of Cabeza de Vaca's crew on the day they had come ashore the previous November. As for Cabeza de Vaca, the islanders said he was still in the oyster bays of the mainland but was very sick. Castillo and Dorantes agreed that they would try to collect him there if they could.

There's no clue in either account of what was said by way of thanks or farewells when the time came to leave the Indians who had saved their lives when they were naked and had taught them how to find oysters and cattail roots when they were hungry. Relations were more complicated than simply master and slave. For instance, though the Indians helped locate the castaways who were strong enough to travel, they did not offer to ferry the dozen men across to the mainland for free. Even more illuminating is that the castaways still had something valuable to offer in exchange for transportation.

What Castillo and Dorantes chose to offer wasn't a European

bauble or weapon, however. Those were either long since traded for food or were being hoarded for future needs. They paid instead with the fine fur coat confiscated from the chief along the Alabama coast the previous summer. They had, in a sense, fully entered the Native American economy, and with the price settled, the islanders ferried them across Galveston Bay.

As planned, they tried to find Cabeza de Vaca, but not very hard. Hearing that he was very close to death, they left him to his fate and followed the route that Figueroa and the other strong swimmers had taken the previous fall. Unlike that party, they had to stop and make rafts at each river and inlet and though the first stream, now called Oyster Creek, wasn't much of a problem, the Brazos was muddy and swollen with spring rains.

They tugged enough driftwood from the tangled masses along the banks to build two rafts, and the first made its way to the opposite bank without incident. But the second, with five people on board, got caught in a rip. The men couldn't find any purchase on the bottom with their short poles, and the ridiculous craft wheeled its way downstream, out of control. Once it was obvious they were being swept out to sea, two of the five jumped overboard and managed to make it to shore. Two more jumped in and drowned.

The last man clung to the raft until it drifted free of the river's current and out into the gulf. When he stood up he could see some of his fellow Christian conquerors struggling in the water and others on the beach waving or just numbly watching. But he had no paddle, no oar, no mast or sail. For a while he tried to hold his arms up to catch more of the wind at his back, but after only a few moments he dropped them by his side again, exhausted. He had no strength and he stood there, a single starving human body on a makeshift pile of driftwood floating at the desolate edge of the New World. But his God wasn't quite done with him and after a few hours the raft came back ashore, and he had rejoined the others on the trek to Matagorda, where they now sat in a circle on the beach telling their story to Figueroa.

Listening to Castillo and Dorantes describe the journey from Malhado, Figueroa remembered crossing those four rivers himself. He remembered as well the long march down the beach, the hunger, the many inlets to cross. When they told him that two more of their company died of starvation along the way, he wasn't surprised, knowing from experience that there was nothing on that beach to eat but seaweed and a few small crabs that were "almost nothing but shell." Nor would it really have surprised Figueroa to hear that Cabeza de Vaca was either dead already or very soon to die. The last word they had of him from the Indians was that he was desperately ill, "with no hope of surviving." Nothing in fact would have surprised any of them at this point, except possibly the arrival of their own particular instant of death, and that only to the degree that every human being must wonder at the very end how and why their time to die has truly come.

Out of three hundred who came ashore in Florida a year before, there were now only fourteen still alive: nine in Dorantes and Castillo's party plus Figueroa and Esquivel made eleven in the vicinity of the Pass Cavallo, and Oviedo and Alaniz back on Malhado made thirteen. Lastly, at death's door on the mainland opposite Malhado, there was Cabeza de Vaca. For him the only surprise of that spring may have been at his own particular capacity to survive when everyone he knew had abandoned him for dead.

18

The Traveling Salesman

Cabeza de Vaca didn't begrudge Dorantes, Castillo, and his other former comrades their decision to abandon him. The fact was, his own assessment of his prospects were in line with theirs. "If any other thing were to give me hope of survival," he recalled of those months, "that illness alone sufficed to deprive me of it altogether."

Slowly, though, he gained strength, and in April he was sturdy enough to travel with his keepers to a place on the coast where they ate nothing but blackberries. There his health began to rebound in earnest, and by the time the cycle of seasonal gathering came full circle and the band returned to Malhado, the islanders had given him a digging stick and told him in no uncertain terms to go get his own supper and some for them as well.

"I had to dig the roots to eat out from under the water and among the rushes where they grew in the ground," he recalled. Cattails grow in vast stands along the Texas coast and like the plants described by Cabeza de Vaca, become inedible in mid to late winter. Despite the stick, the job was murder on his bare hands. "My fingers were so worn that when a reed touched them it caused them to bleed," he remembered later.

He was also expected to gather firewood, and whenever the band moved their camp, which they did every few days in order to find new supplies of roots, he carried "their belongings on his back." In other words, he did all the things that every able-bodied female Malhado islander did almost every day of her life, and after roughly a year he found it intolerable. "I was unable to endure the life that I had," he said, citing "the great labors they forced me to perform and the bad treatment they gave me."

This "bad treatment" was a stark change from the year before. The tough turn may have been the result of the cannibalism and the stomach plague of the previous winter, but one archeologist thinks Cabeza de Vaca's downfall was the first in a pattern that may have a more general explanation. Lawrence Aten studied the records of captives in the region over several centuries and found that all were treated well at first. "But after a period of time had elapsed during which the natives apparently satisfied themselves that the Europeans were not in possession of some fearsome supernatural powers (for the accounts make it clear that this was on their minds), they were suddenly subjected to all manner of inhospitable treatment."

Other than the manual labor, Cabeza de Vaca didn't elaborate on indignities he endured. If it was anything like the range of abuses described by his former boatmates down the coast, or of captives in the

Galveston area in later periods, it was mostly beatings and gratuitous beard and hair plucking. Whatever his tortures consisted of, by the time the cattail roots sprouted in the winter of 1530 and Cabeza de Vaca and his keepers had once again returned to the mainland for the oyster season, the imperial Spanish treasurer for North America had had enough. As soon as the oyster season was over and his current keepers were making ready to return to the island, he planned to "flee" in the opposite direction and look for another group of Indians he knew of called the Charruco. They lived in the river-bottom forests just inland from the shellfish beds.

The moment came when no one was watching and he took off across the saw grass toward the line of trees where he knew a river came into Galveston Bay. He was entirely alone, with neither clothes nor weapons, but only a few shells that he thought the Charrucos would like. Still, he was moving and alive. And no doubt scared. As it turned out, though, the Malhado Indians made no more attempt to stop Cabeza de Vaca than they had Dorantes and the others the previous spring.

Even if they did want him back, they would have thought twice about going after Cabeza de Vaca once he crossed over into Charruco territory. The Charrucos didn't get along with anybody. Their relations with their neighbors consisted of an endless cycle of raids followed by revenge raids. It was, said Cabeza de Vaca, a state of "continual warfare" that left them pretty much isolated from both the tribes further inland and those on the coast.

The only problem with this situation from the Charruco perspective was that there were many things both on the coast and inland that they wanted to buy and couldn't because no one who saw a Charruco coming their way stuck around long enough to do business. So when this strange hairy man from Malhado showed up, it occurred to somebody that he could make himself useful as well as merely exotic, and they loaded him up with merchandise and sent him off shopping.

Understanding the commerce between the myriad native nations of North America before the arrival of Europeans is an archeological work in progress. What's clear, however, is that high-tech research technologies such as optical emission spectroscopy and atomic absorption spectrophotometry are uncovering ever-more complexity and range of precontact trade patterns. Seven thousand years ago beads made from ocean shells were carried to the Duck River in Tennessee. Twenty-five hundred years ago ornaments made of copper from the Great Lakes were buried in graves in southern Florida. Galena from the Upper Mississippi has turned up in precontact sites in Georgia. Large quantities of obsidian at ancient sites in Ohio came from Yellowstone in Wyoming.

Closer to Cabeza de Vaca's time, in the Mississippi River watershed, De Soto's men in the 1540s saw "turquoises and cotton blankets which the Indians gave them to understand by signs were brought from the west," most likely the Zuñi and Hopi peoples of Arizona and New Mexico. Similarly Coronado, advancing in the opposite direction, met Indians in eastern New Mexico who knew about the Mississippi and said that "one could go along this river through an inhabited region for ninety days without a break from settlement to settlement . . . and that the river was more than a league wide."

Most of what is known about precontact commerce comes from beads, ornaments, shell cups, and arrowheads, but those items are simply the ones that survive in archeological remains, while nondurable products disappeared along with the cultures that exchanged them. De Soto's men, for instance, met up with a band of salt merchants in Arkansas, and Cabeza de Vaca met women carrying corn far from any maize-growing region.

Mississippian shell ornament recovered from the Etowah Indian Mounds Historic Site, Georgia. (Harris Hatcher, photographer)

One of the biggest trades was in buffalo robes. Bison hides were transported in large quantities from the Great Plains to the agricultural peoples to the east and south. A dozen years after the Narváez expedition, Coronado met people who "follow the cows, hunting them and tanning the skins to take to the settlements in the winter to sell . . . some to the settlements at Cicuye (Pecos), others toward Quivira (Kansas), and others toward the settlements which are situated in the direction of Florida." Cabeza de Vaca, who was the first European to describe an American bison, said, "the people that live there come down upon them and live off them and distribute large quantities of their hides throughout the land."

Then there was the drug and weapons trade. Flint suitable for arrowhead production was not always available from local sources, nor was wood for bows or shafts. At one point in his travels Cabeza de Vaca met a single tribe that specialized in supplying bow wood to people who lived in treeless areas. As for drugs, speaking generally of all the peoples he met between Malhado and the Rio Grande, he said "in the entire land they intoxicate themselves with something they smoke and they give everything they have for it." Peyote, tobacco, and various other substances were used ceremonially and perhaps recreationally by the natives of southern Texas. Of the Mariames, with whom he later lived, he said "they are great drunkards, and for this they drink a particular thing."

In this vast economy the Charruco were just bit players. The Texas coastal plain was in an economic eddy of sorts. To the north and east were the Mississippians with their corn, copper, and *Busycon* shell trade. To the northwest were the turquoise, feather, cotton, and dyestuff trades of the Zuñi, Havasupai, Pima, and Pueblo peoples. Buffalo occasionally wandered all the way to the Texas coast, but that trade too was primarily the province of others to the north.

Notwithstanding their relative poverty, the Charruco possessed some things in abundance that their neighbors wanted and vice versa. According to Cabeza de Vaca they loaded him up with "pieces of snail shells," presumably for bead making. He also carried a good supply of "snail hearts," most likely the central spiral of the conch, which was made into augerlike tools or cut into disc-shaped beads, and other shells "with which they cut a fruit that is like frijoles, with which they perform cures and do their dances and make celebrations."

Lastly, Cabeza de Vaca carried something he described as "beads of the sea." Some have suggested these may have been pearls collected during the oyster-eating season, though it's not clear why he wouldn't have identified them as such. Other goods that the nearby Karankawa traded were shark teeth, smoked fish, "marine curios," and pottery, which they distinctively decorated and sealed with tar collected from the beach.

"And in exchange and as barter for it," said Cabeza de Vaca, "I brought forth hides and red ochre with which they smear themselves and dye their faces and hair, flints to make the points of arrows, paste, and stiff canes to make them, and some tassels made from deer hair which they dye red." The flints in particular were valued on the Texas coast, where there were no natural supplies of stone that could be chipped.

It was a good business, and one that allowed Cabeza de Vaca a great deal of freedom. He became, according to his own description, something of a celebrity among the peoples he encountered, to the point that "those who did not know me desired and endeavored to see me because of my renown."

His fame was increased by the oddness of his ethnic identity and the fact that the profession of a solo itinerant peddler was itself rare. Most trade moved through chains of exchange that took place when whole villages met at various neutral grounds such as the seasonal oyster harvest. Commerce between warring nations, meanwhile, was more often facilitated by neutral third groups than by individual merchant-diplomats. There were some ethnic groups that, gypsylike, specialized entirely in trade: "strangers and merchants who in their trading passed through many provinces," is how De Soto's men described a group they encountered in Arkansas. When there were solo traders, they were far more likely to be women, whose nearly universal status as noncombatants allowed them to cross political boundaries more freely than men.

The question of how far Cabeza de Vaca wandered during his trading expeditions has generated some rather sniping debate among scholars over the centuries. All Cabeza de Vaca says is that he went "along the coast forty or fifty leagues," and "inland as far as I desired." At another point he says that a custom of newlywed men being forbidden from speaking to their in-laws was "common from the island [of Malhado] to more than fifty leagues inland," which can be interpreted to mean he got at least 150 miles inland. To the great plains of Oklahoma, some have suggested. To Austin and the hill country, say others. To Nacogdoches for the red ochre, wrote Cleve Hallenbeck, a writer seemingly on a mission to get Cabeza de Vaca as deep into the heart of Texas as he could. They're all essentially guesses, most of them poohpoohed by more conservative historians who think Cabeza de Vaca got his trade goods from middle-women rather than at their original inland sources.

Despite his success and freedom, it wasn't an easy life. There were countless nights when he camped alone, cold and hungry. "Great dangers," he recalled, "as well as storms." Winters were simply too harsh to consider traveling, and he spent them holed up with the Charruco in their snug huts. Then, with the arrival of spring, he was off. Alone again, but moving from village to village, and alive. Years slipped by this way: 1529, 1530, 1531, 1532 . . . He mentions no women; he remembers no names.

He never lost his intention of someday going forward to Spanish Mexico, however. Once a year, he went down to Malhado Island to try to convince Lope de Oviedo to make the attempt with him. Like himself, Oviedo and Alaniz had been left behind by Castillo and the others when they headed west along the beach in the spring of 1529. Alaniz had died not long after that, but Oviedo recovered and Cabeza de Vaca desperately wanted him to agree to try to make it to Pánuco.

"Every year he kept me from going, saying that we would go the following year," complained Cabeza de Vaca. Finally, though, Oviedo agreed to leave Malhado after Cabeza de Vaca promised to carry him across any inlets and rivers. To make the decision even easier, he arranged for them to travel with a group of friendly women from a tribe called the Deaguenes. Oviedo also took comfort from the fact that the first hundred miles or so was familiar ground to Cabeza de Vaca, who in his annual peregrinations as a peddler made his way regularly to the Pass Cavallo. In the spring of 1533, when the blackberry season was over, they set off down the long barren beach that had proven so deadly to their fellow expeditioners three years before.

There were people waiting for them when they arrived at the tip of the Matagorda Peninsula, where the great sandbar finally pinches down to a tenuous finger stuck out into the ripping tide on its way in and out of Matagorda Bay. Whether word was sent across the mile-wide Pass Cavallo by smoke signal, or whether it was a regularly scheduled trading session is unsaid, but the Indians had come from the other side specifically to see the Deaguenes women with whom the two Spaniards were traveling. They were the Quevenes, and they scared the daylights out of Oviedo.

At first it seemed that the Quevenes had incredibly good news. There were three foreigners like themselves living further down the coast, they said. They even knew the names: Castillo, Dorantes, and Esteban. But when they started to recount what had happened to all the others who had come that way, Oviedo began to wonder if he'd made the right decision to leave Malhado, where even if life wasn't comfortable it had at least become reliable. The Quevenes announced that other than the three just mentioned, everyone who had traveled down the coast from Malhado three years before was dead, as was Esquivel, the last of the survivors from the boats of Narváez and the friars. Some were killed for trying to escape, some because of dreamt omens. Others, the Quevenes announced, had been executed on a whim, for "amusement."

To Oviedo, all this made Malhado look pretty good in hindsight, especially when the Quevenes said gleefully that even though Castillo, Dorantes, and Esteban were still alive, they were constantly being "kicked and slapped and cudgeled" by the boys and men of the groups they were living with. Not that the Quevenes were being judgmental about the mistreatment of prisoners. To the contrary, "in order that we might see that what they had told us about the bad treatment of the others was true," recalled Cabeza de Vaca, they started beating up Oviedo every chance they got. When that grew tiresome, "they threw mud balls at us, and each day placed arrows at our hearts, saying that they wanted to kill us as they had killed our other companions."

During one such friendly moment, Oviedo decided not to get into a canoe with these people. From the look of the place, Cabeza de Vaca had told him they were only at the mouth of the bay that was called Espíritu Santo on the rudimentary maps that he and the other officers had consulted back in Spain so long ago. This meant that by their own estimation, another five hundred miles of mud-ball throwers or worse lay between them and the Spanish settlements at Pánuco. On the other hand, Oviedo thought, the friendly Deaguenes women were waiting for him not far back. He could return with them to Malhado and never have to see a Quevenes again. What did he have waiting in Mexico or Spain that was worth the risk of going on? Not enough, he decided.

The only hard part was telling Cabeza de Vaca.

"I entreated him repeatedly not to do it," recalled Cabeza de Vaca.

They stood at the tip of the beach and argued. Cabeza de Vaca had waited three years for him, he reminded Oviedo. He would take care of him, he promised. Hadn't they come more than a hundred miles already? These Quevenes were bluffing, didn't he see that? And with the three ahead, there would be five of them who could together make the trip.

Cabeza de Vaca may have spoken once more of duty to King and God as he had in the Florida Panhandle to the mutinous caballeros, but they were years beyond the point where the titles and positions that had once meant so much made any difference. Narváez had been right after all when he had said the rules by which one man commanded another no longer applied in the New World. Or if not right, he was at least accurate: "I pointed out many things, but I was unable to detain him by any means," Cabeza de Vaca recalled later.

"And thus he returned, and I remained alone with those Indians, who were called Quevenes."

19

Pecans and Prickly Pears

Cabeza de Vaca watched Oviedo head back down the beach toward Malhado. So be it. God keep you. Then he turned his own mind west, consoled by the thought of Castillo, Dorantes, and Esteban somewhere just across the bay. Despite all their petty tortures and death threats, the Quevenes had given him a clue as to how he might meet up with the other three. They said the season of nuts was underway over on the mainland, and within two days the various Indians with whom the other Narváez survivors were living would begin to gather in the pecan groves along a nearby river.

That river was the lower Guadalupe, near its confluence with the San Antonio River. From fifty or sixty miles in every direction, bands of Indians came in out of the relentless sun of the Texas coastal plain to the shady river bottom, with its ancient groves of gracefully spreading trees. They left their homes in time to be at the Guadalupe by the first frost of the winter, when the ripe nuts began to drop like manna. Some years the crop failed due to a killing frost in the spring, or a prolonged drought, and the people rapidly dispersed in search of other sustenance. But when the harvest was good, as it was that winter of 1533 when Cabeza de Vaca arrived from Malhado, the nut eaters stayed in the groves for nearly two months.

Among those who harvested pecans were the Mariames, with whom Dorantes was living. They were a band of about two hundred people who actually didn't migrate to the nut season but spent most of the year in the lower Guadalupe Valley; it was their home territory. Their collection of round, mat-covered shelters wasn't a village so much as a campground that they packed up and moved every few days as the local nuts were consumed. They had killed Esquivel and perhaps some of the other Spaniards, but Dorantes seems to have come to some sustainable relationship with them. Esteban and Castillo, meanwhile, lived with the Yguases, a group similar in size and living habit that traveled to the river from slightly further south and west.

The coastal Quevenes, who now had custody of Cabeza de Vaca, were apparently not full participants in the nut harvest. But they did get close enough to the territory in the next few days for Cabeza de Vaca to encounter a nut gatherer who told him that other Spaniards had arrived in the groves. If Cabeza de Vaca could manage to sneak away from the Quevenes and get to the edge of the woods, this person promised, he would take him to the other Spaniards. Hope could now hang on the slightest of threads and Cabeza de Vaca decided to go along with the plan simply because the nut-gatherer "had a different language from that of my Indians."

Four years had passed since Dorantes, Castillo, and Esteban had left Cabeza de Vaca for dead on Malhado. They rarely, if ever, even thought of him separately from the hundreds of other comrades who had perished. There was plenty to worry about in their own day-to-day effort to stay alive without dwelling on the fates of their shipmates. Dorantes, in particular, recalled that not a day went by during the time he was alone with the Mariames when he didn't fear for his own life, "seeing that they killed their own sons without pity or mercy just because of a delirious dream."

The men and boys of both bands reveled in terrorizing the foreigners among them. Dorantes remembered that his keepers would always "look fiercely at him and sometimes, even many times, would come running at him (and at the others where they were) and would point an arrow at their chests pulling the bow clear to their ear." They held it there, chipped flint scratching bare breast, watching for beads of sweat or other signs of panic on the faces of the newcomers.

"And afterward they would laugh," Dorantes recalled, "and ask: Were you afraid?"

The answer was yes, he was afraid. He was always afraid. So he braced himself for the usual abuse when he saw a youth running up to him in the camp. But instead of pulling his beard or sticking an arrow to his throat, this time the boy had news: there was another stranger in the forest. He got up and hurried through the shady grove, wondering if it would be Castillo or Esteban, both of whom he expected to see at some point during the harvest. And then suddenly there before him was Cabeza de Vaca, a friend seemingly back from the dead after four long years of watching comrades die.

Dorantes and Cabeza de Vaca had worked well together on some of the reconnaissance missions in the happier first months of the expedition in Florida, and it was a moving moment for both men. In a long memoir of disappointment and dissolution, Cabeza de Vaca said the reunion under the spreading pecan trees by the muddy

Guadalupe "was one of the days of greatest pleasure that we have had in our lives."

They thanked God and traded news. All Cabeza de Vaca could offer that Dorantes didn't already know was that Alaniz was dead and Oviedo had gone native. Dorantes, on the other hand, filled Cabeza de Vaca in on everything he had learned about the disappearance and presumed death of Narváez, the failure of the five swimmers to get through and find help, and the final fate of everyone but himself, Castillo, and Esteban.

The latter two were already in the groves with their masters, the Yguases, and Dorantes immediately took Cabeza de Vaca to find them. That there was no difficulty arranging this meeting raises questions about the nature of the servitude of the Narváez survivors. Just as Cabeza de Vaca had first "fled" from Malhado and then revisited them annually without suffering any retribution, Dorantes now arranged a meeting under the watchful eyes of members of the tribe he had himself fled from only ten months before.

It's possible that there were no hard feelings between Dorantes and his former tormentors. Or that his current masters, the Mariames, protected him. One thing is for certain, though: he felt actively enslaved. When Cabeza de Vaca announced to his fellow survivors that he intended to keep moving on toward Pánuco, they insisted that under no circumstances should he tell the Indians of his plans. If the Mariames or Yguases even suspected for a moment that he was thinking of escape, they said, he would be killed immediately.

Bide your time, they advised, this is not the best season for breaking away. Come summer, both the Mariames and the Yguases would themselves be traveling a good distance west, in the direction of Pánuco, to feast in the prickly pear patches. That was the time to pass over to other Indians from "further on," they explained. They had planned it all out, and even knew who to look for once they got to the prickly pears. The Avavares, who dealt in bows from the interior and came to the prickly pear harvest from the opposite direction than the Mariames, would help them slip away. The only reason they hadn't done it the previous year, Dorantes explained, was that the Mariames and Yguases with whom they were traveling had never collected in one place long enough for the three to make their move.

Cabeza de Vaca reluctantly agreed to lay low until the prickly pear season. In the meantime, he said, "They gave me as a slave to an Indian with whom Dorantes was staying, who was blind in one eye, as was his wife and a son that he had as well as another person who was in his company, to the effect that all of them were blind in one eye."

Wild pecans in Texas are edible for nearly six months, but the harvesters always made much quicker work of them than that. By mid-winter, the Yguases and others who had come to the river bottom from points further along the coast were beginning to drift back to their spring homelands. Castillo and Esteban went off with their respective masters, while Dorantes and Cabeza de Vaca remained in the Guadalupe Valley with the Mariames. Keep low and stay alive, they told one another as they parted, and we'll meet next summer in the prickly pear patch . . .

Then it was back to grubbing for a living. "Most commonly," one expert on the Indians of Texas has written, "the hunter and gatherer is supremely well adapted to the particular locale, living what some anthropologists have termed the life of the 'first leisure class.'" But a life of leisure and surplus was not the impression that Dorantes and Cabeza de Vaca had of their time among the Mariames. "The greater part of the year they suffer extreme hunger, and every day of their lives they must work at it from morning till night," they remembered.

Occasionally there was more substantial fare when Indians set grass fires and drove whole herds of deer into a killing ground. Or when the young Mariames men chased individual deer across the prairie with almost unimaginable endurance until the animal collapsed in exhaustion and could be killed by hand.

Still, it was never enough. Cabeza de Vaca said they ground up the bones of whatever they had so as to be able to eat them as well. "Their hunger is so great that they eat spiders and ant eggs and worms and lizards and snakes and vipers that kill men when they strike," he recalled. "And they eat earth and wood and everything that they can find and deer excrement and other things that I refrain from mentioning." Black bears eat deer dung, biologists theorize, in order to give them a temporary ability to digest grass. "I believe assuredly that if in that land there were stones they would eat them," Cabeza de Vaca concluded.

The constant references to hunger in the two surviving accounts have caused modern scientists to wonder if there may have been an unusual drought during the years in question. The relentless deprivation "simply does not fit with the archaeological evidence, in terms of faunal remains (animals, fish, marine or freshwater shell, snails, etc.) that occur in sites in the area where [Cabeza de Vaca] must have traveled," wrote Thomas Hester, one of the preeminent archeologists of the region. Later on their journey, the four Narváez survivors met a nation of buffalo hunters who specifically complained that there had been no rain in two years.

Be that as it may, there was at least enough water in the Guadalupe Valley for plagues of mosquitoes to breed. One of Dorantes's and Cabeza de Vaca's many jobs was to build immense smudge fires of rotten wood and make sure they didn't go out during the night. The smoke burned the throats and eyes of sleepers, but that was a small price to pay: Cabeza de Vaca saw one group of hunters who ran out of wood while out on the treeless plain and returned to the river bottom "in such a condition from the mosquitoes that it seems that they have the sickness of St. Lazarus." A later prisoner in the same region found himself confronted by so many mosquitoes that he was "obliged to hide under water to my neck and I passed the night in this manner." But when Cabeza de Vaca and Dorantes tried moving down to the shore for relief, their masters "would remind us with blows to return to light the fires."

Of course the "hunger so great" that Cabeza de Vaca thought drove the Mariames to root around in rotten logs may have been instead an acquired taste for ant eggs and a love of life on the move. Later Spanish missionaries to the area complained that "in order to be at liberty in the woods or on the beach, they prefer to suffer hunger, nakedness and lack of shelter, which they do not suffer when they are in the mission." And Simars de Bellisle noticed that the Indians often chose to go without food for several days at a time rather than go out in the rain. Cabeza de Vaca said, "They are a very happy people; in spite of the great hunger they have, they do not on that account fail to dance or to make their celebrations."

Many of these "celebrations" no doubt had religious significance that was lost on the Spaniards. Still, times of plenty were worthy of joyful noise making. The Karankawa of later centuries danced and sang after a successful hunt ended in a feast of fresh meat. In April, and sometimes again in May, the receding waters of the Guadalupe trapped a huge bonanza of fish in slowly drying ponds behind the natural levees. Then the Mariames gleefully gorged for days on end, but as they had no method—or no desire—to preserve the excess, most of the fish was left to rot on the floodplain.

Better than all the other good times of the year, however, was the prickly pear harvest. "Many times when we were with these people we went three or four days without eating, because nothing was available," Cabeza de Vaca remembered. "To cheer us up, they told us that we should not be sad, because soon there would be prickly pears, and we would eat many and drink of their juice, and our bellies would be very big, and we would be very content and happy and without any hunger whatsoever."

This effort by the Mariames to lift the spirits of men whose beards they were so recently plucking out is typical of the myriad mysterious inconsistencies within the Narváez narratives, where violence comes and goes without explanation, interspersed with small kindnesses. Feast followed famine followed feast in the Mariames's year, and around the time of the fish parties, the unassuming little prickly pears that grew here and there in the valleys where the four survivors were living bloomed their greasy yellow flowers. It was time to get ready to move south and west, to where the plant was more abundant. The happy season was nearing.

When the smell of rotten fish filled the air as the last pockets of floodwaters dried, the Mariames women took down their houses and loaded themselves and their two Spaniards for the trek to come. They started the journey a little earlier than their neighbors to the west, the Yguases, as they had farther to go. The Yguases holding Esteban and Castillo, in turn, began traveling a bit earlier than the next group to the southwest, the Atayos. But by the middle of June, cactus eaters from all over what is now southern Texas and northeast Mexico were on their way across the hot, dry plain to their favorite prickly pear stands.

There wasn't a large contiguous cactus region, but rather many pockets throughout southwest Texas and northeastern Mexico where great concentrations of tree-sized prickly pears grew in dense thickets.

As with the pecan groves, various migratory peoples returned annually to the same locations generation after generation, where they met and traded with other groups who had come from other directions.

The location of the particular cactuses favored by the Mariames and the Yguases has been at the center of a long debate over the Narváez survivors' route from the pecan groves forward. Dozens of articles and books published in the last century and a half delve into everything from the biology of the prickly pears, pecans, pine nuts, and buffalo, to hearsay and history about "old Indian trails" and the size of mountains that the Spaniards may have seen back in Europe. In the early twentieth century one writer went so far as to spend three October nights sleeping naked near the Llano River to prove that the Narváez survivors could have done similarly in 1534. "I duplicated the conditions," said Cleve Hallenbeck, "except that I left out the fires. These might have attracted the attention of some ranch-hand."

The problem is not that the Narváez sources are murkier in their descriptions of Texas than they are about Florida or the Mississippi. The sources clearly state that the route was close enough to the coast that the Mariames and Yguases were able to drown herds of deer by driving them into saltwater bays. The controversy arose, historiographer Donald Chipman argued in an influential 1987 study of the various studies, because some Texans were unhappy that the wandering conquistadors crossed too rapidly into what is today Mexico. In the 1930s in particular, the Dallas *Morning News* published a series of articles intended to restore "Cabeza's Texas citizenship," as they put it. The writer, an eminent geologist of the time, vowed that he would not "sit complacently by and see the very beginnings of our history taken from us, the scene of its story wrongly transferred across the Rio Grande into a foreign country, Mexico."

In recent years, however, perhaps more confident about their state's contributions to American history, opinion among Texas historians and other students of the Narváez expedition has coalesced around a route that runs within about a hundred miles of the coast and that crossed the Rio Grande in the vicinity of what is now the man-made Falcon Reservoir. This puts the prickly pears in the neighborhood of the lower Nueces River, possibly between the modern towns of Alice and Falfurrias, Texas.

Once out of the slightly rolling topography in the vicinity of the river, the groups traveled across a vast, hot savannah, nearly unbroken to the horizon. It was not, however, featureless. This was centuries before overgrazing by cattle and the ending of regular burning by the Indians transformed much of the region into the mesquite-choked wasteland it is today. In the months when the four survivors traveled west, the wide grasslands were a riot of wildflowers. Day after day the four hundred or so Mariames moved across this garden in a snaking, mile-long ribbon of humanity. At times they may have walked along side by side by side, the better to drive before them and capture any small game. Other times they wandered semi-independently in smaller groups or alone.

Periodically the land would begin to dip, imperceptibly at first, and then roll a bit as they neared another chalky river or creek, carving its way from the hill country to the gulf. It was better sleeping down in these bottoms, where the trees produced enough wood for smudge fires and there was water for drinking, cooking, and swimming.

Then it was back out in the sun and the wildflowers again. Silent at times, laughing at others, singing to infants, they walked their ancient trail west. Here and there in the distance deer and antelope played, but that year there was apparently no major game drive. Dorantes said the drives only occurred when the wind was off the sea to the south, and that such hunts only happened rarely, and "by chance."

Elsewhere on the savannah, other winding lines of humanity converged on the prickly pear harvest. There were the Yguases bringing Castillo and Esteban, and from the other side, the Avavares with their supplies of bow wood and other trade goods. The survivors' accounts don't describe the prickly pear thickets, but other sources from before the "great freeze" of 1899, before "root rot" and overgrazing, do not suggest the familiar little clumps, tucked into hollows here and there or hugging the fence lines. Early travelers speak instead in terms of "vast ramparts and towers of prickly pear that seemed to form walls and mountains in their terrible array." Or acres of "impenetrable thickets higher than a man on horseback," that produced "an immense quantity of fruit."

Into these strange and thorny mazes the various harvesters went to collect the purple tunas, as the fruits are called, which ringed the pads of the cactus in great profusion like so many sore thumbs on a monstrous green palm. With sticks they beat new paths into the interior, an activity that over time increased the density of the patches as broken-off pieces of cactus took root and grew into new plants. Prickly pears that size have trunks like trees, thorns like hypodermic needles. The fruits themselves are covered with barbed peach fuzz that's almost worse than the thorns. But no one cared: everybody's skin was too tough, and the pulpy, juicy, bittersweet taste was too delicious to be bothered by such a minor annoyance.

"The best season that these people have is when they eat the prickly pear," said Cabeza de Vaca, "because then they are not hungry, and they spend all their time dancing and eating of them, night and day." What they didn't eat immediately, they dried in the sun and packed into special baskets made for the purpose.

Botanical drawing of the prickly pear (Opuntia macrorhiza) *from the "Report on the United States and Mexican Boundary Survey." (U.S. House of Representatives, 1859)*

Once the Mariames and the Yguases had reunited in the pear patches, the four Narváez survivors also grew optimistic about life. In the mottled shade of the thickets, or around the fire at night, they caught up on the months they had been separated, and made their plans. Like their captors they were in a fine mood, though one fraught with worry and surging with adrenaline as the time for their long-awaited escape approached. When the Avavares bow traders finally arrived from points west there was only a day or two more to go. They were "on the point of fleeing," said Cabeza de Vaca.

Then, in the midst of the feasting, the Mariames and the Yguases got into a terrible fight. All Cabeza de Vaca remembered of the cause of the fracas is that "the Indians who held us fought amongst themselves over a woman, and they punched each other and struck one another with sticks and wounded one another in the head." That may well be enough said on the matter: males periodically hitting each other over the head for the sake of females is what sociologists might call a cultural universal. But other clues about Indian society on the Texas coastal plain suggest more than a simple love story gone wrong. For one thing, women (particularly those without children) were free to change sexual partners at will. "The women leave for no reason at all and marry others," Cabeza de Vaca told the historian Oviedo, adding that "a marriage lasts only as long as they are happy."

More significantly, the altercation may have grown out of a business deal gone bad, as both the Mariames and the Yguases customarily purchased their wives from enemy nations. The usual price was a bow and two arrows, or a fishing net the length of a man. Their own daughters, said Cabeza de Vaca in a startling passage, they killed.

> When female children are born, they allow dogs to eat them, and cast them away from there. The reason they do this, according to what they say, is that all the people of the land are their enemies, and with them they have continual war, and if by chance they should marry off their daughters, their enemies would multiply so much that they would be captured and enslaved by them, and for this reason they preferred rather to kill them than that there be born of them those who would be their enemies. . . . We asked them why they did not marry them themselves and also among one another. They said it was an ugly thing to marry them to their relatives, and that it was much better to kill them than to give them either to a relative or to an enemy.

Boys, too, were sometimes killed by their parents, typically as a result of dreamt omens. During the years he was with the Mariames, Dorantes saw "eleven or twelve children killed and [or] buried alive.

These were all boys because, miraculously, they never do this to females." Of course, if Cabeza de Vaca's characterization is taken literally, there may have been no young girls around to inhabit dreams.

If everything the Narváez survivors said is true, it's amazing there were any Yguases or Mariames around at all. In addition to the violent means of population control, children reportedly were breast-fed until the age of twelve, which would have the effect of suppressing the fertility of their mothers. There was also a taboo on sex for two years after a woman gave birth as well as during menstruation. During these times of female abstinence, Cabeza de Vaca reported, a woman's husband "takes another man, and the aberrant person goes about like a woman and serves in every way that the woman has to do for her husband."

Even though the Narváez survivors lived with the Texas Indians for years, and learned to speak their language, one has to question whether the gulf between watcher and watched was too great for accurate cultural observations. It's worth noting, however, that the Narváez survivors didn't often overgeneralize. Regarding female infanticide, for instance, Cabeza de Vaca stressed that "these Indians and others, their neighbors who are called the Yguases, alone practice this custom, without any others of the land keeping it." He contrasted the Mariames with other native groups, saying, "They don't love their children as much as the ones about whom we spoke earlier." The "ones" he meant were the Malhado islanders, who he said "love their children and treat them better than any other people in the world."

Furthermore, nothing they describe falls outside the bounds of what is known from other sources. In particular, theirs is just one of hundreds of accounts of North American cultures that included men and women whose sexual identity defies easy definition. In Native America there were cross-dressers who took on the occupations of the opposite sex but didn't engage in homosexual sex. There were people who had homosexual sex but didn't cross-dress. There were people who some-times did one thing for part of their life, or part of the time, and another thing at other times. Some cross-dressers went to war, others didn't. Some held positions of honor and power, some were treated poorly.

"In the time that thus I was among these people, I saw a wicked behavior, and it is that I saw one man married to another, and these are effeminate, impotent men," said Cabeza de Vaca in his most extended description of Indian homosexuality. "And they go about covered like women, and they perform the tasks of women, and they do not use a bow, and they carry very great loads. And among these we saw many of them, thus unmanly as I say, and they are more muscular than other men and taller; they suffer very large loads."

For the most part, therefore, scholars take the Narváez survivors' descriptions of life among the Indians at face value. There's not a lot of choice in any case, as theirs are virtually the only accounts of these people that survive. And as with the Malhado islanders, the Apalachee, the Timucua, and the Safety Harbor peoples, there is no one alive today who identifies him- or herself as a Mariames or Yguases, or even a Karankawa; no one to add oral history or traditional knowl-edge to the accounts from the 1530s.

As it turned out, Cabeza de Vaca and his three companions got to observe the Mariames and Yguases for a whole year longer than they had hoped. Whatever caused the fight between their hosts, whether true love or bride commerce, once the head-punching ended and the dust cleared, everyone in both camps quickly took down their houses and moved away. It was a truce, ironically enough, brokered by women.

"When the natives quarrel they strike one another, but a bow or arrow should be used for no reason whatsoever in the fight," Cabeza de Vaca told Oviedo many years later, and "[t]hose who should separate them must be women—and never men in any case."

The combatants went their separate ways, taking with them their separate slaves, and the long lines of humanity snaked again over the prairie and down into the shaded hollows. Back to the pecan groves of the lower Guadalupe River. Back to the winter homelands of Mariames for Cabeza de Vaca and Dorantes. Back to Yguases land for Castillo and Esteban. Away from Pánuco, just when all four survivors had thought they would be heading toward it.

20

The Burning Bush

The winter of 1533–34 didn't go well for Cabeza de Vaca. The previous year's hunger may have been due to a drought, as some have suggested, but if so, the drought continued unabated. More importantly, his relations with the Mariames deteriorated. Three times he ran away, and each time, he said, they "went looking for me and put forth great effort to find and kill me." They didn't kill him, but by the time the winter foraging season at last gave way to the spring fish feasts, and then once more to preparations for the annual trip to the cactus grounds, he was no longer living with the same group of Indians as Dorantes.

From different corners of the coastal plain the long lines of villagers slowly converged once again, as they had for millennia. At the back of one, loaded again with a woman's burden, Cabeza de Vaca soldiered along alone. He thought of Oviedo turning around after he had spent years waiting for him to leave Malhado and wondered if he was still alive back there. He thought of his own past year, repeatedly running for his life from the Mariames and wondered if he could survive another year like that. He thought of the fact that twice already Dorantes, Castillo, and Esteban had failed to escape after being separated in the prickly pear grounds and wondered if it would happen again this year. He thought of Narváez telling him that in the end, when all the trappings of empire are stripped away, it was every man for himself.

Somewhere along the route to the prickly pear harvest Cabeza de Vaca made up his mind that this year he was going to go forward toward Pánuco even if it meant going without Castillo, Esteban, and Dorantes. He didn't know for certain if they were still alive, but if they were and somehow couldn't go with him, so be it. He had traveled alone before and knew he could do it again.

For most of the prickly pear harvest of 1534, however, it seemed as if his concerns were misplaced. The other two Spaniards and the Moroccan had in fact survived the winter. The Mariames and the Yguases, meanwhile, had patched up or forgotten their differences of the previous summer. All were reunited in the pear patches, gorging on the pulpy tunas by day and making music by the fire half the night, still sticky with the acrid juice of the day's feasting. Under a waxing desert moon, the four survivors planned their escape anew. They would sneak out of the camp on the first day of the next new moon, when there would be only the first visible sliver of a crescent to light the way. The date, Cabeza de Vaca thought, would be the first of September, 1534.

The actual date of the September new moon in 1534 was on the eighth of the month. If, as seems likely, his memory was more accurate about the phase of the moon than the exact calendar date, the planned escape day was the ninth. Through the last weeks of August and into September all went well, and the moon shrank away to nothing over the Texas prickly pear patches. When the day arrived, they were still together, ready to flee. But that very morning, for reasons of their own, the Mariames and the Yguases began to break camp and go their separate ways. Once again, the survivors' plans were in jeopardy.

The escape was supposed to coincide with the end of the harvest, so that when the four refugees fled toward the southwest their keepers would be concerning themselves with preparations for their own seasonal journey back east. But this year the harvest wasn't as abundant as some years, and the Mariames and Yguases apparently decided to head homeward early. There were remote thickets that they traditionally harvested at the end of the summer that they weren't even going to bother visiting that year because there was little or no fruit.

It was near one of these places that Cabeza de Vaca hurriedly told the other three castaways that he would meet them in roughly two weeks' time. "I told my companions that I would wait for them at the prickly pear grounds until the moon was full," he recalled. "I informed them that if they did not come during the time we agreed, I would go alone and leave them behind. And thus we parted, and each one went off with his Indians." It had taken him longer, but he had arrived at the same point as Narváez: "One for all and all for one" was now just "be there if you can."

Dorantes was the first to make his way to the appointed thicket. He was particularly good at losing his captors, having already slipped away from the Quevenes and from the Yguases. When he saw opportunity about a week after they had all been separated, he disappeared from the camp of the Mariames and "went secretly and headed inland, to a place where the prickly pears were usually eaten."

To his surprise, there were people already there; a group of Indians called the Anagados had arrived that same day. Fortunately for Dorantes, though, they were "great enemies" of the Mariames, which may explain why the latter didn't bother to come after him. Three or four days later, Esteban and Castillo arrived, and they, too, took up with the Anagados.

The full moon was now only a few days away, and Cabeza de Vaca was still with his own keepers. This may have been part of the plan, as his band had headed past the appointed pear patch in the direction they were all hoping to travel. But planned or not, when Castillo, Dorantes, and Esteban saw smoke signals rising from somewhere "further on" they thought it might be Cabeza de Vaca and decided to go find him.

There was, as usual, a hitch. The Anagados, who had been so happy to take the three strange travelers in, were not as pleased to let them go. They hated the Indians Cabeza de Vaca was with and weren't interested in letting three prime new slaves slip into their hands. It was a potentially disastrous impasse: with the full moon approaching, none of them doubted Cabeza de Vaca would go on without them as he had promised.

Finally, they struck a deal. Castillo would stay with the Anagados as a hostage, and Esteban and Dorantes could go to the smoke signals and bring Cabeza de Vaca back. The only problem with the plan was the smoke signals disappeared, and the two got hopelessly confused in the flat sameness of the parched plain. By the end of the day they were thirsty and desperate, marching around in circles unable to find their way forward to Cabeza de Vaca or even, it seemed, back to the Anagados camp. "They had endured great hardship," Cabeza de Vaca recalled of their eventual arrival at dusk in the camp of his captors. "They had been wandering lost."

The problem of retrieving Castillo resolved itself the next day when Cabeza de Vaca's band decided for mysterious reasons to go make peace with the Anagados. It seems likely this rapprochement was brokered somehow by the arrival of Dorantes and Esteban, perhaps by dropping hints of plentiful prickly pears back at the Anagados camp. However it was engineered, the four survivors didn't waste any time making good their escape, but "left that day without being noticed, nor knowing where they were going; just with confidence in Providence and looking for those prickly pears that grew on the land even though the season was just over."

In their years of captivity they had learned a lot about how to survive in that climate. They knew to dig holes in the ground, into which you could squeeze the sweet juice of the prickly pear fruit and then slurp it back up. And how to bury and bake the cactus pads to make them edible. How to find snails and insects to eat. But they had also learned that the people from whom they were running might follow and recapture them, and that their best defense was affiliation with another group of Indians. So when they again saw "spires of smoke" on the horizon, they made straight for them.

At dusk they saw someone in the distance, but as soon as he saw the four of them he turned and fled. "We sent the black man after him," Cabeza de Vaca recalled, and Esteban raced ahead through the dry grass, dodging cactuses, waving his arms, and calling out.

This is the first mention in the narratives of Esteban acting as the group's advance man, a job he did with increasing frequency. Almost all that is known of this "black, Arab, native of Azzemmour, Africa" is that he came on the expedition as a slave of Dorantes. He's not even mentioned by name by either source until he is one of only a dozen or so survivors left on Malhado, and then always with the diminutive

Estebanico or little Esteban, in keeping with his status as a slave and perhaps his youth. More often, he's simply called "the black."

His social rank among the four survivors may have been a factor in his selection at this point to run forward and attempt to parley with the fleeing Indian. It's hard to imagine, though, that such distinctions still functioned with much power among the survivors after so many years of near-naked starvation, during which both he and his putative master, Dorantes, were fellow slaves. More likely Esteban went after the man in the distance because he was the best linguist of the group and had the youngest legs, to boot. Later in the journey, Cabeza de Vaca says, "The black man always spoke to [the Indians] and informed himself about the roads we wished to travel and the villages that there were and about other things that we wanted to know."

By that time all four castaways spoke one or more native languages, picked up from the small itinerant nations of the Texas coast with whom they had been living. Of more use once they were on the run, they had also gained some facility with the sign language that functioned as a lingua franca in Native America. "We asked and they responded by signs as if they spoke our language and we theirs," recalled Cabeza de Vaca at one point, "because although we knew six languages, we could not make use of them in all areas because we found more than a thousand differences."

When Esteban finally caught up with the man in the distance, he turned out to be a member of the bow-trading Avavares, the people whom they were hoping to find. Their winter territory was to the west and south rather than back to the east from which the Narváez survivors had come. As befits international traders, the Avavares were multilingual, and the man could speak the Mariames language. Esteban explained that he and his companions had come peacefully in search of the people whose smoke they had seen earlier in the day.

The sun was dropping below the horizon when they arrived within sight of the little collection of mat- and skin-covered tents. Their new friend had rushed ahead with word of their impending arrival, and not since they had first washed up on Malhado Island five years before were the survivors so warmly welcomed by a group of Indians. Four Avavares who were waiting to greet them on the outskirts of town grandly led Esteban and Dorantes to the house of one "physician," presumably a place of great honor, and put Cabeza de Vaca and Castillo in the house of another.

The choice of housing was not accidental. The Avavares had heard rumors of the four before they arrived or remembered them from trading sessions with the Mariames, Yguases, and others. But what they had heard wasn't how poorly the bearded strangers were treated or how lousy they were at harvesting roots and pecans. What they had heard was that these strange wanderers could heal the sick.

As early as the first year after the shipwreck, back on Malhado, they had dabbled in medicine. Cabeza de Vaca only mentions the incident in passing, but it is fascinating for what it says about the islanders' perception of the world as a place where even inanimate objects are infused with mysterious power that needed only to be channeled by a willing intermediary. Or, in the case of the castaways, by unwilling intermediaries.

"They tried to make us physicians without examining us or asking us for our titles, because they cure illnesses by blowing on the sick person, and with that breath of air and their hands they expel the disease from him," he recalled. "And they demanded that we do the same and make ourselves useful. We laughed about this, saying that it was a mockery and that we did not know how to cure."

One of the local healers then took Cabeza de Vaca aside and explained the universe to him. "The stones and other things that the fields produce have powers," he said. Therefore "it was certain that we, because we were men, had greater virtue and capacity." More to the point, the shaman pointed out that the strangers had best start healing if they wanted to keep eating: "They took away our food until we did as they told us," Cabeza de Vaca griped.

It was a convincing line of reasoning. In addition to the blowing and massaging, the local methods of healing included some localized incisions and blood-sucking, placing of hot rocks on areas of pain, and if necessary some cauterizations with fire. To these the Spaniards added a bit from their own tradition. "The manner in which we performed cures was by making the sign of the cross over them and blowing on them, and praying a Pater Noster and an Ave María, and as best we could, beseeching our Lord God that he grant them health and move them to treat us well."

The mix proved potent, and Cabeza de Vaca performed a few more cures in the pecan groves during the spring of 1533. Those early medical successes hadn't made the Mariames any friendlier, but now, among the Avavares, they were treated as shamans worthy of special reverence. As a result, their already strange lives began to veer into the realm of the bizarre.

It started that first evening, when a few Avavares came to Castillo complaining of headaches. He made the sign of the cross over them, said a few words on their behalf to the Christian God, and "at that point the Indians said that all the sickness had left them." They rushed home and returned with great loads of prickly pears and even a piece of venison to offer as gifts. Soon others in the village began to feel in need of medical assistance. They came to Castillo, too, and went home happy. "And each one brought a piece of venison," remembered Cabeza de Vaca, "and there were so many of them that we did not know where to put the meat."

Once all the sick were healed, the Avavares began to dance and sing. Cabeza de Vaca thought at the time that it was a "celebration held on account of our arrival," and the four travelers certainly enjoyed it as such, continuing to give "great thanks to God because each day his mercy and blessings were increasing." Modern anthropologists, on the other hand, are more inclined to describe the performances as unidentified "ceremonial activity." Either way, the Avavares danced all night long under the Texas stars and the September moon, and then slept it off in the morning. All through the next night they danced and sang and then a third night after that.

Cabeza de Vaca's intention when he had told the other three that he was leaving on the night of the full moon with or without them was clearly to get going and keep moving until he reached the Spanish settlements. But when the dancing and singing at last wound down and he asked the Avavares about the lay of the land ahead, the news wasn't propitious. In summer the region was full of people and prickly pears, they told him, but that season was over. All the easy fruit had been picked and the bands had dispersed to their winter quarters. The Avavares, too, would be leaving shortly.

It was only early fall, but the cold months were "already upon us" said Cabeza de Vaca. The four discussed their options, and between the chilly nights and the warmth of the Avavares they came to a hard decision. The Avavares were planning to move vaguely in the direction they wanted to go, which is to say south and west, but any real progress toward the Spanish settlements would have to wait until the following year's prickly pear season. They consoled themselves with the thought that at least the Avavares were fun and friendly, easy to cure, and generous with the venison.

But once again the winter and spring turned out to be more famine than feast. Only two days after the dancing ended, the local prickly pear harvest was exhausted, and the Avavares packed up their houses and made ready to move on to a streambed about a week's travel away.

Unlike some of the other groups with whom the survivors had lived, the Avavares didn't have distinct summer and winter territories separated by a migration route. Rather, they roamed around the watershed of the lower Nueces River, in the general vicinity of Alice, Texas. As locals, they were late-harvest prickly pear specialists who knew of fruits in remote places after most of the migratory bands of the high season had moved on.

They fully expected, therefore, to find a few last remaining prickly pear fruits along the way to their new campsite. But due to the poor harvest that year, there were none to be had. The venison, so freely given only a week before, was gone. As a result, within two weeks Cabeza de Vaca was again feeling empty. "After traveling five days with very great hunger," he complained, "[w]e arrived at a river where we put up our houses."

Despite the new respect with which the four were treated, it was a hard season. Their backs were all raw, covered with great, oozing sores that were excruciatingly painful when they carried the great loads of firewood that needed to be constantly replenished. In his spare time, Cabeza de Vaca manufactured a few combs, bows, nets, and mats in order to trade for more food, and he was never happier than when he was given the job of scraping and softening hides as, he said, "I scraped it very clean and ate of those scrapings, and that sufficed me for two or three days."

The draws and gullies of the lower Nueces were not filled with the gracefully spreading pecans that the Mariames enjoyed on the Guadalupe River, so the Avavares and their new medicine men spread out in search of scrub ebony, which produces pods of seeds about the size of peas. These hang from the tree usually until December but are most palatable earlier in the season. They may also have sought mesquite, the beans and pods of which were important to the diet of people to the south.

Everyone, young and old, wandered the valley looking for the plants, which is what Cabeza de Vaca was doing when he heard the rattle of a diamondback, felt the puncture of its fangs, and after a few hours of stumbling around looking for help, lay down and died. At least, that's what the Avavares announced must have happened to him when he failed to show up at camp at the end of a long day of foraging.

One might expect Castillo, Dorantes, and Esteban to set off immediately in search of their comrade, but they had lived with death so long now that they figured they would either find him during the next day's foraging expedition, or not, and that either way it wouldn't make a difference. If he was alive and could move, he would see the smoke from their fires and come in toward camp. If he was indeed killed by a viper, there was no point in wasting energy looking for another corpse. Half-starved on a winter night, no one had the energy to leave the fire.

Still, though, they held out hope for Cabeza de Vaca. They had assumed him dead before, only to have him turn up in the pecan groves after three years. Of course that time he had been with Indians, and this time he was alone, naked, and half-starved on a cold, open prairie where even these people who were native to the place went hungry for days on end. When four nights had passed with no sign of Cabeza de Vaca, they gave up on him and assumed that they were the last three survivors of the Narváez expedition.

"All took great pleasure in seeing me," was Cabeza de Vaca's memory of their reaction when he stumbled into camp at the end of five days with a singed-off beard and a story that he had not been killed by a viper but saved by a burning bush.

Cabeza de Vaca didn't explicitly describe the event in miraculous tones, saying only that it "pleased God that I found a tree aflame, and warmed by its fire I endured the cold." He'd spent his nights sleeping in a hole surrounded by campfires, one of which ignited his grass bedroll and burned off his beard.

Nonetheless, Cabeza de Vaca's return from his four days and four nights of fasting in the wilderness marked a decided turn toward the mystical and miraculous in his story. The cures became immediately more significant; headaches relieved are replaced by the "crippled and very ill" picking up their beds and walking. Native groups from miles around began to appear in search of help. And then, in a village not far from where the Avavares had set up their own shelters, Cabeza de Vaca raised a man from the dead.

21

The Traveling Medicine Show

Castillo didn't want to attempt that particular cure. The four were still living with the Avavares, moving from camp to camp among the gullies and flatlands between the Nueces River and the Rio Grande. As word spread of their healing powers, delegations from neighboring nations began appearing with their sick in tow or with requests for visits from the new shamans. These supplicants called the four healers "children of the sun," said Cabeza de Vaca without explaining how they may have gotten this notion. People called the Cuthalchuches and the Maliacones came to see them, as well as the Atayos, and the Coayos. It was from a group called the Susolas that a request for help came for "one who was very near his end."

They specifically asked for Castillo, who was originally the most sought after of the four healers. But he was also, said Cabeza de Vaca "a very cautious physician, particularly when the cures were threatening and dangerous." Specifically, Castillo worried that it was only a matter of time before his own sins, whatever they may have been, would cause one of his attempted healings to fail. This man sounded too far gone for a sinner's feeble prayers and cross signings, and Castillo balked.

Cabeza de Vaca, on the other hand, was less conflicted. He had performed some minor cures for the Susolas before and had been richly rewarded by them at that time. "And thus I had to go with them," he wrote. Neither Dorantes nor Esteban were attempting cures at that point, but they went along as well. By the time they and an Avavares escort got to the Susolas village, however, the patient's house had been taken down. This was a sure sign that his family considered him dead. A mat of reeds had been laid over the body, and family and friends were standing around weeping.

Nor was the Spaniards' diagnosis any better than that of the locals. "When I arrived, I found the Indian, his eyes rolled back in his head, and without any pulse, and with all the signs of death," Cabeza de Vaca recalled. "So it seemed to me, and Dorantes said the same."

Nevertheless, Cabeza de Vaca removed the mat and began to pray. He prayed for the health of the dead man and of all the people in the village. He mentions no sign of progress from the patient. He muttered some Latin and made the sign of the cross and blew on the man "many times." Still, there was nothing to suggest that a resurrection was imminent. At this point the dead man's relatives presented his bow to Cabeza de Vaca, along with a basket of crushed prickly pears, and he left the corpse to go and attend to those in the village who had only one foot in the grave. These were sufferers from something identified as "sleeping sickness," and they responded with the usual rapidity to Cabeza de Vaca's ministrations. Two more baskets of prickly pears were brought, which he in turn presented to his Avavares escort, and they all returned home. The dead man, at that point, was still dead.

That evening, however, someone ran into the Avavares camp with news that over in the Susola camp the corpse had revived. He was walking and healthy. It was, quite naturally, a sensation throughout the surrounding countryside, and in its aftermath a flood of supplicants arrived to see the strange healers. So many came that Dorantes and Esteban were forced to begin performing minor cures to pick up the slack. "We all became physicians," said Cabeza de Vaca, "though in boldness and daring I was the most notable among them."

The debate over what to make of the miraculous cures performed by the conquistador-shamans in Texas and northern Mexico during 1534 and 1535 began almost as soon as Cabeza de Vaca published his memoir. Before the twentieth century, the question was more often about what the miracles may have signified than about whether they actually occurred. Some criticized the survivors for overstepping their positions as laypersons, while others saw the healings as incontrovertible evidence that the conquest of the Americas was God's will.

Current responses more often include an inference that both the illnesses and the cures were vaguely psychological in nature. These generally start from Claude Lévi-Strauss's proposition that shamanism is a kind of collective reality-altering exercise, in which the most important factor isn't what the shaman does by way of treatment but that everyone agrees he or she has medicinal power. "[Cabeza de Vaca] and his followers no doubt did cure some psychosomatic maladies," wrote Rolena Adorno in an example of this line of thought, "yet this point is subordinate to a more fundamental one: it is not that they became great shamans because they performed cures, but rather that they performed cures because they were great shamans."

As the four became more comfortable with their new roles as celebrity healers, they worked to maintain their hold over the Indians. They specifically tried to magnify the mystical power of their physical differences from the Indians by having the dark-skinned Esteban do most of the talking while the three Spaniards remained aloof and silent. Such self-conscious "otherness" is in keeping with anthropologist Michael Taussig's notion that the power of shamanism "lies not with the shaman but with the differences created by the coming together of shaman and patient." He warns, however, that trying too hard to explain what "actually" happens in shamanistic healings leads to what he calls "the unstated ritual of academic explanation, turning chaos into order."

Whatever the "reality" of the faith-healing situation in southwest Texas in the spring of 1535, it's important to remember that most European medicine at that time was hardly more scientific than the Native American variety. Castillo, Dorantes, Esteban, and Cabeza de Vaca may have been worldlier than their patients in that they had traveled farther, but they didn't doubt the possibility of miracles at crucial moments in the lives of a believer.

That said, Cabeza de Vaca went out of his way to stress that he did not himself see the New World Lazarus up from the grave. Similarly, though the average sixteenth-century Christian didn't question the physical existence of Satan and his various demons, the four travelers were at first incredulous when the locals told them of a small, bearded "bad thing" who lived in a cleft in the ground. This creature periodically came out at night—sometimes as a woman, sometimes as a man—to torment mortals and perpetrate strange sorceries.

"We laughed a great deal about these things that they told us, making fun of them," said Cabeza de Vaca. But when they were shown people with three great scars along their torsos where the "bad thing" had cut into them with a flint knife, removed a piece of their entrails, and then healed them with a wave of his hand, the four shamans ceased laughing and began preaching.

"We gave them to understand that if they believed in God our Lord and were Christians like us, they would not be afraid of him," remembered Cabeza de Vaca. What's more, he promised, "as long as we were in the land, he would not dare to appear in it."

Not surprisingly, the Avavares loved hearing that the "bad thing" was banished, and the four refugees were given total freedom for the first time since the shipwreck on Malhado. They still had to collect their own food whenever there weren't enough medical gratuities flowing in, but they could go where they wanted and no one pulled out their beards.

The downside, if there was one, was that they were now immensely valuable to their hosts, as their promise to keep the tricksterlike "bad thing" at bay highlighted. Their impact wasn't just spiritual either. The baskets of prickly pears presented by grateful patients made the four healers useful economically to the Avavares as well. This explains why, when the prickly pears were once again covered with waxy yellow blossoms, the four decided not to announce their intention to move on. Despite the good treatment and relative freedom, it was better to slip away.

They used the old strategy, heading southwest as close as possible to the time that they knew their hosts were preparing to migrate in the opposite direction toward the prickly pear harvest. It was early summer of 1535 when they made the move, and from that point on, they never stayed with one group of Indians for longer than a few weeks.

They stopped first with some friends of the Avavares called the Maliacones, who were a long day's journey away. With these people they traveled "further ahead," which is to say southwest across the high flat prairie for another full day until they joined with a group called the Arbadaos. The Maliacones had hoped to join the Arbadaos in harvesting mesquite beans or Texas ebony pods, but the expected bounty wasn't yet ripe, and the Arbadaos were barely getting by on cooked prickly pear pads. They were, said Cabeza de Vaca, "very sick, and emaciated and bloated, so much so that we were astonished." The Maliacones took one look at the situation and turned around and went back home, encouraging the four shamans to return with them. But, having promised themselves never to backtrack again, they stayed with the starving Arbadaos.

Hungry as they were, the Arbadaos weren't desperate enough to eat their pets, and they sold two dogs to Cabeza de Vaca in exchange for the deerskin he was wearing, along with some fishing nets and other items he had manufactured. Before the purchase the four travelers were "so weak that they did not dare walk a league more," but after eating the animals they felt revived and asked the Arbadaos about the road ahead. In what was the beginning of a routine of sorts, the Arbadaos were sad to see them go but pointed out the route to another village "further on."

On those hot open flats in June, storms appear on the horizon hours before they arrive overhead, giant flashing banks of thunderheads darkening immense swaths of territory. Then, when the rain itself comes in on a hot wind, visibility drops very quickly to nothing, or near enough to nothing, in a place where landmarks are as subtle as a smudge of cottonwood or pecan tops on the horizon. It was on a day like this that the four chose to leave the Arbadaos, and the rain eventually poured in such great torrents that it felt at times as though they "walked in water." They lost the path and wandered hopelessly around in the mud until at last they gave up looking for the route at all and simply followed the water downhill into a "very great woods." Despite the wet, they got a fire going, dug an oven in the ground and filled it with prickly pear pads, which they ate the next morning before setting off again.

Forward. They went always forward toward the southwest, until at last they wandered into a small encampment where the people said go forward more, which they did, and came to a town of fifty houses. These may have been the Cuchendados, the last group of Indians they met for whom a specific name is known. If they were not the Cuchendados but some other group, as some have argued, they were the first of an even longer list of peoples who treated the four wanderers generously and helped them along their way but whose national names are lost to history. For fifteen days in this town of fifty houses the four travelers rested their own bodies and healed those of others.

Here, some twenty to twenty-five miles north of the Rio Grande, at the very bottom of Texas, the pace of events in the two surviving narratives begins to quicken. The sporadic, repeatedly stalled efforts to escape that typified the previous six years were at last over. With each new cure performed, their confidence grew. With each gift of food— the menu now included mesquite beans, pounded and mixed with handfuls of earth and water into a muddy paste, or baked into bread— their bodies strengthened. By the time they waded across what is now the border between the United States and Mexico, optimism had leaked into them.

"Wider than the Guadalquivir in Seville," was their impression of the Rio Grande when they saw it. They had pushed through the thick band of tall grasses lining the river and stood with their ankles in the gritty water. It was wide where they crossed, somewhere near the present site of the Falcon Reservoir dam. But it was not deep. "The water was up to their knees, then the thighs, and two lance-lengths more and it was up to their chests," they later remembered, "but there was no danger."

They were traveling with just a few local women as guides, though as usual, word of their approach had gone ahead. That evening, as the sun dropped red below the horizon, they were met on the outskirts of a town by a throng of people shaking holy rattles. These gourds, the people believed, had fallen from the gods of the sky and washed down the river to them. They were slapping their thighs in excitement and awe as they came out of a hundred dwellings, pushing at each other to get close enough to rub their hands on the strange travelers.

Cabeza de Vaca feared for a moment that he would be crushed in the push, and Dorantes and the others were amazed that no one's eyes were poked out in the delirious, throbbing tumult. Before that could happen, though, the shamans were lifted onto many hands, "and without letting our feet touch the ground," Cabeza de Vaca remembered, "they carried us to their houses." It was a far cry from the last time he had been carried on Indian shoulders, shivering and near death from the beach of Malhado, worried that he was soon to be sacrificed to some heathen deity. Now, five years later, the healed had become the divine healers.

In the next weeks they traveled through three or four similarly sized villages south of the Rio Grande and were met in a like fashion by adoring crowds. The adulation was infectious, and the four men's new-found optimism began to coalesce into the nearly forgotten, virile and viral idea that they were masters of their own destinies in this strangest of new worlds. In this reempowered, imperial frame of mind they made an astonishing decision.

They would not go to the pathetic little outpost on the Rio Pánuco, after all. Pánuco had been their goal ever since the courage and long-bows of the Apalachee had driven the expedition into the sea nearly seven years before. But now, when the Spanish outpost was at last only a few weeks' journey down the coast, they turned away from Pánuco and headed inland, into the mountains toward the Pacific Ocean.

"We did this because by crossing through the land we would see many of its particularities, because if God our Lord were served by tak-ing some one of us out of there and bringing him to the land of the Christians, he could give an account and description of it," said Cabeza de Vaca in his memoir. In other words, they had come full circle. They were no longer simply survivors trying to get home by the shortest route, but were once again royal servants acting for the glory of God and the good of the empire. It's even possible that, through Narváez, they were aware of rumors circulating as early as mid-1527 of rich cities named Coluntapan and Nuxpalo somewhere to the north of Mexico and that they hoped to find them.

At least the good of the empire was what Cabeza de Vaca wanted the king to think was the main reason for the course change when he was reading the memoir and considering how to reward the survivors for their hardships. Another reason they turned inland, Cabeza de Vaca confessed, was that they were terrified that the Indians who lived along the coast would be more like the Quevenes and Mariames than like their new disciples. What they didn't know—couldn't have known or it seems impossible that they would have done it—was that their grand gesture for God and King added twenty-five hundred miles and two major mountain ranges to their journey.

The turn from the coast happened not long after they had re-stored vision to the residents of the third or fourth town below the Rio

Grande, which was inhabited mostly by people who were blind in one eye and many who had no sight at all. Interestingly, this time Cabeza de Vaca says nothing in his personal memoir about restoring sight, though in the context of his having recently seen a burning bush, raised the dead, told the crippled to walk, banished a demon, and compared his cuts and abrasions to those of Christ, the average reader is unlikely to notice the omission. For once, therefore, it is the joint report prepared by the survivors that makes greater claims about the miracles performed, saying first that all the cataracts were removed and then immediately backtracking a bit, noting in a startlingly modern way that even "if the Christians did not cure all of them, at least the Indians believed they could cure them."

In terms of their own vision, the four travelers from another hemisphere saw something from that village that they had not laid eyes on since leaving Cuba. In the distance, rising like a mirage out of the dry coastal plain, there were mountains. Mountains! Here was a sign at last that they were nearing something different. Mexico City was in the mountains. Gold came from mountains. It may well have been the blue and purple outline of these peaks of the Sierra de Cerralvo, running northwest to southeast against the horizon, that more than anything else drew the four travelers inland.

The formerly blind were also anxious to lead them that way, to a village a day's march away. It belonged to friends of theirs, they explained along the way, but as soon as they arrived they ransacked the houses and stole all the valuables they could lay hands on. It began suddenly and was quite shocking, and Esteban hastily tried to explain that they didn't want trouble. The blind who now could see just laughed at him and said not to worry. These were their relatives; this was their custom.

And apparently it was, for the depredations were not resisted. Not surprisingly, perhaps, it was also customary among these people to hide their valuables whenever the extended family was on its way over. When the initial mayhem of searching and grabbing had subsided, therefore, and the four travelers had performed their customary curing of the sick, the robbed villagers happily produced shell beads, red ochre, and other gifts for the bearded shamans that they had squirreled away in anticipation of their cousins' confiscations. It all ended up in the hands of the people from the blind town anyway, as the shamans had their own custom by now, which was to pass everything they received as payment along to their guides of the moment. The ex-blind went home laden and happy, and the new villagers began to discuss with the strange healers where they might all go to recoup their losses.

"Ritualistic" thievery of this sort became, with minor variations, a pattern that followed the four shamans as they made their way along the foothills of the Sierra de Cerralvo. Their new guides from the recently ransacked town were not at all happy with the lowland route the four had chosen, having argued that there was a larger population of relatives in a town up in the mountains where the ransacking was sure to be fruitful. But they were determined to follow the shamans wherever they went, hoping to recoup their recent losses.

When the traveling medicine show reached the San Juan River, which drains the region between the Sierra de Cerralvo and the main ranges of the Sierra Madre Oriental to the west, the Indians once again tried to direct the four toward easy pickings. They "tried hard to take [us] towards the sea because they figured on getting even by doing what had been done to them. They told [us] there were a lot of people who would give the Christians many things." Upstream, on the other hand, they said there were no people and no food for many miles.

But the shamans were determined to go up the nearly dry river, and by this time their followers were in such awe of them that they wouldn't even take a drink from the women who were carrying water without permission. They all marched glumly up the river. But though the Indians' devotion was fervent it wasn't deep, and when scouts who had gone ahead reappeared to say that, indeed, there were no people in that direction, everyone but the four Narváez survivors turned around and headed home.

Suddenly left without their multitude, Cabeza de Vaca, Esteban, Castillo, and Dorantes loaded themselves up with as much as they could carry and trudged on alone up the narrow valley. The going along the riverbed was relatively easy, but there were steep, arid mountains now on both sides of them, long flat-topped walls of eroding stone with only occasional breaks revealing more mountains behind. Summer is the rainy season in the Chihuahuan desert, which isn't to say there's a lot of rain, but the century plants and sotol were still in bloom, and they walked at times below the cartoonish flowers towering to sixteen feet or more over their heads. In terms of geography, this was the decisive turn inland; Pánuco now was directly behind them. They were heading northwest, keeping their eyes open for a pass through the Sierra Madre to their left.

Four solitary walkers, they were committed now to some plan of their own that mystified the Indians as much as it has confused half a millennium of historians. But if they had any doubts about the decision, they consoled themselves with the knowledge that they were on a well-worn trail, belying their former escort's exaggerations about the emptiness of the land ahead. And sure enough, out of the late afternoon haze two fuzzy specks approached from the opposite direction and materialized into a pair of women. They, too, were burdened down with heavy loads, which in their case turned out to be corn flour.

Maize! They hadn't seen cultivated food since their last paltry supplies of parched corn from Florida had run out years ago on Malhado Island. Where the cargo came from is a mystery, as they were nowhere near any known agricultural regions. They talked a while in the afternoon sun, sitting on their haunches, resting their backs. There was a village further up the riverbed where they might find more corn, the traveling women said to the wandering men. Then, parting company, the women continued downstream while the men marched on with renewed vigor. As promised, near sunset they approached a wooded area, an oasis of shade and water, in which there was a town of about twenty houses.

The townspeople were not happy to see them. To the contrary, they were "weeping and with great sorrow," said Cabeza de Vaca, "because they already knew that wherever we went all the people were sacked and robbed by those who accompanied us." Only when they became convinced that the four strangers were alone did they produce some prickly pears for the travelers to eat.

Their relief was premature. The corn-trading women took news of the village back to the people downstream and the following dawn they appeared en masse and sacked the little town in the oasis. The residents were unprepared, had hidden nothing, and howled with distress. These were not their cousins come for some time-honored redistribution festival, this was not their tradition. They were thoroughly displeased by the unplanned potlatch.

But they were willing to learn. The raiders told their victims to quit moaning, their turn would be next. These four wanderers were the Children of the Sun who had come among them with the power to cure and to kill, the pillagers told the distressed villagers, along with what Cabeza de Vaca called "other lies even greater than these."

Then, having explained the system, the pillagers took their loot and returned down the river, leaving the new hosts to make plans to recoup their losses in the next big town to the north. In that town, which was three days' journey away, the villagers outnumbered the ransackers, thus limiting the damage. The new people were good sports about it all, however, and after the traditional fracas, their own medical men gave the Narváez survivors two holy gourd rattles. These served to further signify their mystique as they traveled forward. Village to village they now went, from uncontested pillage to uncontested pillage. "And in that manner they advanced eighty leagues more or less"—some 250 miles—"skirting the mountain range going inland, due north."

As the above quote typifies, the narratives move more rapidly now than at any other place in the story. Largely gone are Cabeza de Vaca's ethnographic descriptions of mystical tricksters, menstrual taboos, and marriage patterns. Gone are the tribal names learned during the months and years stuck at the bottom of the social ladder on the Texas coast. Even food, their old obsession, is now mentioned only in passing, as the travelers' diet progressed from prickly pear to piñon nuts, rabbits, and finally to the corn country of the more settled peoples of north-central Mexico. As Cabeza de Vaca himself confessed, "We went through so many types of people and such diverse languages that memory is insufficient to be able to recount them."

What remains in the narratives, however, are tales of miraculous cures performed and unusual gifts received, interspersed with thumbnail descriptions of landscapes and estimated distances passed. They were trekking relentlessly now across the middle of the continent, a mostly arid journey described only in the vaguest terms—"through the foothills of the sierra, we went inland more than fifty leagues," or "up that river a fifteen-day journey without resting."

By triangulating from clues like these, their route has been fairly well established by Alex Krieger and other researchers, though not surprisingly there are ongoing quibbles over details. But the mountain described as a "sierra of seven leagues and the stones in it were iron slag" that they crossed in late July or early August of 1535 is agreed by nearly all to be the Sierra de la Gloria, in the Sierra Madre Oriental, just southeast of the Mexican steel town of Monclova. They were traveling roughly parallel to the Rio Grande, one to two hundred miles to its west, heading in the direction of the "big bend" of that river.

In a small camp at the foot of the seven-league mountain, an Indian presented Dorantes with a gift that confirmed in their minds that they were moving in a propitious direction. It was a thick copper bell, cast or engraved with the image of a face on it. The bell, they were told, came "from the north, across the land towards the South Sea." The givers may have been traders, like the corn women, as they were camping in only four mat huts and spoke a different language than the locals. They came from further inland, they explained, and were on their way home. And yes, they would be honored to take the four powerful strangers with them.

Looking at the cast bell and the cotton blankets of their new guides, Cabeza de Vaca and his companions jumped to the conclusion that there was an advanced culture further ahead: "Where this rattle came from, since it was not of gold, there must be a mine and smelting." But ironically, given today's skeptical climate regarding the morality of excavating native artifacts, the bell was more likely looted from the ruins of the vanished people of Casas Grandes, a city in the eastern foothills of the western range of the Sierra Madre.

Once a flourishing copper-producing center with a large trading network, Casas Grandes's culture had stagnated and collapsed for mysterious reasons a century before the arrival of Europeans in the Americas. Its people, like those of Mesa Verde and Canyon de Chelly to the north, ultimately deserted the place. The "mound of the offerings" and other places at Casas Grandes show evidence of what post-Columbian archeologists call "pre-Columbian vandalism." But the pre-Columbian vandals didn't get it all, as post-Columbians at the site have found some fine copper bells, including at least one with a human face on it like the one described by Dorantes.

On they went, toward the current border with Texas in the neighborhood of Presidio, curing the sick, collecting followers. Not all the medicine was mystical in nature, though its success seems miraculous nonetheless. On the banks of "a very beautiful river," Cabeza de Vaca cut open a man's chest with a flint scalpel and removed an arrow point that had been lodged in his cartilage for many years. The first incision wasn't deep enough, but with a second slice he was able to see the arrowhead. The patient tried not to show pain as Cabeza de Vaca wedged one rock under the other and popped it out. Then, with a bone needle he sutured the incision closed. "And two days later, I removed the two stitches from the Indian and he was healed. And he said that he felt no pain or discomfort whatsoever."

Like the raising from the dead incident, this cure heightened the wandering shamans' fame to a new, regional level. More people tagged along than ever before: "Never less than two thousand souls," they estimated. "So great a company that in no manner could we make use of them," remembered Cabeza de Vaca.

But use was made. Each of the four shamans now had their own personal entourage of followers, including women who prepared individual houses for them at each campsite and may have had other duties as well. During the days, young men with bows ranged up in the hills and returned to the camp in the evening with venison, quail, and other game. At higher elevations, even though they were in the middle of the Chihuahuan desert, there were grassy valleys thick with jack-rabbits. There the multitude spread out in a great line, and the startled animals would jump up sometimes right into the hands of the walkers. Everyone carried a special small club, a few spans of the hand long, sug-gesting that such communal game drives were a part of life before the arrival of the strange shamans.

Likewise, the presence of "the lord of the people who went with us" and distributed the bounty, shows that as strange as the events were, the mass migration did not upend the existing political structure of the Indians. These "lords" also managed the looting, which became ever more stylized as the horde made their way north. They were traveling well-known routes, and four runners—one to symbolically represent each of the shamans—were always sent ahead to gather people along the roads. The residents of each new town now brought their belong-ings out for presentation, rather than having their houses ransacked. The Narváez survivors passed the bounty on to the "lords," who then distributed it to the rank and file.

It was a fat time, followed rather suddenly by an equally lean one. Ninety miles or so after crossing a large river—either the Rio Babia or the Rio Sabinas—the grassy plains abruptly gave way to 150 miles of mountainous deserts. They had entered the dessicated ranges just south of Big Bend, a place hardly habitable today, yet most of their entourage continued to travel with them.

The desert mountains "were so dry there was no game in them," remembered Cabeza de Vaca, "and because of this we suffered much hunger." Hunger and thirst were old enemies by now, things to be mindful of but not to be feared. They were still on a road, after all, how-ever barren it might be. And they had guides from further on who had heard of the westering miracle workers; an envoy from the other side of the desert was waiting for them at the beginning of the deadliest stretch. Forward was progress, forward was hope, backward was unthinkable.

They were in the deep, dry canyons now, badlands and cliffs, popular among snakes and tarantulas. They were in the dust, and the heat that radiated up off the ground felt even hotter than that coming down from above. Or they were on high mesas, close to the sun in lonely lands, ringed with the azure sky. From there, when they looked up from their trudging feet, they could see thunderheads that promised rain, and once in a while even gave it. More often, though, the clouds trailed low-lying virga, which looked for all the world like water falling but dried in the air before hitting the superheated earth.

Many in the multitude with them began to weaken as the days became weeks without adequate food or water. Some fell ill, some fell behind. But the shamans, who after so many years and miles were honed to a level of endurance that bordered on senselessness, simply tucked their heads down once again and plodded forward, semiconscious. But moving. Always moving.

Here and there on the walls by the trail they saw strange artwork in the rock, ancient figures and glyphs that said little more than that others had passed that way and survived. Or had survived at least that far. And at last, cutting through the crumbling land like a green bandage across a massive burn, was a great river.

Again there was the tall, thick grasses, the acrid smell, the intense hum of insects and birds announcing that here was a place where life was reliable. Again the chalky water was up to their knees, then their thighs and chests. But there's nothing in the accounts to suggest that the four men suspected it was the same river—the Rio Grande—that they had crossed once before, some four hundred miles downstream.

They didn't care what river it was. What was important was that after crossing the Rio Grande, the killing desert peaks of the eastern

Sierra Madre, which Cabeza de Vaca called "bitter and difficult in the extreme," finally ended. They cared as well that not far past the river there was a village of a hundred huts belonging to kind people, who were waiting to welcome them and their collapsing horde of followers.

And most of all, they cared that these new people, nice as they were, steadfastly refused to lead them any further in the direction they wanted to go.

22

Six Hundred Hearts of Deer

Like virtually everyone they had encountered so far since wrecking their boats on Malhado six years before, the new Indians were a migratory people who carried their houses with them when they traveled. They had come from far away to see the miraculous strangers, they said, and as usual, they brought with them many gifts. Baskets and baskets of piñon nuts were presented, which the four promptly turned over to their exhausted guides from south of the river. There were more nuts, in fact, than either they or their entourage could possibly use, but when Cabeza de Vaca tried to return some to the Indians who gave them, they were told it was positively against tradition to take back something once it had been given away. Half of the nuts rotted on the ground, or were eaten by birds.

These nut-givers also respectfully insisted that the only people who lived toward the west, where the shamans wanted to go, were unfriendly and far away. They wouldn't even dispatch the usual four-person advance team in that direction to herald the coming of the four, even though Cabeza de Vaca "ordered them to send people." It was a tense time; the four shamans were accustomed to nearly constant progress by this point and were not in a mood to delay with fall again on the way and winter not far behind it. As a compromise, the piñon nut people finally allowed two women to go forward as envoys, mostly because one of them spoke the language of the people to the west, having been taken captive from there in a previous skirmish. Only women, they explained, could mediate in times of war.

The following days were excruciating. They weren't entirely stuck; the company moved along toward the place where the women were expected to return with news from the west. But it was at a snail's pace, in part because the further they traveled, the more the new additions to their entourage began to fall ill. Worst of all, when they finally arrived at the rendezvous point, the women were nowhere to be seen. This was proof, said their hosts, that there was no one ahead in that direction, and they refused to go further.

One day passed, then another, with no sign of the women. Out of frustration, when the diplomats still hadn't returned after a third day, the Spaniards offered a compromise. If you won't go west, they said, take us north to circumvent your enemies. It didn't work: no friendly people in that direction, they were told, and nothing to eat or drink. Other than this unwillingness to go west, the piñon nut people were quite pliable. "The most obedient people we found throughout the land," said Cabeza de Vaca, "and of the best nature." But Dorantes had had enough.

In a fit of anger, he told one of the people in his personal entourage to explain that the piñon nut people would all start dying pretty soon if they kept up with their resistance. Cabeza de Vaca, too, decided to get tough. According to his memoir, he became so disgusted at the delay that he "went one night to sleep in the countryside, apart from them."

Sure enough, the day after the death threat the men of the town went off to hunt as usual, but they came home from the work at noon, sick as dogs. Within two days, two people were dead and more than three hundred stricken. In his version, Cabeza de Vaca upped the number of casualties to eight dead on the day after he stayed away from the main campsite.

Not surprisingly, the piñon nut people caved in. "They went to where I was," recalled Cabeza de Vaca, "and they were there the entire night without sleeping and with very great fear and speaking to me and telling me how terrified they were, begging us to not be angry anymore, and that even though they knew they would die on the road, they would take us wherever we wanted to go."

This was obviously welcome news, but Cabeza de Vaca and Dorantes now began to worry that the plague had gone too far. The entire camp was terror stricken. No one laughed, sang, or even wept when their family members passed away. No one would look the strangers in the eye, but would only approach with their faces downward, as if confronting a deity. When one young girl started to cry, she was taken away and scratched from her shoulders to the bottom of her legs with the teeth of a rat, a procedure which Cabeza de Vaca was led to understand was punishment for daring to weep in front of the dangerous shamans, but which may have been part of a traditional cure; rodent teeth were found by archeologists in a "shaman's kit" discovered in the region.

"We feared that all of them would die, or that they would abandon us out of fear," he recalled. More importantly, if the terror spread, "all the people from there onward would do the same."

The whole system that had allowed them to travel so successfully since leaving the Avavares was in jeopardy of collapsing. So the four shamans didn't simply pray for the end to the plague in a perfunctory way. They got down on their knees and "beseeched God our Lord to remedy it."

And for once it didn't work; the sick did not rise immediately from their beds and proclaim their symptoms gone. A whole day passed before the tide of death turned a bit, and the ill began to revive. The people's fears were further relieved when the two women at last returned with news that their enemies were not massed nearby after all. Almost everyone in that direction had already gone north to hunt the buffalo, the women reported. The crisis atmosphere receded.

This isn't to say that the piñon nut people were now anxious to accommodate the shamans. To the contrary, they wanted to be left alone, having seen enough of this new religion. They were still not quite well, they pointed out to the travelers, and they had come from such a long way away. It would be best, therefore, if the four powerful shamans would just go north by themselves to the buffalo grounds, where there would be plenty of people to whom they could minister. As for themselves, they would stay where they were or go back east to their homes.

But the four were in no mood to negotiate. They had been moving in a northwesterly direction ever since turning inland after the town of the blind, so that by now their latitude was equal to, or even higher than, that of Malhado and Apalachee. It was again autumn. The days were notably shorter, and the nights were growing clear and cold. They didn't need to see the buffalo plains to the north-northeast with winter coming on: "The Christians said no, that they were to take them towards the west, because that was the right route."

No one wanted another full-blown showdown, and a compromise was quickly worked out. Castillo and Esteban went forward with the women to collect what people they could find to the west and bring them out onto the trail to greet the other two, who would follow along behind. Only twenty or thirty of the timid piñon nut people needed to escort Cabeza de Vaca and Dorantes. The sick and the weak, meanwhile, could stay where they were to continue their rehabilitation. "The Indians were relieved to hear this," the survivors later recalled.

Castillo didn't get very far before racing back to Cabeza de Vaca with news of the territory ahead. The woman who spoke the language of the western people had taken them directly to the village where her father still lived, about a day and a half's journey away. It was at a place where the river came out from between some mountains, which could mean one of the many famous towering canyons of the Rio Grande. But it wasn't the landscape that excited Castillo, it was the architecture. For the first time since leaving Florida, the buildings looked permanent rather than portable. What's more, the people were farmers.

Cabeza de Vaca was ecstatic at the news. "He had seen maize," he recalled of Castillo's report. "This was the thing that gladdened us more than anything else in the world."

While Castillo was delivering the news, Esteban succeeded in rounding up a respectable welcoming committee from among the enemies of the piñon nut people. Most of "the cow people," as the Spaniards came to call them, were gone north for the buffalo hunt as the women had reported. But those left behind loaded themselves with robes and beans, along with squashes both for eating and for carrying water, and followed Esteban out of their town and down the dusty road.

It was a tense moment when the processions met. Just as the piñon nut people had insisted all along, the two groups were sworn enemies. But there was oil to throw upon the waters in the form of worldly goods offered to the four healers by the new suppliants and passed along to the old entourage—the same oil that had been greasing the travelers' wheels since they first encountered the blind town so many months ago.

Once all the gifts were distributed, things settled down. There wasn't much time for old hostilities to build, as the piñon nut people were anxious to see the last of the strange shamans. Unlike the departure from so many other groups along the journey, there was no weeping or gnashing of teeth. They just picked up their loot and went away "very content."

They partied all night long in the cow people town. Despite the early indications, however, it was not the beginning of a time of plenty for the travelers. In the light of morning it was obvious the cow people's agriculture was marginal at best; what corn they had turned out to be imported. But the move to the cow people did mark a return to the steady forward momentum that had come worrisomely close to stalling out during the previous three weeks. The cow people didn't want to go to the corn country themselves, but they told the travelers how to get there. It was a long and hungry journey, they warned, and suggested it would be much better to come with them to the Great Plains, to the buffalo kill, where meat was plentiful.

"But we did not want to follow the road of the cows because it is toward the north, and this for us was a great detour," recalled Cabeza de Vaca, "because we always held it for certain that going the route of the setting sun we would find what we desired."

So after two days they set off with a few guides along the road that had been described to them. Up the Texas side of the Rio Grande they trekked, sometimes through flat valleys, sometimes through narrow canyons. Their endurance was now almost as legendary among the Indians as their healing: dawn till dark they traveled with little to eat but an occasional piece of deer fat from a supply they carried with them and some splintery beans the cow people picked from trees along the way. Of all the things they had eaten in the past seven years, the four wanderers found these beans the least appetizing.

Finally, at the end of seventeen days, they reached a point where

View of the Rio Grande from the "Report on the United States and Mexican Boundary Survey." (U.S. House of Representatives, 1859)

the trail split and one road went west across the river through a pass in the mountains. This may have been the place that later became known as El Paso del Norte, and then later just El Paso, but more likely it was a bit south, near Banderas, Mexico. This was their last chance to go to the bison ranges, their guides said, but they turned west, wading across the Rio Grande for the last time.

For twenty days, more or less, the three Spaniards, one African, and assorted Indian guides and hangers-on walked through the mountain-ous highlands of northern Chihuahua. They passed near the ruins of Casas Grandes, where Castillo's bell may have originated. Then the trail climbed up into the pine forests, over range after purple range of the massive western chain of the Sierra Madre. It was two hundred miles or so of rough road, though at least it was periodically shady, and cooler at the higher elevations. Neither source describes the stage as either harder or easier than any of their previous difficult passages; as if the narratives themselves are now rushing for the finish line, they give no details of these breathtakingly dramatic stretches of territory except to say that the people they met survived on jackrabbits and "powders of grass."

At the end of the mountains they dropped into a fertile valley, a land of flat-roofed adobe houses, whose owners had great stores of dried corn. They had crossed the continental divide, leaving the desert behind at last. "And from here we passed through more than one hundred leagues of land, and we always found permanent houses and many stores of maize and frijoles," remembered Cabeza de Vaca, in a typical summation. "And they gave us many deer and many robes of cotton, better than those of New Spain."

This was Yaqui country, and every few days there was a prosperous town, where they stopped to rest and heal the sick. The cycle of gifting and curing resumed at full force, as people from thirty miles in every direction gathered to be touched and cured by the strangers from the northeast. Infant hands holding two or three kernels of corn were held out toward them along the road as they passed, in the hope that if one of the healers should take the gift it would ensure that the child would be safe from disease and suffering. Healthy people asked only that the sign of the cross be made over them. Lions did not quite lie down with lambs, but Cabeza de Vaca says warring nations made peace with one another at the bequest of the travelers.

"A thousand or 1,500 people came," he and Dorantes later estimated, "and sometimes over 3,000, until they arrived on the plains near the coast."

The gifts, meanwhile, became more varied and extravagant.

Turquoises, coral beads, and some green stones that Cabeza de Vaca thought were emeralds, but which most likely were not. The locals explained that the precious stones were purchased in the far north in exchange for parrot feathers. In one town, Dorantes was presented with more than six hundred hearts of deer, each one carefully split and dried. It was so memorable that the shamans named the place the el pueblo de los coraçones—the village of hearts.

It was now December of 1535, coming on to winter, and they had crossed the continent. They were only twenty or thirty miles from the Gulf of California, and when they learned from the locals that salt water was at hand and that there was no maize on the coast itself, they knew it was at last time to turn definitively south toward Cortés's territory. After three days resting in the village of hearts they set out, but soon reached a river that was too swollen from rain for them to cross.

For two long, muddy weeks they waited to cross that swollen stream, which was the Rio Yaqui. "It rained there for fifteen days," they later remembered, "and it was around Christmas time." During those days they worked their way slowly downriver, hoping to find a safe place to ford. Mostly, though, they bided their time, healing and blessing the multitudes, and waiting for the water to drop. All in all, it was an unwanted delay.

But while they were there, Andrés Dorantes noticed something that stopped him cold. One of the supplicants who had traveled to the riverside to meet the shamans had a strange object hanging around his neck on a thong of deer hide. Dorantes called him over for a closer look and took the amulet in his hand. It was a buckle like one he himself had once possessed many years before—a buckle that could only have come from the sword belt of a Spaniard.

23

Peace in the Valley

Castillo tried to hide his excitement. He turned the buckle over and over in his hands, but there was no doubt about its authenticity. The man also had a horseshoe nail "hanging around his neck like a jewel," and Castillo took that as well. He called out, and the other three rushed over to see the items. Where were these things from, they asked, and were told that men with beards had arrived from the sky with horses and swords. The owner of the buckle pantomimed for them how he had seen people killed with lances.

The news wasn't as good as it could have been; there was no mention of a town or settlement of Europeans nearby. "We found ourselves greatly disturbed and saddened," Cabeza de Vaca recalled, "believing that those men would not be but those who had come by the sea to explore."

If the buckle did come by sea, it was most likely on one of several voyages up the Pacific coast that Cortés sponsored in the early 1530s. That same summer of 1535 that the four Narváez survivors were crossing the Sierra Madre and working their way south, Cortés himself was exploring the waters between Baja California and Mexico in search of the rumored island of pearls inhabited by the ever-elusive Amazons. Failing that, there might be the long-sought strait between the two oceans.

Sword buckles and horseshoe nails were not typical trade goods, suggesting that the original owner of the items Dorantes found had come to an unhappy end (along with his horse). A more likely source than Cortés's own voyage of 1535, which reported no mishaps, was one he had funded a few years earlier that went awry when its flagship ran aground. Everyone from that vessel who made it ashore was killed by the local people and their possessions are known to have been incorporated into the local economy because an overland expedition the following year found people wearing, among other things, a necklace of belt buckles.

That overland expedition, which took place in 1533, may well be the most likely source of all for the buckle. Officially an exploration of the northern frontier but essentially little more than a slaving raid, it progressed to the banks of the very same river on which the four Narváez survivors were camped. A daily journal kept by its commander is sprinkled with comments such as "a few people were captured," "the old man who was taken in the first village was the guide for further on," and "no people were taken because they were too canny."

The commander wasn't terribly astute. "I arrived at the river in secrecy. I went into a town; they weren't expecting me; some people were taken," he wrote. Then, less than two sentences later, he was mystified: "I sent for peaceful Indians. They didn't come."

More important than the specific origin of the buckle Dorantes found is the impact that expeditions like the one above had on the region that the four Narváez survivors were about to enter. When the waters of the Yaqui River finally receded and they waded across, the itinerant shamans almost immediately found themselves in a thoroughly terrorized countryside. They were traveling now through placid river valleys, some thirty miles from the sea, bounded on the left by the high Sierra Madre and on their right by lower coastal ranges. Judging from the similar country they had come through north of the Yaqui River, it should have been teeming with prosperous farmers, but it wasn't.

"We traveled through much land and we found all of it deserted," said Cabeza de Vaca, "because the inhabitants of it went fleeing through the sierras without daring to keep houses or work the land for fear of the Christians."

Cabeza de Vaca, in particular, was startled by the devastation he saw. Despite his years lost in North America, his experience of the imperial project was limited to a single winter spent on the already fully "pacified" islands of Cuba and Hispaniola, followed by a few months marching up the peninsula of Florida in a hapless army that only rarely engaged the enemy and never succeeded in establishing a permanent beachhead. After that, as has been seen, he was just one of a dwindling number of survivors, whose life depended on his ability to avoid offending the local population.

In other words, he had never witnessed the frontier of a successful conquest like the one spreading inexorably north from Mexico. Though the four were in a good mood, walking now with what they recalled as "great desire and joy because of the news of the Spaniards ahead," the reentry was nonetheless a bitter education:

> It was a thing that gave us great sorrow, seeing the land very fertile and very beautiful and very full of waterways and rivers, and seeing the

places deserted and burned and the people so emaciated and sick, all of them having fled and in hiding. And since they did not sow, with so much hunger they maintained themselves on the bark of trees and roots . . . They even told us how other times the Christians had entered the land and had destroyed and burned the villages and carried off half the men and all the women and boys, and that those who had been able to escape out of their hands now went fleeing, as we saw them so terrorized that they dared not stop in any place, and they neither wanted nor were able to sow or work the land; rather, they were determined to let themselves die, and they considered this better than waiting to be treated with as much cruelty as they had been up to that point.

The transformation of Cabeza de Vaca from loyal royal treasurer to vocal critic of his fellow conquistadors has contributed greatly to his mystique over the centuries. But he never became a radical, like Narváez's old chaplain, Las Casas. When he finally did get back to the corridors of power he never questioned Spain's right to use its military superiority to spread its ideals to the oppressed evildoers and make a little profit too. He only advocated for a more compassionate conversion, if possible, under the leadership of none other than himself.

But that was all much later, after the feasts and fiestas with Cortés in Mexico City and a voyage back to Spain during which, almost unbelievably, his ship was nearly captured by pirates. In the short run, for Cabeza de Vaca and his companions the burned villages and starving people south of the Rio Yaqui presented dangerous new dilemmas. The problem wasn't just that the collapsed economy made food scarce; they were used to hunger. Far more frightening was the realization that they were in a barely occupied war zone, and it wasn't at all clear whether the refugees and resistance fighters among whom they were now traveling would perceive them as friends or foes.

"We feared that when we arrived at the ones who held the frontier against the Christians and were at war with them, they would treat us cruelly and make us pay for what the Christians were doing to them," said Cabeza de Vaca.

It was with trepidation, therefore, that they agreed to travel to a secret refugee camp nestled in the Sierra Madre to the west of the valley. It was out of their way, tucked on "top of a high rugged crag, for fear of the Christians," and Cabeza de Vaca recalled that it was a long and strenuous climb up a twisting path. There was little sign of human habitation on the hike up, but as soon as the path dropped into a small alpine valley, they were thronged by people from all around the region.

Given the harshness of the situation in the lowlands, the four were "not a little amazed" to be treated with respect and deference by these people, who presented them with two thousand loads of corn. But as long as the old routines continued to function, the four shamans figured they may as well stick to them. From the mountain camp, therefore, the usual messengers were sent ahead, one to represent each of the shamans. The refugees had reported that the nearest Indian town was three days south, and the envoy was told to gather as many people as they could find and wait there for the arrival of the main party.

The leaders of the refugee camp also announced that the nearest Spanish outpost was about a hundred miles to the south, in the vicinity of San Miguel de Culiacán, or modern Sinaloa. A hundred miles! Only a week away, maybe less. They would leave tomorrow, Cabeza de Vaca and his companions told the refugees. Get ready to go.

As it turned out, however, a hundred miles was too close to the advancing Spanish frontier for the old shaman routine to work as well as it had among people with no previous experience of Europeans. As planned, Castillo, Dorantes, Esteban, and Cabeza de Vaca set off the day after their advance team, heading down the path from the mountain hideaway with as many of the refugee population as they could convince to go along. Also in the group were many who had traveled with them from as far away as the village of hearts and perhaps beyond, making a total of six hundred people picking their way down the steep defile.

Not long after reaching the valley floor, they passed places where people with horses had recently camped, inspiring the Spaniards to push on even harder. But they encountered no one, Spanish or Indian, until around midday when their own advance team hurried up from the direction of the towns ahead.

"What news?" Cabeza de Vaca and the others called out as soon as the envoys were in earshot. But the scouts were "so upset they could hardly talk." When they finally did speak, the news was bad: there were no people in the towns ahead and none in the land around either. Everyone was in hiding, "fleeing to avoid being killed or made slaves by the Christians."

But had they seen any other Spaniards?

They had. Just the previous night they had crept near enough to a camp to see the horses and armored men. But what had terrified them was not the sight of the Spaniards themselves, but that they had with them great numbers of "Indians in chains."

For most of the refugees traveling with them, this was enough said. By the tens and hundreds they turned around and fled north, back toward the mountain hideaway. Something had to be done, and done quickly, or the four shamans would soon be left to find their way south alone.

The result was a final, stunning upending of the expected vision of colonial reality. Only months before, the wandering shamans had promised that the all-powerful Christian God would protect the cactus eaters of Texas from the depredations of the "bad thing" who lived in the clefts of the earth and caused peoples' hair to stand on end. But here on the frontier they promised their followers the opposite; not protection *for* new Christians, but protection *from* old Christians. Cabeza de Vaca explicitly assured the restless followers that he and his comrades would "make the Christians they feared return to their settlement and not harm them and to be their friends." It was a promise they no doubt hoped to keep, and one that made the refugees "very pleased."

"And to reassure them," said Cabeza de Vaca, "we slept there that night."

At dusk the following day, the unlikely band reached the place near the Sinaloa River where the envoys had seen the chain gang, but there was nothing remaining of the slavers' camp but some dead fireplaces and the stakes where the horses had been tied up. The trail was clear enough, however, beaten down by a company of about twenty riders and their stumbling chain gang of captives.

Oddly, given that there is almost nothing like it elsewhere in his memoir, Cabeza de Vaca groused at this point that he asked Castillo and Dorantes to try to catch up with the slavers but that they refused to go. Both men were younger and fitter than he himself, he said, but claimed they were too tired to make the effort.

That left Esteban, who at any rate had been their usual advance man during the long journey from Texas. But this time Esteban didn't go forward alone as he usually did, and one has to wonder if it occurred to Cabeza de Vaca immediately or only after some thought that it might not be the best idea to send a near-naked black-skinned man to look for rapacious slave hunters in a war-ravaged frontier. Cabeza de Vaca's memoir was not a diary written at the time of the events, yet at this point in the story there's the whiff of a shift in his perception of his Moroccan traveling companion. Both geographically and socially, the four survivors were on their way back to whatever they had been before the Apalachee pushed them into the sea, and whatever measure of equality Esteban had gained during the long years of shared hardship began to ebb away.

With the trail of the horsemen visible in the dirt ahead, Esteban was not given the choice to decline what Dorantes and Castillo were afforded. "The next day in the morning I took with me the black man and eleven Indians," said Cabeza de Vaca flatly.

Esteban the enigmatic—black skinned, Moroccan, Arabic speaking, Christianized, slave of Arabs perhaps, slave of Spaniards, slave of Quevenes, slave of Yguases, front man and translator for the wandering faith healers. He is the least discussed yet most intriguing character in the entire expedition, and if he was at all given to introspection it must have been an interesting journey that he took with Cabeza de Vaca on the trail of the slavers.

For three days Esteban, Cabeza de Vaca, and the small contingent of Indians followed the signs, hurrying as best they could to close the gap, until finally, finally, the long-imagined moment was at hand. The four horsemen of the slaving party sat in their saddles dumbfounded by the sight before them. For nearly two weeks they and their companions had been scouring the countryside in search of people and had seen none. Now, here before them in broad morning daylight were thirteen who made no effort to run away. And that was the least of it.

"They remained looking at me a long time, so astonished that they neither spoke to me nor managed to ask me anything," recalled Cabeza de Vaca. It was April of 1536, eight years to the month since their landing in Florida.

The slavers' camp was only a mile or two away, at a spring near the Sinaloa River, and the captain of the slavers, Diego de Alcaraz, was there when his subordinates brought the strange little company in. He was naturally as amazed as his men had been at the appearance of

Cabeza de Vaca and Esteban, and everyone got down on their knees and prayed.

Alcaraz wasn't so overwhelmed, however, that he forgot why he was in that God-forsaken stretch of territory. After hearing the outlines of the adventure, he didn't ask what he could do for Cabeza de Vaca and Esteban; he asked rather what they could do for him. His men and horses were hungry, he explained, having found no inhabited villages in half a month. It wasn't just the soldiers who needed sustenance, either. There were the new captives, still in their chains, and a sizable contingent of porters who had come up from the south with them. If Cabeza de Vaca had as much influence over the Indians as he claimed, Alcaraz suggested, perhaps he could convince the locals to come out of hiding and bring food.

Did Cabeza de Vaca pause and think before announcing that, yes, he knew where there were hundreds of Indians?

On Cabeza de Vaca's advice a party of three horsemen and fifty foot soldiers set off immediately, led by Esteban, and returned five days later with Castillo, Dorantes, and a huge crowd of followers. "There came 600 men and women, some with suckling babes in their arms, with jars full of corn that they had hidden in the mountains," they later recalled.

The inevitable clash wasn't long in coming. When he saw the six hundred from the mountain hideaway, Alcaraz wanted more, and Cabeza de Vaca sent messengers into the hinterland around the Sinaloa River to call the people out of hiding. Another six hundred soon arrived, bearing their corn in sealed clay containers that had been buried in the ground for safekeeping. With twelve hundred Indians now gathered where previously he and his men had found none, Alcaraz announced that he intended to enslave at least some—if not all—of the gathered. Cabeza de Vaca was apparently surprised by the turn, and a "great dispute" erupted between the Spaniards who had ridden horses up from the south and the four who had walked barefoot down from the north.

At the first sign of trouble, the Narváez survivors urged the majority of their entourage to return to their homes, plant their crops, and otherwise "secure themselves." But ironically, the Indians now refused to leave, saying that if they couldn't deliver the four shamans to another group of followers, they would surely die. Nor were the erstwhile shamans able to explain that despite their previous promises they had no real power to protect the Indians from their Christian brethren. "Going with us," Cabeza de Vaca recalled of the Indians, "they feared neither the Christians nor their lances."

For Alcaraz's part, the novelty of the four wanderers' influence over the Indians had worn off. It had become, in fact, an annoyance, and he decided to disabuse the pathetic hoards of their heathen misconceptions about their mystical half deities.

"They made their interpreter tell them that we were of the same people as they, and that we had been lost for a long time, and that we were people of ill fortune and no worth," recalled Cabeza de Vaca, who with obvious satisfaction went on to say the Indians didn't accept the argument that the naked healers from the east could be the same people as the armored thieves from the south.

But the four wanderers had gotten what they wanted most, which was to be back in the world of Spanish power. And in that world Alcaraz had the upper hand, and he simply shuffled the troublesome quartet off under guard to his superiors. As they were departing, the four ex-shamans finally managed to convince the Indians to go home and take up their old lives, explaining cheerfully that they themselves were on their way to "the chief of the Christians" to put an end to the slaving and marauding.

As for the slaver Alcaraz, the joint report of the survivors says somewhat blandly that he went into the mountains to take up where he had left off looking for more slaves to add to those he had already captured. Cabeza de Vaca's personal version of the end of their careers as spiritual leaders, however, is markedly more bitter and incendiary:

> The Christians sent us off under the guard of an alcalde who was named Cabreros and three other Christians with us, from which it is evident how much men's thoughts deceive them, for we went to them seeking liberty and when we thought we had it, it turned out to be so much to the contrary. And in order to remove us from conversation with the Indians, they led us through areas depopulated and overgrown so that we would not see what they were doing nor their conduct, because they had conspired to go and attack the Indians whom we had sent away reassured and in peace. And they carried it out just as they had planned it.

Whether or not Alcaraz did, in fact, succeed in carrying out his diabolical plan to round up the followers of the four shamans is not clear. He turned up a few weeks later in the Spanish outpost of San Miguel, where the four were resting, with the news that all the Indians to the north had resumed their farming. They were building churches, he reported, carrying crosses in their hands, and sharing their food with the erstwhile slavers. Peace, both accounts say, broke out across the whole northern frontier through which the four had passed.

To the south of San Miguel, however, war with the Indians still raged, and the four traveled the next three hundred miles with an escort of twenty armed cavalry and six slavers who were driving a gang of five hundred chained-up Indians. They were all heading down the Pacific coast toward Compostela, where the governor of the region lived. This was the notoriously brutal Nuño de Guzmán, who like

Narváez had been in Cuba in the early days, and who took up where the latter had left off as the principal thorn in the side of Cortés in Mexico. The year Narváez sailed from Spain, Guzmán was appointed governor of Pánuco, that long-sought destination of the survivors, and when Narváez disappeared, Guzmán carved out an empire called Nueva Galicia, which stretched from coast to coast just north of Cortés's New Spain.

When the four survivors arrived at his residence in Compostela in the summer of 1536, therefore, Guzmán was one of the most powerful men in the Americas. He gave them clothes from his personal supply, but they found them strangely too confining to wear. He gave them beds, but they could only fall asleep lying on the ground. For two weeks he entertained them, listening eagerly to their descriptions of the lands to the north, descriptions that included the hardships, yes, but also delicious hints of emeralds and pearls, metals and advanced civilizations.

Guzmán was more than casually interested. The great veins of rich Mexican and South American ores that ultimately turned the irregular shipments of plunder to Europe into a reliable river of silver and gold had yet to be discovered. Cortés's cousin Francisco Pizarro, meanwhile, had recently toppled the Inca Empire, reinforcing the old wisdom that the conquest of rich new civilizations was the most reliable route to ultimate colonial success. Guzmán, with his position astraddle the northern frontier of Spanish influence, harbored hopes that he might be the next big winner.

Rumors of wealth to the north—of a "new Mexico" waiting to be discovered and annexed—were already circulating in the conquered portions of Mexico and in Spain before the four survivors turned up. Something of a race to discover the secrets of the north was underway between Guzmán's land parties and the voyages of Cortés, who was limited by the king to exploration by sea. As early as 1527—the year Narváez sailed—a New World pilot named Luis Cárdenas had written to the king telling him of a rumored city called Coluntapan, far across a desert to the north of Mexico City, and another beyond it named Nuxpalo, "where they arm themselves with silver and use metal swords." Another rumor in circulation in the 1530s was of a place to the north called Topira, where in addition to "large numbers of native chickens," the emerald-bedecked Indians were said to "make general use of gold and silver, with which they cover their houses."

Guzmán himself possessed a slave named Tejo, who filled his master's ears with stories of rich provinces to the north that he had visited as a child. "The Indian said he was the son of a trader who was dead, but that when he was a little boy his father had gone into the back country with fine feathers to trade for ornaments, and that when he came back he brought a large amount of gold and silver," said Pedro de Castañeda, who was a member of the Coronado expedition to North America a few years later. Tejo accompanied his father on one or two such trading missions, where he "saw some very large villages, which he compared to Mexico and its environs." Best of all, after crossing a desert some forty days' travel wide, Tejo said he and his father "had seen seven very large towns which had streets of silver workers."

Seven was the right number, tailor-made to titillate the imaginations of the would-be conquerors. The idea among Spaniards that somewhere in their travels they would find seven great cities was older than Columbus's first voyage of discovery. It was based on a myth that seven Portuguese bishops of the Church had escaped by sea in the year 714, after Roderick lost his Christian kingdom to the invading Moors. The archipelago on which they landed was supposed to be somewhere in the Atlantic, along with the equally mysterious islands of Saint Brendan, Saint Ursula, and Hy-Brasil, not to mention any possible remains of Atlantis. Even before 1492, the Portuguese hoped to find the Seven Cities, as did various fifteenth-century voyagers out of Bristol, England. A 1424 map identified the islands as "Antillia," from which the real islands Columbus discovered in the Caribbean got the name Antilles, even though the Seven Cities did not materialize there. Similarly, the Virgin Islands were named for Saint Ursula.

The real importance of the seven lost cities as a driving force for the conquistadors is debatable, and the current trend among scholars of the period is to discount its actual power over decision makers like Guzmán or Cortés. Some even dismiss the very existence of Tejo and his tales of the Seven Cities as an after-the-fact fabrication by a disgruntled Castañeda. The Seven Cities, like the Fountain of Youth or the search for the Amazons, is one of the more lacquered facets of the romantic image of the conquistadors. But the notion of seven rich kingdoms was undeniably always there, lurking in the background, and seemingly corroborated by overlapping traditions among some of the Mexican Indians of seven mystical caves of origin.

There's no evidence that the four Narváez survivors ever suggested they had seen the Seven Cities during their travels through the unknown north, and in light of the hardships of their journey, it's one of the richer ironies of the story that their return to Spanish territory helped fan the smoldering speculation about the north into a frenzy. The more so because Cabeza de Vaca and his companions had nothing to show for their efforts: the bag of "emerald" arrowheads and other gifts from their disciples were all lost during the hasty departure from the Rio Sinaloa, said Cabeza de Vaca. There's no further mention in either account of the cast bell, suggesting that it, too, was gone. All that seems to have made it south with them was Esteban's mystical gourd rattle and a buffalo skin.

But given the events that followed, it's obvious that Cabeza de Vaca, Castillo, Dorantes, and Esteban did nothing to overtly dispel the idea that they had seen signs of great wealth to the north. By the time they finally entered Mexico City on July 23, 1536, they were celebrities. In towns and outposts along the road from Compostela, people had turned out in the streets to see them pass. And in the great city itself there were bullfights and jousting tournaments two days after they arrived. It was the feast day of Saint James: Santiago, the patron saint of Spanish warriors. And though they had, by then, become accustomed to wearing European clothes, the four agreed to make an appearance in front of the church "dressed in skins as they had arrived from the land of Florida."

There were banquets with Cortés, whom Cabeza de Vaca referred to by his title, the Marquis del Valle. His wings had finally been clipped a bit by the emperor, who just the previous year had sent Antonio de Mendoza to take over the day-to-day government as the first viceroy of New Spain. But Narváez's old nemesis was still immensely wealthy and powerful. By no means had he given up hope of leading new conquests northward. Like Guzmán, therefore, Cortés was more than just casually interested in what they knew about *el Norte*.

But the real power was now Viceroy Mendoza, and there were banquets and interviews with him as well. Guzmán and Cortés could dream of sending great expeditions north, but their moments of royal favor had passed. Cortés had permission to explore the "island" of [Baja] California that he had discovered off the west coast of Mexico, but the emperor wasn't about to turn him loose elsewhere. As for Guzmán, his reputation for slaving and brutality was proving too embarrassing for the emperor, and within a year he was removed from his position as governor of New Galicia to be replaced by a young protégé of Mendoza's named Coronado. Practically speaking, therefore, only Mendoza had both the incentive and the legal wherewithal to mount an expedition north.

The viceroy tried to enlist Cabeza de Vaca in the effort, but he wasn't interested. His reluctance wasn't because, having barely escaped with his life, he didn't want to return to the north. In fact, Cabeza de Vaca desperately wanted to return. But like his old commander Narváez a decade before, he felt he had earned the right to be more than someone else's surrogate. As far as anyone in Mexico knew at that time, no one had yet convinced the emperor in Europe to reassign Narváez's old option on North America, and Cabeza de Vaca wanted it for himself. Who better than me? he thought, and made plans to return immediately to Spain and begin the usual lobbying effort.

Nor could Dorantes be convinced to take part in the viceroy's plans. "I consulted with him many times," Mendoza later complained in a letter to the king. "It seemed to me that he could render great service to your Majesty if he were sent with forty or fifty horsemen to lay bare the mysteries of that region. On that account I spent considerable money in providing what was necessary for his journey, and I do not know how it was that the plan fell through and the undertaking was abandoned." Most likely Dorantes had an agreement with Cabeza de Vaca to work together to get the contract for North America for themselves, and he, too, was in a hurry to get back to Spain.

As for Castillo, he wasn't interested in crossing either the ocean or the northern frontier. He was, however, interested in finding a wealthy widow with whom he could settle down, one with an estate and, more importantly in those days when land was cheaper than labor, an allotment of Indian slaves. Mendoza made some appropriate introductions for him.

That left Esteban, and it didn't matter whether Esteban did or did not want to go back north. Now back in "civilization," he belonged once more to Dorantes. And Dorantes sold him.

"The viceroy bought the negro for this purpose from one of those who escaped from Florida," Coronado later explained to the king. "His name is Esteban."

24

Lost in the New World

How much money Viceroy Mendoza paid for the privilege of owning the fourth shaman is not known. Whatever the price, though, the sale of Esteban finally and firmly closed the circle of upended imperial expectations that had begun on the island of Malhado, or even earlier when the Apalachee had forced Narváez to beat his swords into boat nails. Now Cabeza de Vaca and Dorantes were back to being hidalgos looking for favors from the king. Castillo, for his part, was looking to live out his days in peace and comfort. And "the black," as Esteban was usually referred to, was again the property of a white man looking for the treasure of the red man.

"You shall take with you Esteban de Dorantes, as guide," Mendoza wrote in his instructions to Fray Marcos de Niza, a Franciscan whom he had asked to lead a small reconnaissance expedition north in early

1539. "I command him to obey you in whatever you may order him, as he would obey me in person."

By the time Esteban and Fray Marcos started north again from San Miguel de Culiacán on March 7th of that year, Cabeza de Vaca and Dorantes had learned to their dismay that Narváez's much-coveted contract for North America had already been awarded to Hernando De Soto. Cabeza de Vaca would eventually get an appointment as governor of the Plate River region of Argentina, where his attempts at reform resulted in him being sent back to Spain in chains by the indignant colonists who accused him of a litany of abuses. His lawyers and contacts at court barely managed to prevent him being banished to North Africa, but he never again returned to the Americas and focused instead on writing his memoirs.

Castillo, meanwhile, had found his rich wife through an introduction made for him by Viceroy Mendoza. Her name was Isabel de Sanabria, and her first husband had been one of Cortés's original company. Mendoza found Dorantes a suitable wife, too, a woman named María de la Torre.

As for Esteban, if he had any regrets about having to return to the "uncivilized" north he seems to have come to terms with them. He wasn't going as a porter, after all, but as an expert guide. He had acquired a pair of greyhounds and a set of green dishes on which all his meals were to be prepared. He still had with him his magic gourd, covered with bells and two feathers, one red and the other white, to symbolize his mystical powers.

When he and Fray Marcos took their leave of Coronado, who accompanied them for the first part of their journey, they were attended by a large retinue of Indians who had been "liberated and purchased for this purpose" (if that makes any sense).

"I left them in the care of more than one hundred Indians from

Petatlán and from the section whence they had come," Coronado later recalled. "They carried the padre on the palms of their hands, pleasing him in everything they could."

Esteban, too, was well cared for along the way. According to Coronado's man Castañeda, who didn't witness what he reported but presumably heard it from people who did, it wasn't long before Esteban was "loaded with the large quantity of turquoises they had given him and some beautiful women whom the Indians who followed him and carried his things were taking with them and had given him."

Fray Marcos apparently didn't ride at all times on the palms of his company, because after a few weeks of travel in the region to the north of the old mountain refuge camp, he determined to take a rest for Easter. Esteban and his entourage continued ahead with explicit instructions: if Esteban found a place of "moderate importance," he was to send a white cross about the size of a man's hand. If it were "something great," the signal was to be a cross the size of two hands.

"And if it was something bigger and better than New Spain," Marcos instructed—in other words if it was better than Montezuma's Tenochtitlan—Esteban was to send "a large cross."

It didn't take him long. Only four days after they parted, a man arrived in Marcos's camp carrying a cross as big as himself. Fray Marcos should waste no time, the messenger told him, because Esteban had "reached people who gave him information of the greatest thing in the world." There were in fact no fewer than "seven very great cities" ahead, he said, the smallest of which was called Cíbola.

It was a new name, but the right number. Could this at last be them? Despite his excitement, Fray Marcos didn't set off immediately. He wanted to wait a few days for some people he had sent to explore the coast to return. Of course Esteban would wait for him as they had planned.

But Esteban didn't wait. Once Marcos finally set out along the route Esteban had taken, he traveled as fast as he could, but the Moroccan, for reasons of his own, always seemed to stay a few days ahead. He did leave behind hints for the friar. At one place, Marcos found a large cross planted in the ground, which he thought was meant "to indicate that the news of the good country always increases." Another time Esteban left word with the locals that he would wait for Fray Marcos just ahead, beyond the next desert stretch.

Some say they got as far north in this cat and mouse fashion as the Zuñi pueblos of New Mexico, crossing through the great pass now named for Coronado. (The name Cíbola later became associated with those pueblos.) Others argue that however far Esteban may have gotten, Fray Marcos never got north of El Paso.

According to Marcos's report, he hustled along as best he could, through many towns where he remembered seeing everyone wearing turquoise jewelry from their noses and ears, and cotton clothing. Five days in this valley he traveled, four days crossing that desert. He went through towns where the people told him that in Cíbola, ahead, were ten-story buildings. He saw a hide of a beast bigger than a buffalo with one curling horn. He stopped in a town that was "all irrigated and is like a garden."

The last messenger from Esteban told Fray Marcos that the Moroccan was very happy, and that he had entered the final desert passage before the first of the seven great cities. He was more certain than ever, he said, of the "grandeur of the country."

Then, just as Marcos was about to make the last push to Cíbola himself, frantic messengers ran into his camp with news that Esteban's magic gourd rattle had offended the lord of the great first city, who recognized it as the work of his enemies. This king had warned Esteban to take his three hundred-person entourage and leave, the runner said, and when Esteban had refused, the Cíbolans had attacked. The messengers, who were "covered with blood and with many wounds, said they had only escaped by hiding under the bodies of their dead comrades until dark."

"We heard loud voices in the city, and on the terraces we saw many men and women watching," they told Fray Marcos.

And what of Esteban himself? Marcos wanted to know.

"We saw no more of Esteban," they answered. Esteban had disappeared.

When Fray Marcos got back to New Spain, he told Viceroy Mendoza that after hearing of Esteban's presumed downfall he was afraid to go on to Cíbola alone. But in order to be certain of what lay ahead he overcame his fears and went as far as a hill overlooking the city. It was indeed bigger than Montezuma's Tenochtitlan, the friar swore, "on a plain at the skirt of a round hill."

And so beautiful, he remembered, that he remarked on it to the two Indians who had taken him to see it. The other six cities, they assured him, were even larger and lovelier.

Before turning and fleeing south, Friar Marcos made a small cross. He mounted it in a cairn of rocks he collected there on his overlook above the city of Cíbola. He thought the place ought to be called the New Kingdom of San Francisco, in honor of Saint Francis, the patron of his order. He claimed both it and the other six cities in Mendoza's name for Christ and for the emperor in Spain.

But though Coronado was soon marching north and east from Mexico with an army of five hundred conquistadors, and Hernando De Soto was already on the ground at the opposite corner of North America getting ready to march his company of six hundred north and west from Florida, no one ever found the beautiful cities again.

Notes

A NOTE ABOUT SOURCES

"And now we come to the list of authors cited, such as other works contain but in which your own is lacking. Here again the remedy is an easy one; you have but to look up some book that has them all, from A to Z as you were saying, and transfer the entire list as it stands. What if the imposition is plain for all to see? You have little need to refer to them, and so it does not matter; and some may be so simple minded as to believe that you have drawn upon them all in your simple unpretentious little story. If it serves no other purpose, this imposing list of authors will at least give your book an unlooked for air of authority. What is more, no one is going to put himself to the trouble of verifying your references to see whether or not you have followed all these authors, since it will not be worth his pains to do so."

—CERVANTES, *Don Quixote*

As mentioned in the prologue, there are essentially two surviving first-hand accounts of the Narváez expedition. The first and best known is the memoir of the treasurer, Álvar Núñez Cabeza de Vaca, originally published in Zamora, Spain, in 1542. It is by far the most important document, though it's compromised a bit by having been written long after the fact in an attempt to gain some recognition and remuneration from the king and public for the suffering of its author. It has been translated into English at least six times, most recently by Rolena Adorno and Charles Pautz. I have generally relied on their translation, both because of its grace and because it appears with the Spanish text on the facing page. Unless otherwise noted, all quotations attributed to Cabeza de Vaca (and the associated page references) are from the Adorno and Pautz translation of the 1542 Zamora edition.

The second major source of information on the expedition is a report prepared by the survivors of the expedition for the colonial authorities in Hispaniola and Spain. Unfortunately, the original of this document has been lost, but the early historian of the Spanish colonial enterprise (and friend of Narváez) Gonzalo Fernández Oviedo y Valdés included what is generally considered to be a relatively faithful paraphrasing of it in the thirty-fifth book of his massive *General and Natural History of the Indies*. This, too, has been translated into English multiple times. In order to avoid confusion between Oviedo the historian and Lope de Oviedo, one of the Narváez expeditionaries, and to avoid the repetitive awkwardness of explaining the uncertain provenance of the text, I have chosen throughout the book to refer to this text as the joint report, though I acknowledge that this runs the risk of understressing the paraphrased nature of Oviedo's version. In the notes below, however, the joint report is referred to as Oviedo, and unless otherwise noted, all quotes are from that prepared by Basil Hedrick and Carroll Riley.

For other sources than those already mentioned, every effort has been made to credit them in the bibliography and, for direct quotes, in the notes that follow. Two secondary sources stand out for special notice, however. The first is Adorno and Pautz's multivolume companion to their translation. While I have not always been convinced by the historical arguments in this encyclopedic textual analysis of the Cabeza de Vaca memoir, it is nonetheless a baseline of sorts for academic studies of the Narváez expedition and will remain so for a long time coming. The second source that deserves special acknowledgment is Alex Krieger's doctoral dissertation on the route of the Narváez survivors through Texas and Mexico, which was originally written in the 1950s and influenced generations of scholars before it was finally published in 2002.

I was already buried away in the story of the Narváez expedition before either of these two important works were published, and suffice it to say that I would most likely still be lost today somewhere between the Florida Panhandle and the village of hearts if their authors had not finished their books before I did mine. I am grateful to all three, as well as to all those mentioned in the bibliography and specific notes that follow. In those notes, I have only listed titles in cases where more than one source by the author appears in the bibliography.

CHAPTER NOTES

Introduction:

"This alone is what a man . . . ," Cabeza de Vaca, in Adorno and Pautz translation, p. 21.

"To serve God and the king . . . ," Díaz del Castillo, as quoted in Elliott, *Imperial Spain,* p. 65.

Chapter 1: A Continent to Call His Own

In an early version of this book, the telling of Narváez's early career in Cuba and his subsequent difficulties and obsession with Cortés stretched to several hundred pages. Fortunately for most readers, that is now largely gone. Those who do desire more may want to begin with Hugh Thomas's *Conquest* for the best modern overview of the Cortés saga, but don't neglect rereading Díaz del Castillo's personal account or Cortés's own letters to the emperor. The first chapters of Wright's *Early History of Cuba* are useful for Narváez's early life in the Caribbean, as are the historical works of Las Casas, Oviedo, and Martyr. See also Weddle, Elliot, Kamen, Floyd, Fernández-Armesto, and Leonard as well as Thomas's other works for further background on Spain and the Caribbean in the period. Hoffman's *New Andalucia* is the best source on the disastrous Ayllón expedition.

"I tell you . . . ," Díaz del Castillo, p. 281.

"Santa María, Santa María," Díaz del Castillo, p. 286.

"When finally I came up . . . ," Cortés, *Letters,* p. 105.

"Defended himself like a gentleman," quoted in Goodwyn, p. 151.

"Holy Mary protect me . . . ," "very deep . . . ," and "we stood there for some time . . . ," and other firsthand descriptions of battle in Cempoallan, Díaz del Castillo, pp. 288ff., unless otherwise noted.

"Jeering," "Haughty," Díaz del Castillo, pp. 262ff.

"You should regard highly the good luck . . . ," López de Gómara, as translated by Goodwyn, p. 155. Same story is told in Díaz del Castillo, along with Cortés's reply.

"entreating for justice . . . ," Oviedo, Davenport translation, p. 124.

"This is what he found," Oviedo, Hedrick and Riley translation, p. 2.

"their love of great deeds . . . ," J. H. Parry, *Spanish Seaborne Empire,* p. 84.

"I, Pánfilo Narváez . . . ," translation of one of Narváez's petitions to the king appears, along with other interesting documents, in the appendix to Buckingham Smith's translation of the Cabeza de Vaca account.

"I'd like to see the clause . . . ," as quoted in Thomas, *Conquest*, p. 564.

"Consider that to other persons . . . ," Goodwyn, p. 154.

"to serve your majesty . . . ," appendix to Buckingham Smith's translation of the Cabeza de Vaca account, pp. 207–8.

"From one sea to the other," as quoted in Adorno and Pautz, vol. 2, p. 32.

CHAPTER 2: THE COMPANY GATHERS

In addition to the general sources mentioned above, see Restall's discussion of the diversity of the conquistadors and Kamen's work on conversos and the Inquisition, and Thomas's *Slave Trade*. The best work on Ayllón is undoubtedly Hoffman's *New Andalucia*. The story of Princess Anna's annulment is detailed in Adorno and Pautz, with the caveat that the only evidence of Cabeza de Vaca's role in the affair was hearsay.

"I ask Your Majesty . . . ," appendix to Buckingham Smith's translation of the Cabeza de Vaca account, p. 289.

"Neither holy, nor Roman . . . ," from Voltaire's *Essai sur les moeurs*, as quoted in Bartlett's *Familiar Quotations*.

"Narváez, and other captains who want them . . . ," Oviedo, Davenport translation, p. 276.

"untitled, middle-ranking nobility," Adorno and Pautz, p. 298.

"and thus the poor volunteer . . . ," Oviedo, Davenport translation, p. 276.

"Other dues belonging to us," from "Instructions given to Cabeza de Vaca . . . ," appearing in the appendix to Buckingham Smith's translation of the Cabeza de Vaca account, pp. 218–23.

CHAPTER 3: ACROSS THE OCEAN SEA

Morison, Peterson, and Leonard were particularly useful for details of life at sea in the 1500s. The conquest of the Canaries and the early history of the Caribbean is discussed in Sauer, Floyd, Morison, Weddle, Fernández-Armesto, Bishop, Helps, Wright, and Adorno and Pautz, as well as in Las Casas, Martyr, and Oviedo. As in the previous chapter, see Hoffman's work on Ayllón.

"Seek to write to their sons . . . ," Oviedo, Davenport translation, p. 276.

"Why, the coasts and islands . . . ," Isaiah, 60:9.

"First intoxicating years . . . ," Elliott, *Imperial Spain*, p. 183.

"To be young . . . ," Leonard, p. 27.

"Old and worn out ships . . . ," Oviedo, Davenport translation, p. 276.

"Sea of mares," Oviedo, as quoted in Morison, *Admiral of the Ocean Sea*, p. 160.

"A ship is a very narrow and stout prison . . . ," and other comments by Father de la Torre are quoted in Leonard, p. 153.

"There are fish they call flying fish . . . ," as quoted in Peterson, pp. 84–85.

"and valorous Don Quixote . . . ," Cervantes, p. 102.

"one hero kills twenty men . . . ," this and the quote that follows are from Leonard, p. 67. Leonard, for that matter, is the source for most of the material regarding the book craze in sixteenth-century Spain.

"We were amazed . . . ," Díaz del Castillo, p. 190.

"What news? What news . . . ," Las Casas, *Selected Writings*, translated and edited by George Sanderlin, p. 5.

"a house for public women . . . ," Martín, p. 20.

"acting under the King's banner," letter dated June 12, 1527, as quoted in Weddle, *Spanish Sea*, p. 204.

"our whole safety . . . ," Cortés, p. 123.

"horses and Negroes . . . ," Díaz del Castillo, p. 37.

"He ordered a captain . . ." and other quotes regarding the hurricane, Cabeza de Vaca, p. 25ff.

"Fortune favors the brave," Cortés, p. 128.

"crossbow shot in width," Weddle, p. 22.

Chapter 4: Into the Gulf

For this and the chapters that follow, see the many works of Milanich, Mitchem, Willey, Hudson, Swanton, and the others listed in the bibliography with titles suggesting ethnographic and archeological interpretations of the pre-Columbian cultures of Florida. I am especially grateful to Milanich and Mitchem for their generous help via e-mail. Also, the various De Soto narratives translated in Hodge and in Clayton et al. were indispensable. And don't neglect Garcilaso, "the Inca" for sheer reading pleasure if nothing else. The Ponce de León story is told in scraps here and there all over, but most of the useful material has been collected together and translated in large sections in Fuson.

"Because there was a feeling . . . ," Wright, p. 163.

"because they said . . . ," Cabeza de Vaca, Adorno and Pautz translation, pp. 32–33.

"so thick a cat . . . ," Morison, *Southern Voyages*, p. 128.

"not without much danger," Cabeza de Vaca, Adorno and Pautz translation, p. 33.

"Cuba ran east-west like it . . . ," Herrera, as translated by Fuson, p. 111.

"The other ship had been lost . . . ," Cabeza de Vaca, Adorno and Pautz translation, p. 273.

"And he called . . . ," Cabeza de Vaca, p. 35.

"Decorated," Biedma, account in Clayton et al., p. 61.

"called it La Florida . . . ," Herrera, as translated by Fuson, p. 98.

"many of them very thoroughly . . . ," Las Casas, as translated by Fuson, p. 98.

"bastard son . . . ," Thomas, *Conquest*, p. 65.

"people with large, broad ears . . . ," Velázquez, as quoted in Leonard, p. 46.

"Vain belief . . . ," Pastor Bodmer, p. 106.

"from a distance," Herrera, translated by Bolton, p. 8.

"was believed to be a native . . . ," Herrera, as translated by Fuson, p. 108.

"if I understand correctly . . . ," Columbus, *Journal*, October 13.

"the women of the Lucayan islands . . . ," Martyr, p. 251.

"made from a tree-trunk . . . ," Columbus, p. 95.

"the name of Hernando Cortés . . . ," Herrera, as quoted in Bolton, p. 10.

"temperature of the region was very disagreeable . . . ," Fuson, p. 165.

"scandalized all the land . . . ," Ponce de León, as quoted by Wright, p. 79.

"These Indians carried . . . ," Díaz del Castillo, p. 15.

CHAPTER 5: THE REQUIREMENT

The classic work on the mental and theological gymnastics of the Spanish in their attempts to justify to themselves and the rest of the world that their imperialism was, in fact, in the interests of "civilization" is Hanke's *Spanish Struggle for Justice*.

"dwelling with an open shed . . . ," Hodge, p. 19.

"The town was seven or eight houses . . . ," Gentleman of Elvas account, Clayton et al. translation, p. 57.

"major town . . . ," Mitchem, "Safety Harbor Redefined," p. 88.

"many fishing nets . . . ," Oviedo, Hedrick and Riley translation, p. 8.

"Spaniards were so accustomed . . . ," Hanke, p. 6.

"In behalf of the Catholic . . . ," the version of the *requirimiento* carried by Narváez appears in its entirety in the appendix of the Buckingham Smith translation of Cabeza de Vaca's memoir.

"calm the conscience," as quoted in Thomas, *Conquest*, p. 72.

"My lords it appears . . . ," Oviedo, as quoted in Hanke, p. 33.

"I promised your Majesty . . . ," Cortés, p. 32.

"I have not come for any such reason . . . ," Pizzaro, as quoted in Hanke, p. 6.

"to subdue Saracens . . . ," papal bull *Dum diversas* of 1452, as quoted in Thomas, *Conquest*, p. 59.

"Thanks to God they saw . . . ," Rodrigo Rangel account, Clayton et al., p. 255.

"Since we did not have an interpreter . . . ," Cabeza de Vaca, as translated by Adorno and Pautz, p. 37.

Chapter 6: In Tocobaga's Charnel House

Again, Milanich and Mitchem are the place to start on matters relating to pre-contact and early-contact Florida. Also see Hudson and Calvert for descriptions of Spanish armies of the period.

"wore poor and rusty coats . . . ," Gentleman of Elvas account, Clayton et al. translation, p. 50.

"We showed them maize . . . ," Cabeza de Vaca, as translated by Adorno and Pautz, p. 37.

"incontrovertible evidence," Milanich, *Archeology*, p. 108.

"a temple, on the top . . . ," Gentleman of Elvas account, Clayton et al. translation, p. 57.

"Buzzard-men," Swanton, p. 729.

"two days until the flesh . . . ," Milanich, *Florida Indians*, p. 76. See also Swanton, *Indian Tribes*, p. 722.

"that his people had fled . . . ," Solís de Merás, p. 225.

"this governor was very given . . . ," Rangel account, Clayton et al. translation, p. 256.

"The reader must understand . . . ," Rangel account, Clayton et al. translation, p. 257.

"The reader must understand . . . ," Rangel account, Clayton et al. translation, p. 257.

"The dog charged . . . ," Las Casas, as translated by Andrée Collard, p. 91.

"The [native] king's brother . . . ," Martyr, p. 285.

"The conquistadors in the Indies . . . ," Rangel account, Clayton et al., p. 257.

"their right hands . . . ," Gentleman of Elvas account, Hodge, p. 219.

"But to delay further the death . . . ," and "half-baked . . . ," Garcilaso de la Vega, p. 63ff.

"a dense deposit of charred wood . . . ," Willey, p. 149.

"hardware of some type . . . ," Milanich and Hudson, p. 64.

Chapter 7: Leaving Safety Harbor

"They indicated to us . . . ," and "a good-sized plot . . . ," Cabeza de Vaca, Adorno and Pautz translation, p. 39ff.

"without seeing a single Indian," Oviedo, Hedrick and Riley translation, p. 10.

"In case he did not find the port . . . ," Cabeza de Vaca, Adorno and Pautz translation, p. 37.

"both ships should get . . . ," Oviedo, Hedrick and Riley translation, p. 9.

"He had already miscalculated . . . ," and other quotes regarding decision to divide forces, Cabeza de Vaca, Adorno and Pautz translation, p. 37ff.

"an attribute of nobility . . . ," Elliott, *Imperial Spain*, p. 222.

"it is better to die . . . ," Díaz del Castillo, p. 286.

"astrology meant as much . . . ," Schama, p. 36.

"auguries, portents, and . . . ," Fernández-Armesto, p. 41.

"A free mixture . . . ," Kamen, p. 5.

"Part pagan . . . ," Bolton, p. 3.

"I shall hammer in the nail . . . ," Elliott, *Spain and Its World*, p. 34.

"fight and conquer . . . ," Cabeza de Vaca, Adorno and Pautz translation, p. 275.

"fatuous," and "the most incompetant," Morison, *European Discovery*, pp. 518–19.

"grasping bungler," Cabeza de Vaca, Covey translation, p. 9.

"aggressive and brutal," Weddle, p. 116.

"a man of little ability . . . ," Hallenbeck, *Journey and Route*, p. 17.

"On this all abandoned any hope . . . ," Cortés, p. 34.

"had nothing to rely on . . . ," Cortés, as quoted in Thomas, *Conquest*, p. 222.

CHAPTER 8: ACROSS THE WITHLACOOCHEE

In addition to the archeological sources mentioned above, see Johnson and
    Kohler for a study of what little is known of the Alachua peoples.

"many plaits and slashes," Gentleman of Elvas, Clayton et al. translation, p. 57.

"They loved color . . . ," Hudson, p. 67.

"I, the King . . . ," a full translation of Cabeza de Vaca's instructions appears in
    the appendix to the Buckingham Smith translation of Cabeza de Vaca's
    relation, p. 218.

"Obstructed by woods and swamps . . . ," Gentleman of Elvas account, Clay-
    ton et al. translation, pp. 59–60.

"during this entire time . . . ," Cabeza de Vaca, Adorno and Pautz translation,
    p. 47.

"we were all accustomed . . . ," Díaz del Castillo, p. 134.

"we were most certainly new . . . ," Cabeza de Vaca, Adorno and Pautz transla-
    tion, p. 47.

"Apalachee . . . ," Oviedo, Hedrick and Riley translation, p. 12.

"They gestured to us . . . ," and related quotes, Cabeza de Vaca, Adorno and
    Pautz translation, p. 47ff.

"good-looking Indian women," Díaz del Castillo, p. 367.

"who were not old nor the most ugly . . . ," Rangel account, Clayton et al.
    translation, p. 289.

CHAPTER 9: THE SOUND OF FLUTES

Though many of his own observations of Native American cultures have come
    into some disrepute, the nearly encyclopedic collection and translations of
    first impressions in Swanton's work for the Smithsonian were invaluable.

"The forepart of their bodies . . . ," Ribault, as quoted in Swanton, *Indians of
    the Southeastern United States*, p. 532.

"The most part of them have bodies . . . ," Laudonnière, as quoted in Swan-
    ton, *Indians of the Southeastern United States*, p. 532.

"They let their nails grow . . . ," Le Moyne, as quoted in Swanton, *Indians of
    the Southeastern United States*, p. 537.

"flat land with hard sand . . . ," Oviedo, Hedrick and Riley translation, p. 12.

"many large and small lagoons," Cabeza de Vaca, Adorno and Pautz trans-
    lation, p. 57.

"extreme need," Oviedo, Hedrick and Riley translation, p. 12.

"almost from sunrise . . . ," Bartram, p. 310.

"from carrying their weapons . . . ," Cabeza de Vaca, Adorno and Pautz translation, p. 55.

"twenty pipers . . . ," Le Moyne, Hulton et al. translation, p. 121.

"irresistibly moving . . . ," Bartram, p. 206.

"a kind of flute . . . ," Bartram, p. 396.

"Messengers from Ucachile . . . ," Rangel account, Clayton et al. translation, p. 264.

"Every day they came out . . . ," Gentleman of Elvas, Hodge translation, p. 158.

"hieroglyphics . . . ," Bartram, as quoted in Swanton, *Indian Tribes*, p. 533.

"many pieces of stuff," Le Moyne, in Swanton, *Indian Tribes*, pp. 456 and 511.

"it seemed to us . . ." and other quotes related to encounter with Timucua, Cabeza de Vaca, Adorno and Pautz translation, p. 51ff.

"numberless . . . ," Díaz del Castillo, p. xxx.

"As to what you say . . . ," Gentleman of Elvas account, Clayton et al. translation, p. 134.

CHAPTER 10: IN THE LAND OF THE APALACHEE

In addition to the archeological and anthropological texts already mentioned, see Hann, *Apalachee*. Also of particular value were the many essays in *Mississippian Emergence* (Smith, ed.), *Columbian Consequences* (Thomas, ed.), *Forgotton Centuries* (Hudson and Chaves Tesser, eds.), as well as articles by Scarry and McEwen, Bullen, Mitchem, Knight, and Larsen.

"The Spaniards attacked it daringly . . . ," Oviedo, Hedrick and Riley translation, p. 12.

"In the end . . . ," and other quotes related to Apalachee, Cabeza de Vaca, p. 55ff.

"It is useless . . . ," Swanton, p. 358.

"based on organized squadrons . . . ," Dye, "Warfare in the Sixteenth-Century Southeast," in *Columbian Consequences*, D. H. Thomas, ed., vol. 2, p. 214.

"large and good houses," Garcilaso de la Vega, p. 184.

"very populous . . . many open districts . . . ," Gentleman of Elvas account, Clayton et al. translation, p. 71.

"large-scale corporate labor . . . ," Smith, *Mississippian Emergence*, p. 4.

"war chief" etc., Widmer, "Structure of Southeastern Chiefdoms," in Hudson and Chaves Tesser, p. 141.

"head peace town . . . ," Hann, "The Apalachee of the Historica Era," in Hudson and Chaves Tesser, p. 329.

"from another area . . . ," Oviedo, Hedrick and Riley translation, p. 13.

"painted all over . . . ," Hann, *Apalachee*, p. 93.

"the Indians were in the marshes . . . ," Oviedo, Hedrick and Riley translation, p. 14.

"they now engaged us in daily skirmishes . . . ," Alonso de Carmona, as quoted by Garcilaso de la Vega, p. 258.

"perfect," Gentleman of Elvas account, Hodge, *Spanish Explorers*, p. 148.

"are of such large build . . . ," Cabeza de Vaca, Adorno and Pautz translation, p. 63.

"These Indians of Apalachee . . . ," Alonso Carmona, in Garcilaso de la Vega, p. 258.

"made of certain canes . . . ," Gentleman of Elvas account, Hodge, *Spanish Explorers*, p. 148.

"entering the chest . . . ," Garcilaso de la Vega, p. 234.

"the base of a poplar tree . . . ," Cabeza de Vaca, Adorno and Pautz translation, p. 63.

"the thickness which the arrows pierced . . . ," Oviedo, Hedrick and Riley translation, p. 18.

"concluded without becoming a live war . . . ," and other quotes regarding ball game: Hann, *Apalachee*, p. 76ff. A complete translation of Friar Pavia's report on the ball game appears in the appendix of Hann, *Apalachee*.

"The Indians are exceedingly ready . . . ," Gentleman of Elvas account, Hodge, *Spanish Explorers*, p. 148.

"The Indians made war on us . . . ," Cabeza de Vaca, Adorno and Pautz translation, p. 61.

"were beginning to wound . . . ," Oviedo, Hedrick and Riley translation, p. 14.

"had a great deal of maize . . . ," Cabeza de Vaca, Adorno and Pautz translation, p. 61.

"how else to explain . . . ," Hoffman, "Narváez and Cabeza de Vaca in Florida," in Hudson and Chaves Tesser, p. 65.

Chapter 11: Chest-High in Hell

"They can shoot arrows at two hundred paces . . ." and other quotes regarding the march to the Bay of Horses, Cabeza de Vaca, Adorno and Pautz translation, p. 63ff.

"harassed more by their own rage . . . ," Garcilaso de la Vega, p. 176.

"one knee on the chest . . . ," Alonso Carmona, as told to Garcilaso de la Vega, p. 379.

"occupied themselves . . . ," Garcilaso de la Vega, p. 376.

"bound up the hurts . . . ," Díaz del Castillo, p. 59.

"oil, dirty wool, and incantations . . . ," Garcilaso de la Vega, p. 524.

"tepid wine . . . ," Casis, p. 284.

"best evidence . . . ," Milanich and Milbrath, p. 101.

"many," Oviedo, Hedrick and Riley translation, p. 17.

"each day more . . . ," Oviedo, Hedrick and Riley translation, p. 15.

"began to steal away," Cabeza de Vaca, Lopez-Morillas translation, p. 30.

"began to leave secretly," Cabeza de Vaca, Favata and Fernández translation, p. 46.

"altogether powerless, without strength . . . ," Cabeza de Vaca, Adorno and Pautz translation, the aborted desertion appears on p. 69. The remaining quotes on the incident are from that translation.

"searching and thinking . . . ," Oviedo, Hedrick and Riley translation, p. 17.

Chapter 12: Into the Gulf . . . Again

The PhD dissertations of both Mitchem and Hutchinson were vital to the discussion of the Tatham mound.

"We held it to be certain . . ." and other quotes about the building of the boats, Cabeza de Vaca, Adorno and Pautz translation, p. 69ff.

"riddled with arrows," Oviedo, Hedrick and Riley translation, p. 18.

"typical of a downward blow," Mitchem, "Safety Harbor Redefined," p. 483.

"the only descendants . . . ," Milanich, *Florida Indians and the Invasion*, p. 231.

Chapter 13: Father of Waters

"without any one of us . . . ," and other quotes regarding the boat trip, Cabeza de Vaca, Adorno and Pautz translation, p. 75ff.

"look to see . . . ," Cabeza de Vaca, Adorno and Pautz translation, p. 275.

"a fire burning . . . ," Hann, "Florida's Terra Incognita," p. 80.

"very quickly . . ." Oviedo, Hedrick and Riley translation, p. 19.

"beads, rattles, and some corn," and "many of the Indians were quite cut up,"
    Oviedo, Hedrick and Riley translation, p. 20.

"naked as eve . . . ," I. A. Wright, p. 35.

"this is the flesh . . . ," Martyr, p. 30.

"a comrade deserted . . . ," Rangel account, Clayton et al. translation, p. 235.

"In fear of being made to pay . . ." Gentleman of Elvas account, Hodge, p. 238.

"had news of how the boats . . . ," Biedma account, Clayton et al., p. 232.

"In that town . . . ," Rangel account, Clayton et al., p. 292.

CHAPTER 14: CASTAWAYS

"We could not determine . . ." and other quotes regarding the disappearance
    of Narváez, Cabeza de Vaca, Adorno and Pautz translation, p. 87ff.

"lighter and could move faster," Oviedo, Hedrick and Riley translation, p. 22.

"this alone is what a man . . . ," Cabeza de Vaca, Adorno and Pautz transla-
    tion, p. 21.

"to remain . . . ," Cabeza de Vaca, Adorno and Pautz translation, p. 69.

"It is no longer time . . . ," Cabeza de Vaca, Adorno and Pautz translation,
    p. 91.

"some very novel things . . . ," Cabeza de Vaca, Adorno and Pautz translation,
    p. 21.

"so that they might walk . . . ," Oviedo, Hedrick and Riley translation, p. 31.

"very muscular," Díaz del Castillo, as quoted in Davenport and Wells, p. 126.

"very thin and ill . . . ," and other quotes describing the disappearance of
    Narváez, Oviedo, Hedrick and Riley translation, p. 31.

"I believe Pánfilo," Oviedo, Hedrick and Riley translation, p. 14.

CHAPTER 15: THE ISLE OF BAD FORTUNE

There is a wide range of scholarly literature on the Native American cultures
    of precontact and early-contact Texas. For this and the following chap-
    ters, see especially Aten, Bolton, Campbell and Campbell, Gatschet,
    Highley and Hester, Krieger, and Ricklis.

"fallen on top of one another . . . ," and other quotes relating to the arrival on
    Malhado, Cabeza de Vaca, Adorno and Pautz translation, p. 91ff.

"tinklers," Highley and Hester, p. 32.

"clothes were the standard . . . ," Fernández-Armesto, p. 82.

"For the love of God . . . ," Cervantes, p. 274.

"sacrificed before us . . . ," Díaz del Castillo, p. 102.

CHAPTER 16: FIGUEROA'S ATTEMPT

"All together we agreed," and other quotes relating to the winter on Malhado, Cabeza de Vaca, Adorno and Pautz translation, p. 103ff.

"Other defects" and other quotes relating to the winter on Malhado, Oviedo, Hedrick and Riley translation, pp. 25ff.

CHAPTER 17: THE NEWS FROM MALHADO

"With their arrows . . . ," Folmer, pp. 218–19.

"When they see fit . . . ," Wolff, p. 14.

"most maligned . . . ," Ricklis, p. vii.

CHAPTER 18: THE TRAVELING SALESMAN

See Hickerson, Hudson and Tesser, Smith, Creel, Claasen and Sigman, and D. H. Thomas.

"I was on the other side . . ." and other quotes relating to Cabeza de Vaca's time alone on the Texas coast are in Cabeza de Vaca, Adorno and Pautz translation, p. 119ff.

"But after a period . . . ," Aten, p. 94.

"The children would tease . . . ," Oviedo, Hedrick and Riley translation, p. 40.

"turquoises and cotton blankets . . . ," Gentleman of Elvas account, Clayton et al. translation, p. 148.

"a very large river . . . ," Castaneda account, Hodge, *Spanish Explorers*, p. 330.

"head smashed in . . . ," Krech, p. 144.

"follow the cows . . . ," Castaneda account, Hodge, *Spanish Explorers*, p. 362.

"in the entire land . . . ," Cabeza de Vaca, Adorno and Pautz translation, p. 189.

"they are great drunkards . . . ," Cabeza de Vaca, Adorno and Pautz translation, p. 141.

"marine curios," Swanton, *Indians of Southeastern United States*, p. 737.

"strangers and merchants . . . ," Garcilaso de la Vega, p. 449.

"no one could depend . . . ," Oviedo, Hedrick and Riley translation, p. 42.

CHAPTER 19: PECANS AND PRICKLY PEARS

In addition to the ethnographic and archeological works cited above, see
    Callender and Kochems.

"because they had a different language ..." and other quotes regarding his
    time among the pecan harvesters appear in Cabeza de Vaca, Adorno and
    Pautz translation, p. 127ff.

"seeing that they killed their own sons ... ," Oviedo, Hedrick and Riley trans-
    lation, pp. 42–43.

"Most commonly ... ," Hester, in Thomas, ed., *Columbian Consequences*,
    vol. 1, pp. 193–94.

"The greater part of the year ... ," Oviedo, Hedrick and Riley translation,
    p. 43.

"simply does not fit ... ," Hester, "Artifacts, Archeology," p. 1 (Web page).
    www.english.swt.edu/css/TRHESTERCDU.HTML.

"so many mosquitoes ... ," Folmer, p. 216.

"in order to be at liberty ... ," Gilmore, in Thomas, ed., *Columbian Conse-*
    quences, vol. 2, p. 234.

"I duplicated the conditions ... ," Hallenbeck, *Journey and Route*, p. 159.

"It may seem superfluous ... ," Baskett, p. 246.

"We had clinched ... ," Wood, p. 242.

"Cabeza's Texas citizenship," Chipman, "In Search," p. 138.

"Vast ramparts ... ," Campbell and Campbell, p. 7.

"The women leave for no reason ... ," Oviedo, Hedrick and Riley translation,
    p. 77.

"A marriage lasts ... ," Cabeza de Vaca, Favata and Fernández translation,
    p. 71.

"When female children ... ," Cabeza de Vaca, Adorno and Pautz translation,
    p. 137ff.

"eleven or twelve children ... ," Oviedo, Hedrick and Riley translation, p. 42.

"takes another man ... ," Oviedo, Hedrick and Riley translation, p. 78.

"these Indians and others ... ," Cabeza de Vaca, Adorno and Pautz transla-
    tion, p. 141.

"love their children ... ," Cabeza de Vaca, Adorno and Pautz translation,
    p. 109.

"In the time ... ," Cabeza de Vaca, Adorno and Pautz translation, p. 191.

"When the natives quarrel ... ," Oviedo, Hedrick and Riley translation,
    p. 293.

"Whereupon it was necessary . . . ," Cabeza de Vaca, Adorno and Pautz translation, p. 147.

Chapter 20: The Burning Bush

"went looking for me . . ." and related quotes, Cabeza de Vaca, Adorno and Pautz translation, p. 149ff.

"went secretly . . . ," Oviedo, Hedrick and Riley translation, p. 45.

"it was God's will," Oviedo, Hedrick and Riley translation, p. 153.

"the black man always spoke . . . ," Cabeza de Vaca, Adorno and Pautz translation, p. 233.

"They tried to make us physicians . . . ," Cabeza de Vaca, Adorno and Pautz translation, p. 113ff.

"at that point . . ." and related quotes, Cabeza de Vaca, Adorno and Pautz translation, p. 155ff.

"ceremonial activity," Campbell and Campbell, p. 29.

"I scraped it very clean . . . ," Cabeza de Vaca, Adorno and Pautz translation, p. 173.

"all took great pleasure . . . ," Cabeza de Vaca, Adorno and Pautz translation, p. 159.

Chapter 21: The Traveling Medicine Show

"children of the sun" and related quotes, Cabeza de Vaca, Adorno and Pautz translation, p. 165ff.

"Cabeza de Vaca and his followers . . . ," Adorno, "The Negotiation of Fear," p. 173.

"lies not with the shaman . . . ," Taussig, p. 460.

"The water was up their knees . . . ," Oviedo, Hedrick and Riley translation, p. 50.

"and without letting our feet touch the ground . . . ," Cabeza de Vaca, Adorno and Pautz translation, p. 195.

"notwithstanding their fear . . ." and related quotes, Oviedo, Hedrick and Riley translation, p. 51ff.

"We did this . . ." and related quotes, Cabeza de Vaca, Adorno and Pautz translation, p. 201ff.

"pre-Columbian vandalism," Epstein, p. 475.

Chapter 22: Six Hundred Hearts of Deer

"ordered them to send people . . ." and related quotes, Cabeza de Vaca, Adorno and Pautz translation, p. 215ff. Also see Oviedo, Hedrick and Riley translation, p. 57ff.

Chapter 23: Peace in the Valley

See the Hammond and Rey translations of the Coronado documents. Adorno and Pautz's treatment of the Guzmán material in particular was also indispensable, as were Krieger, Bolton, and Sauer.

"hanging around his neck . . ." and related quotes, Oviedo, Hedrick and Riley translation, p. 64ff.

"We found ourselves greatly disturbed . . ." and related quotes, Cabeza de Vaca, Adorno and Pautz translation, p. 239ff.

"a few people . . . ," Hedrick and Riley, *Documents*, pp. 16–23.

"top of a high rugged crag . . . ," Oviedo, Hedrick and Riley translation, p. 63.

"where they arm themselves . . . ," letter from Cardenas to the emperor, as quoted in Sauer, "Discovery of New Mexico," p. 271.

"large numbers of native chickens . . . ," letter from Coronado to Mendoza, Hammond and Rey, p. 42.

"The Indian said he was the son . . . ," Castaneda account, Hodge, pp. 285–86.

"dressed in skins . . . ," Adorno and Pautz, vol 2., p. 420.

"Having here with me Andres . . . ," Hammond and Rey, p. 51.

"The viceroy bought the negro . . . ," Hammond and Rey, p. 47.

Chapter 24: Lost in the New World

"you shall take with you Esteban . . . ," Hammond and Rey, p. 59.

"liberated and purchased . . . ," Fray Marcos narrative, Hallenbeck, *Journey of Fray Marcos*, p. 15.

"I left them in the care . . . ," Hammond and Rey, p. 43.

"loaded with the large . . . ," Castaneda account, Hodge, p. 289.

"moderate importance . . ." and related quotes, Hallenbeck, *Journey of Fray Marcos*, p. 18ff.

Bibliography

Adorno, Rolena. "The Discursive Encounter of Spain and America: The Authority of Eyewitness Testimony in Writing History." *William and Mary Quarterly* 49 (April 1992).

———. "The Negotiation of Fear in Cabeza de Vaca's Naufragios." *Representations* 33 (1991): 163–99.

Adorno, Rolena, and Patrick Pautz. *Álvar Núñez Cabeza de Vaca: His Account, His Life, and the Expedition of Pánfilo de Narváez*, 3 vols. Lincoln: University of Nebraska Press, 1999.

Aiton, Arthur S., and Agapito Rey. "Coronado's Testimony in the Viceroy Mendoza Residencia." *New Mexico Historical Quarterly* 22 (1937).

Allen, John L. "From Cabot to Cartier: The Early Exploration of Eastern North America, 1497–1543." *Annals of the Association of American Geographers* 82, no. 3 (1992): 500–21.

Anderson, Edward F. *Peyote: The Divine Cactus.* Tucson: University of Arizona, 1996.

Apalachee Province. "Apalachee and Spanish Residential Styles in the Late Prehistoric and Early Historic Period Southeast." *American Antiquity* 60, no. 3 (July 1995): 482–95.

Arnold, J. Barto, and Robert Weddle. *The Nautical Archeology of Padre Island: The Spanish Shipwrecks of 1554*. New York: Academic Press, 1978.

Aten, Lawrence E. *Indians of the Upper Texas Coast*. New York: Academic Press, 1983.

Augier, F. R., and S. C. Gordon. *Sources of West Indian History*. London: Longman Group, 1962.

Axtell, James, and William C. Sturtevant. "The Unkindest Cut, or Who Invented Scalping." *William and Mary Quarterly*, 3rd ser., vol. 37, no. 3 (July 1980): 475–92.

Bandelier, Adolph Francis. *Contributions to the History of the Southwestern Portion of the United States*. Cambridge, Mass.: John Wilson & Son, 1890.

Bannon, John Francis. *The Spanish Borderlands Frontier, 1513–1821*. Albuquerque: University of New Mexico Press, 1974.

Bartram, William. *Travels of William Bartram*. New York: Dover, 1955.

Baskett, James Newton. "A Study of the Route of Cabeza de Vaca." *Texas Historical Association Quarterly* 10 (1907).

Berlandier, Jean Louis. *The Indians of Texas in 1830*. Translated by Patricia Reading Leclercq. Washington, D.C.: Smithsonian Institution, 1969.

Bishop, Morris. *The Odyssey of Cabeza de Vaca*. New York: Century, 1933.

Blakely, Robert, ed. *The King Site: Continuity and Conflict in 16th Century Georgia*. Athens: University of Georgia, 1988.

Bloom, Lansing B. "Who Discovered New Mexico?" *New Mexico Historical Review* 15 (April 1940).

Bollaert, William. "Observations on the Geography of Texas." *Journal of the Royal Geographical Society of London* 20 (1850).

Bolton, Herbert. *The Spanish Borderlands*. New Haven: Yale, 1921.

Booker, Karen M., Charles M. Hudson, and Robert L. Rankin, "Place Name Identification and Multilingualism in the Sixteenth-Century Southeast." *Ethnohistory* 39 (Autumn 1992).

Buker, George. "The Search for the Seven Cities and Early American Exploration." *Florida Historical Quarterly* 71 (1992).

Bullen, Ripley P. "Southern Limit of Timucua Territory." *Florida Historical Quarterly* 47: 414–19.

Burke, Peter. *The Renaissance Sense of the Past*. New York: St. Martin's Press, 1969.

Cabeza de Vaca, Álvar Nuñez. (For bibliographical information on Adorno and Pautz translation, which was the primary one used for this book, see entry for Adorno and Pautz, above.)

———. *Cabeza de Vaca's Adventures in the Unknown Interior of America* (the narrative). Translated and edited by Cyclone Covey. Albuquerque: University of New Mexico Press, 1998.

———. *Castaways* (the narrative). Edited and with an introduction by Enrique Pupo-Walker. Translated by Frances M. Lopez-Morillas. Berkeley: University of California Press, 1993.

———. *Relation of Alvar Nunez Cabeza de Vaca*. Translated and edited by Buckingham Smith. New York, 1871.

———. *The Account: Alvar Nuñez Cabeza de Vaca's Relación*. Translated by Martin A. Favata and Jose B. Fernández. Houston: Arte Público Press, 1993.

Callender, Charles, and Lee M. Kochems. "The North American Berdache." *Current Anthropology* (August–October 1983).

Calvert, Albert F. *Spanish Arms and Armour*. London: John Lane, 1907.

Campbell, T. N. "Coahuiltecans and Their Neighbors." *Handbook of North American Indians 10 Southwest*. Washington, D.C.: Smithsonian Institution Press (1983): 343–58.

Campbell, T. N., and T. J. Campbell. "Historic Indian Groups of the Choke Canyon Reservoir and Surrounding Area." Southern Texas Center for Archeological Research, University of Texas at San Antonio, Choke Canyon Series 1, 1981.

Casis, Lilia M., trans. "Letter of Don Damian Manzanet to Don Carlos De Siguenza Relative to the Discovery of the Bay of Espíritu Santo." *Texas Historical Association Quarterly*, 1899.

Céliz, Francisco. *Diary of the Alarcón Expedition into Texas, 1718–1719*. Translated by Fritz Leo Hoffmann. Los Angeles: Quivera Society, 1935.

Cervantes Saavedra, Miguel. *The Ingenious Gentleman: Don Quixote*. Translated by Samuel Putnam. New York: Penguin Books, 1976.

Childress, David Hatcher. *Lost Cities of North & Central America*. Kempton, Ill.: Adventures Unlimited Press, 1992.

Chipman, Donald E. "In Search of Cabeza de Vaca's Route across Texas: An Historiographical Survey." *Ethnohistory* 16, no. 1 (Winter 1969).

Chipman, Donald E. *Spanish Texas, 1519–1821*. Austin: University of Texas Press, 1992.

Claasen, Cheryl, and Samuella Sigmann, "Sourcing Busycon Artifacts of the Eastern United States." *American Antiquity* 58, no. 2 (1993): 333–47.

Clayton, Lawrence A., Vernon James Knight, and Edward C. Moore, eds. *The De Soto Chronicles: The Expedition of Hernando de Soto to North America in 1539–1543*. Tuscaloosa, Ala.: University of Alabama Press, 1993.

Clendinnen, Inga. *Ambivalent Conquests: Maya and Spaniard in the Yucatan, 1517–1570*. Cambridge, U.K.: Cambridge University Press, 1987.

Columbus, Christopher. *The Voyage of Christopher Columbus: Columbus' Own Journal of Discovery*. Translated by John Cummins. New York: St. Martin's Press, 1992.

Coopwood, Bethel. "Notes on the History of La Bahia el Espiritu Santo." *Texas Historical Association Quarterly*, 1898.

Coopwood, Bethel. "The Route of Cabeza de Vaca." *Texas Historical Association Quarterly*, 1899.

Cortés, Hernan. *The Letters of Hernando Cortés*. Translated by J. Bayard Morris. New York: McBride & Co., 1929.

Creel, Darrell. "Bison Hides in Late Prehistoric Exchange in the Southern Plains." *American Antiquity* 56 (January 1991).

Cunninghame Graham, R. B. *The Horses of the Conquest*. Norman: University of Oklahoma Press, 1949.

Davenport, Harbert, and Joseph K. Wells, "The First Europeans in Texas." *Southwestern Historical Quarterly*, no. 2 (October 1918).

Davies, R. Trevor. *The Golden Century in Spain*. New York: St. Martin's Press, 1967.

Day, A. Grove. "Mota Padilla on the Coronado Expedition." *Hispanic American Historical Review* 20 (February 1940).

Delgado-Gomez, Angel. *Spanish Historical Writing about the New World*. Providence: John Carter Brown, 1992.

DePratter, Chester B., Charles M. Hudson, and Marvin T. Smith. "The Route of Juan Pardo's Explorations in the Interior Southeast, 1566–1568." *Florida Historical Quarterly* 62 (1983).

Di Peso, Charles. *Casas Grandes: A Fallen Trading Center of the Gran Chichimeca*. Dragoon, Ariz.: Amerind Foundation, 1974.

Díaz del Castillo, Bernal. *The Discovery and Conquest of Mexico*. Translated by Irving Leonard. New York: Farrar, Straus & Cudahy, 1956.

Doolittle, William, E. "Cabeza de Vaca's Land of Maize: An Assessment of Its Agriculture." *Journal of Historical Geography* 10 (1984).

Dowling, Lee. "Story vs. Discourse in the Chronicle of the Indies: Alvar Nunez Cabeza de Vaca's Relación." *Hispanic Journal*, 1984.

Durán, Fray Diego. *The History of the Indies of New Spain*. Translated by Doris Heyden. Norman: University of Oklahoma Press, 1994.

Elliott, J. H. *Imperial Spain, 1469–1716*. Harmondsworth, U.K.: Penguin, 1963. Reprint, London: Penguin, 1990.

———. *Spain and Its World*. New Haven: Yale University Press, 1989.

Emory, William H. *Report on the United States and Mexican Boundary Survey*. Washington, D.C.: House of Representatives, 1857.

Epstein, Jeremiah F. "Cabeza De Vaca and the Sixteenth Century Copper Trade in Northern Mexico." *American Antiquity* 56, no. 3 (1991): 474–82.

Ewen, Charles R., and John H. Hann. *Hernando De Soto among the Apalachee: The Archaeology of the First Winter Encampment*. Gainesville: University of Florida Press, 1998.

Fernández, José B. *Alvar Nuñez Cabeza de Vaca: The Forgotten Chronicler*. Miami: Ediciones Universal, 1975.

———. "Opposing Views of La Florida: Alvar Nunez Cabeza de Vaca and El Inca Garcilaso De La Vega." *Early American Literature* 25 (1990).

Fernández-Armesto, Felipe. *Columbus*. Oxford: Oxford University Press, 1991.

Floyd, Troy S. *The Columbus Dynasty in the Caribbean, 1492–1526*. Albuquerque: University of New Mexico Press, 1973.

Folmer, Henri. "De Bellisle on the Texas Coast." *Southwestern Historical Quarterly* (October 1940).

Forbes, Jack. "Unknown Athapaskans: The Identification of the Jano, Jocome, Jumano, Manso, Suma, and other Indians of the Southwest." *Ethnohistory* 6, no. 2 (Spring 1959).

Foster, William, ed., Warren, Johanna, trans. *The La Salle Expedition on the Mississippi River: A Lost Manuscript of Nicholas de La Salle, 1682*. Austin: Texas State Historical Association, 2003.

Francisco de Vitoria. *Political Writings*. Edited by Anthony Pagden and Jeremy Lawrance. Cambridge: Cambridge University Press, 1991.

Fuentes, Carlos. *The Buried Mirror: Reflections on Spain and the New World.* New York: Houghton Mifflin, 1992.

Fuson, Robert H. *Juan Ponce de León and the Spanish Discovery of Puerto Rico and Florida.* Blacksburg, Va.: McDonald & Woodward, 2000.

Garcilaso de la Vega. *The Florida of the Inca: The First Great Classic of American History.* Translated by J. and J. Varner. Austin: University of Texas, 1980.

Gatschet, Albert. *The Karankawa Indians: The Coastal People of Texas.* Elibron Classics, Peabody Museum, 1891.

Goggin, John M. "Manifestations of a South Florida Cult in Northwestern Florida." *American Antiquity* 12, no. 4 (1947): 273–76.

Gonzales, Laurence. *Deep Survival: Who Lives, Who Dies, and Why.* New York: Norton, 2003.

Goodwyn, Frank. "Pánfilo de Narváez, a Character Study of the First Spanish Leader to Land an Expedition to Texas." *Hispanic American Historical Review* 29, no. 1 (February 1949): 150–56.

Grafton, Anthony. *New Worlds, Ancient Texts.* Cambridge, Mass.: Harvard University Press, Belknap Press, 1992.

Hallenbeck, Cleve. *The Journey and Route of Álvar Núñez Cabeza de Vaca: The Journey and Route of the First European to Cross the Continent of North America, 1534–1536.* Glendale, Calif.: Arthur H. Clark Company, 1940.

———. *The Journey of Fray Marcos.* Dallas: Southern Methodist University Press, 1987.

Hammond, George P. "Don Juan de Onate and the Founding of New Mexico." *New Mexico Historical Quarterly* 1 (1926).

Hammond, George P., and Agapito Rey. *Narratives of the Coronado Expedition.* Albuquerque: University of New Mexico Press, 1940.

Hanke, Lewis. *The Spanish Struggle for Justice in the New World.* Philadelphia: University of Pennsylvania Press, 1949.

Hann, John H. *Apalachee: The Land between the Rivers.* Gainesville: University Presses of Florida, 1988.

———. "Florida's Terra Incognita: West Florida Natives in the Sixteenth and Seventeenth Century." *Florida Anthropologist* 41, no. 1 (March 1988).

———. "Political Leadership among the Natives of Spanish Florida." *Florida Historical Quarterly* 71 (1992): 188–208.

Hedrick, Basil C., Charles Kelley, and Carroll Riley, eds. *The Classic Southwest: Readings in Archaeology, Ethnohistory, and Ethnology.* Carbondale: Southern Illinois University, 1973.

Hedrick, Basil, and Carroll L. Riley. *Documents Ancillary to the Vaca Journey.* University Museum Studies no. 5. Carbondale, Ill.: University Museum, Southern Illinois University, no date.

Helps, Arthur. *The Spanish Conquest in America: And Its Relation to the History of Slavery and to the Government of Colonies.* New York: AMS Press, 1966.

Hendricks, Sterling Brown. "The Somervell Expedition to the Rio Grande." *Southwestern Historical Quarterly* 23 (1919–1920).

Henige, David. "Primary Source by Primary Source? On the Role of Epidemics in New World Depopulation." *Ethnohistory* 33, no. 3 (Summer 1986): 293–312.

Hester, Thomas. "Historic Native American Populations, from the Gulf to the Rio Grande: Human Adaptation in Central, South, and Lower Pecos, Texas." Arkansas Archeological Survey, 1989.

Hester, Thomas R. "Artifacts, Archaeology, and Cabeza de Vaca in Southern Texas and New Mexico." www.english.swt.edu/css/TRHESTERCDU.HTML.

Hickerson, Nancy P. "How Cabeza de Vaca Lived With, Worked Among, and Finally Left the Indians of Texas." *Journal of Anthropological Research* 54, no. 2 (Summer 1998).

Highley, Lynn, and Thomas Hester, eds. *Papers on the Archaeology of the Texas Coast.* Center for Archaeological Research, University of Texas at San Antonio, Special Report no. 11, 1980.

Hodge, F. W. "The First Discovered City of Cibola." *American Anthropologist* 8 (April 1895).

Hodge, Frederick W., and T. E. Lewis, eds. *Spanish Explorers in the Southern United States, 1528–1543.* New York: Barnes & Noble, 1907. Reprint, 1971.

Hoffman, Paul E. *A New Andalucia and a Way to the Orient: The American Southeast during the Sixteenth Century.* Baton Rouge: Louisiana State University Press, 1990.

Horgan, Paul. *Conquistadors in North American History.* New York: Farrar, Straus & Co., 1963.

Howard, David A. *Conquistador in Chains: Cabeza de Vaca and the Indians of the Americas.* Tuscaloosa: University of Alabama, 1997.

Hudson, Charles. *Knights of Spain, Warriors of the Sun: Hernando de Soto and the South's Ancient Chiefdoms.* Athens: University of Georgia Press, 1997.

———. "A Spanish-Coosa Alliance in Sixteenth-Century North Georgia." *Georgia Historical Quarterly* 62, no. 4 (Winter 1988).

Hudson, Charles, ed. *Black Drink: A Native American Tea.* Athens: University of Georgia Press, 1979.

Hudson, Charles, and Carmen Chaves Tesser, eds. *The Forgotten Centuries: Indians and Europeans in the American South, 1521–1704.* Athens: University of Georgia Press, 1994.

Huff, Sandy. *Paddler's Guide to the Sunshine State.* Gainesville: University Press of Florida, 2001.

Hulton, Paul, et al. *The Work of Jacques Le Moyne de Morgues: A Huguenot Artist in France, Florida and England.* London: British Museum Publications, 1977.

Hutchinson, Dale L. "Postcontact Native American Health and Adaptation: Assessing the Impact of Introduced Diseases in Sixteenth-Century Gulf Coast Florida." PhD diss., University of Illinois, 1977.

Jane, Cecil, trans. *Select Documents Illustrating the Four Voyages of Columbus.* London: Hakluyt Society, 1930.

Johnson, G. Michael, and Timothy A. Kohler. "Toward a Better Understanding of North Peninsular Gulf Coast Florida Prehistory: Archaeological Reconnaissance in Dixie County." *Florida Anthropologist* 40, no. 4 (December 1987).

Josephy, Alvin. *America in 1492.* New York: Vintage, 1991.

Kamen, Henry. *Philip of Spain.* New Haven: Yale University Press, 1997.

———. *The Spanish Inquisition: A Historical Revision.* London: Weidenfeld & Nicolson, 1997.

Kemp, Peter, ed. *The Oxford Companion to the Sea.* Oxford: Oxford University Press, 1976.

Knight, Vernon James, Jr. "The Institutional Organization of Mississippian Religion." *American Antiquity* 51, no. 4 (October 1986): 675–87.

Krech, Shepard. *Myth and History: The Ecological Indian.* New York: Norton, 1999.

Krieger, Alex D. "Food Habits of the Texas Coastal Indians in the Early Sixteenth Century." *Bulletin of the Texas Archeological Society* 27 (1956).

———. *We Came Naked and Barefoot: The Journey of Cabeza de Vaca.* Austin: University of Texas Press, 2002.

Larsen, Lewis H., Jr. "Functional Considerations of Warfare in the Southeast during the Mississippi Period." *American Antiquity* 37 (July 1972).

Las Casas, Bartolomé. *Bartolomé De Las Casas: A Selection of His Writings.* Translated and edited by George Sanderlin. New York: Knopf, 1971.

————. *History of the Indies*. Translated by Andrée Collard. New York: Harper & Row, 1971.

————. *A Short Account of the Destruction of the Indies*. Translated and edited by Nigel Griffin with an introduction by Anthony Pagden. London: Penguin, 1992.

* Leonard, Irving A. *Books of the Brave*. Berkeley: University of California Press, 1992. First published 1949 by Harvard University Press.

* Long, Haniel. *Interlinear to Cabeza de Vaca*. Tucson: Peccary Press, 1985.

* Lunenfeld, Marvin. *1492: Discovery, Invasion, Encounter*. Lexington: D. C. Heath, 1991.

* MacLeish, William H. *The Day before America: Changing the Nature of a Continent*. Boston: Houghton Mifflin, 1994.

MacLeod, W. C. "The Distribution of Secondary Cremation and of the Drinking of Ashes." *American Anthropologist* 32 (July–September 1930).

* Malville, J. McKim, and Claudia Putnam. *Prehistoric Astronomy in the Southwest*. Boulder: Johnson Books, 1989.

Mann, Charles C. "1491." *Atlantic Monthly*, March 2002.

* Marcos de Niza. "Discovery of the Seven Cities of Cibola." Translated by Percy M. Baldwin. Historical Society of New Mexico, Albuquerque, November 1926.

* Martín, Luis. *Daughters of the Conquistadores: Women of the Viceroyalty of Peru*. Albuquerque: University of New Mexico Press, 1983.

* Martyr, Peter. *De Orbe Novo: The Eight Decades of Peter Martyr D'Anghera*. Translated by Francis Augustus MacNutt. New York: Burt Franklin, 1912. Reprint, 1970.

McGann, Thomas. "The Ordeal of Cabeza de Vaca." *American Heritage* 12 (1960).

Mecham, J. Lloyd. "The Second Spanish Expedition to New Mexico: An Account of the Chamuscado-Rodiquez Entrada of 1581–1582." *New Mexico Historical Review* 1 (1926).

Milanich, Jerald T. *Archaeology of Precolumbian Florida*. Gainesville: University Press of Florida, 1994.

————. *Florida Indians and the Invasion from Europe*. Gainesville: University Press of Florida, 1998.

Milanich, Jerald T., and Charles Hudson. *Hernando de Soto and the Indians of Florida*. Gainesville: University Press of Florida, 1993.

* Milanich, Jerald T., and Susan Milbrath, eds. *First Encounters: Spanish Explorations*

in the Caribbean and the United States, 1492–1570. Gainesville: University Press of Florida, 1989.

Milanich, Jerald, and Samuel Proctor, eds. *Tacachale: Essays on the Indians of Florida and Southeastern Georgia during the Historic Period.* (See especially "Tocobaga Indians and the Safety Harbor Culture," by Ripley P. Bullen.) Gainesville: University Press of Florida, 1978.

Mitchem, Jeffrey. "Ethnohistoric and Archaeological Evidence for a Proto-historic Provincial Boundary in West Peninsular Florida." Paper presented at the 46th Annual Meeting of the Southeastern Archaeological Conference, Tampa, November 8–11, 1989.

———. "Safety Harbor Redefined," PhD diss., University of Florida, 1989.

Mitchem, Jeffrey M., and Jonathan M. Leader. "Early Sixteenth Century Beads from the Tatham Mound." Citrus County, Florida: Data and Interpretations. *Florida Anthropologist* 41, no. 1 (March 1988).

Moody, Ralph. *The Old Trails West.* New York: Thos. Crowell, 1963.

Morison, Samuel Eliot. *Admiral of the Ocean Sea.* Boston: Little Brown, 1942.

Morison, Samuel Eliot. *The European Discovery of America: The Southern Voyages, 1492–1616.* Oxford: Oxford University Press, 1974.

Morison, Samuel Eliot, and Mauricio Obregón. *The Caribbean as Columbus Saw It.* Boston: Atlantic Monthly Press, 1964.

Nassaney, Michael S., and Eric Johnson, eds. *Interpretations of Native North American Life.* Gainesville: University Press of Florida, 2000. (See especially "Ritual and Material Culture as Keys to Cultural Continuity: Native American Interaction with Europeans in Eastern Arkansas, 1541–1682," by Kathleen H. Cande.)

National Geographic Society. *A Columbus Casebook.* Washington, D.C., 1986.

Newcomb, W. W. *The Indians of Texas.* Austin: University of Texas Press, 1961.

Oviedo y Valdez, Gonzalo Fernandez. "The Expedition of Pánfilo De Narváez" (the Joint Report). Translated and edited by Harbert Davenport. Southwestern Historical Quarterly.

———. *The Journey of the Vaca Party: The Account of the Narváez Expedition, 1528–1536, as Related by Gonzalo Fernández de Oviedo y Valdés* (the Joint Report). Translated by Basil Hedrick and Carroll L. Riley. Carbondale, Ill.: University Museum, Southern Illinois University, 1974.

Parry, J. H. *The Spanish Seaborne Empire.* New York: Knopf, 1970.

Pastor Bodmer, Beatriz. *The Armature of Conquest: Spanish Accounts of the Discovery of America, 1492–1589.* Translated by Lydia Longstreth Hunt. Stanford, Calif.: Stanford University Press, 1992.

Pearson, Fred Lamar, Jr. "The Florencia Investigation of Spanish Timucua." *Florida Historical Quarterly* 51, no. 2; 166–76.

Peck, Douglas T. "Reconstruction and Analysis of the 1513 Discovery Voyage of Juan Ponce de León." *Florida Historical Quarterly* 71 (1992).

Perry, I. Mac. *Indian Mounds You Can Visit.* St. Petersburg, Fla.: Great Outdoors, 1993.

Peterson, Mendel. *The Funnel of Gold.* Boston: Little Brown, 1975.

Phinney, A. H. "Narvaez and De Soto: Their Landing Places and the Town of Espirito Santo." *Florida Historical Quarterly,* 1925.

Pogue, Joseph E. "Aboriginal Use of Turquoise in North America." *American Anthropologist* 14, no. 3 (July–September 1912).

Ponton, Brownie, and Bates H. M'Farland. "Alvar Nunez Cabeza De Vaca: A Preliminary Report on His Wanderings in Texas." *Texas Historical Association Quarterly,* 1889.

Rabasa, José. *Writing Violence on the Northern Frontier: The Historiography of Sixteenth Century New Mexico and Florida and the Legacy of Conquest.* Durham, N.C.: Duke University, 2000.

Reff, Daniel T. "The Introduction of Smallpox in the Greater Southwest." *American Anthropologist* 89 (September 1987).

Restall, Matthew. *Seven Myths of the Spanish Conquest.* Oxford: Oxford University Press, 2003.

Rickard, T. A. "The Use of Native Copper by the Indigenes of North America." *Journal of the Royal Anthropological Institute of Great Britain and Ireland* 64 (July–December 1934).

Ricklis, Robert A. *The Karankawa Indians of Texas: An Ecological Study of Cultural Tradition and Change.* Austin: University of Texas Press, 1996.

Riley, Carroll L. "Blacks in the Early Southwest." *Ethnohistory* 19 (Summer 1972).

———. "Las Casas and the Golden Cities." *Ethnohistory* 23, no. 1 (Winter 1976).

———. "Mesoamerican Indians in the Early Southwest." *Ethnohistory* 21 (Winter 1974).

Rippy, J. Fred. "The Negro and the Spanish Pioneer in the New World." *Journal of Negro History* 6 (April 1921).

Sahagun, Bernardino de. *A History of Ancient Mexico*. Translated by Fanny Bandelier. Glorieta, N.M.: Rio Grand Press, 1976.

Samuels, Peggy. "Imagining Distance: Spanish Explorers in America." *Early American Literature* 25 (1990).

Sauer, Carl O. "The Discovery of New Mexico Reconsidered." *New Mexico Historical Review* 12 (1937).

———. *The Early Spanish Main*. Berkeley: University of California Press, 1969.

Scarry, John F., and Bonnie G. McEwan. "Domestic Architecture in Apala- chee Province." *American Antiquity* 60, no. 3 (July 1995).

Schama, Simon, "They all laughed at Christopher Columbus." *New Republic,* January 6, 13, 1992.

Shaafsma, Curtis, and Carroll Riley, eds. *The Casas Grandes World*. Salt Lake City: University of Utah Press, 1999.

Shelby, Charmion Clair. "St. Denis's Second Expedition to the Rio Grande, 1716–1719." *Southwestern Historical Quarterly* 27 (1923).

Smith, Bruce, ed. *The Mississippian Emergence*. Washington, D.C.: Smith- sonian Institution Press, 1990.

Solís de Merás, Gonzalo. *Pedro Menéndez de Avilés*. Facsimile of the 1923 edition. Translated and edited by J. T. Connor. Gainesville: University of Florida Press, 1964.

Sowell, John. *Desert Ecology*. Salt Lake City: University of Utah Press, 2001.

Steck, Francis Borgia. *A Tentative Guide to Historical Materials on the Spanish Borderlands*. New York: Burt Franklin, 1971.

Swanton, John R. *Final Report of the De Soto Expedition Commission*. Washing- ton, D.C.: Smithsonian Institution, 1985.

———. *Indian Tribes of the Lower Mississippi Valley and Adjacent Coast of the Gulf of Mexico*. Washington, D.C.: Government Printing Office, 1911.

———. *Indians of the Southeastern United States*. Washington, D.C.: Smithson- ian Institution, 1979.

———. *Source Material on the History and Ethnology of the Caddo Indians*. Washington, D.C.: Government Printing Office, 1942.

Taussig, Michael. *Shamanism, Colonialism, and the Wild Man: A Study in Terror and Healing*. Chicago: University of Chicago Press, 1987.

Taylor, Paul S. "Spanish Seamen in the New World during the Colonial Period." *Hispanic American Historical Review* 5, no. 4 (1922): 631–61.

Terrell, John Upton. *Estevanico the Black.* Los Angeles: Westernlore Press, 1968.

Thomas, David Hurst, ed. *Columbian Consequences.* Vol. 1, *Archaeological and Historical Perspectives on the Spanish Borderlands West.* Washington, D.C.: Smithsonian Institution Press, 1989.

———. *Columbian Consequences.* Vol. 2, *Archaeological and Historical Perspectives on the Spanish Borderlands East.* Washington, D.C.: Smithsonian Institution Press, 1990.

Thomas, Hugh. *Conquest, Montezuma, Cortés, and the Fall of Old Mexico.* New York: Touchstone, 1993.

———. *The Slave Trade: The Story of the Atlantic Slave Trade: 1440–1870.* New York: Simon & Schuster, 1997.

———. *Who's Who of the Conquistadors.* London: Cassel & Co., 2000.

Todorov, Tzvetan. *The Conquest of America.* Translated by Richard Howard. New York: Harper & Row, 1982.

Vázquez de Espinosa, Antonio. *Description of the Indies.* Translated by Charles Upson Clark. Washington, D.C.: Smithsonian Institution Press, 1968.

Wagenheim, Kal, and Olga Jiménez de Wagenheim, eds. *The Puerto Ricans: A Documentary History.* Princeton: Markus Wiener, 1999.

Wagner, Henry, Fr. "Marcos de Niza." *New Mexico Historical Review* 9 (1934).

———. "Three Accounts of the Expedition of Fernando Cortes, Printed in Germany between 1520 and 1522." *Hispanic American Historical Review,* May 1929.

Weatherford, Jack. *Native Roots: How the Indians Enriched America.* New York: Fawcett Columbine, 1991.

Weber, David J. *The Spanish Frontier in North America.* New Haven: Yale University Press, 1992.

Weddle, Robert S. *Spanish Sea: The Gulf of Mexico in North American Discovery, 1500–1685.* College Station, Tex.: Texas A & M University Press, 1985.

Welch, Paul D., and C. Margaret Scarry. "Status-Related Variation in Foodways in the Moundville Chiefdom." *American Antiquity* 60, no. 3 (July 1995): 397–419.

Wellman, Paul. *Glory, God and Gold.* Garden City, N.Y.: Doubleday, 1954.

Wesson, Cameron B. "Chiefly Power and Food Storage in Southeastern North America." *World Archaeology* 31, no. 1: 145–64.

● Wilford, John Noble. *The Mysterious History of Columbus*. New York: Knopf, 1991.

● Willey, Gordon R. *Archeology of the Florida Gulf Coast*. Gainesville: University Press of Florida, 1998.

Williams, O. W. "Route of Cabeza de Vaca in Texas." *Texas Historical Association Quarterly*, 1899.

Wolff, Thomas. "The Karankawa Indians: Their Conflict with the White Man in Texas." *Ethnohistory* 16, no. 1 (Winter 1969).

● Wood, Michael. *Conquistadors*. California: BBC, 2000.

Wright, I. A. *The Early History of Cuba*. New York: Macmillan, 1916.

● Wright, Ronald. *Stolen Continents: The Americas through Indian Eyes since 1492*. New York: Houghton Mifflin, 1992.

● Young, Richard A. "Re-reading the Past: Cabeza de Vaca in History, Fiction, and Film." In *Making Contact: Maps, Identity, and Travel*. Edited by Glen Burger. Edmonton: University of Alberta Press, 2003.

● Zwinger, Ann Haymond. *The Mysterious Lands: A Naturalist Explores the Four Great Deserts of the Southwest*. Tucson: University of Arizona Press, 1989.

Acknowledgments

There are so many people to thank, foremost among them the hundreds of scholars, translators, and archeologists whose names appear in the bibliography. There are also numerous librarians in Providence, Boston, New York, and elsewhere, whose names I don't know but without whose assistance I could never have finished the book. Like almost all history, this is a retelling, resting on the foundation built by those who told parts of the story before.

Without my wife, Nina Bramhall, and our son, Natty, to both of whom this book is dedicated, it's hard to imagine anything of this magnitude being worth the effort. What's more, Nina's help with the manuscript was invaluable. Other readers who deserve special gratitude include, as always, my parents, Pat and Peter Schneider, my sisters, Bethany and Rebecca, and Kib and Tess Bramhall. My father went the extra 3,500 miles by prowling with me around much of Texas and northern Mexico. Laurel Schneider, Dan Okrent, Ward Just, and Julie Michaels all lent moral support when it was particularly needed. Will Lucky did too, and threw in teaching me tri-tone substitutions and upper-structure voicing at the same time. Also on the Vineyard, Daniel Prowten and Steve Flanders built a writer's dream garret, with plenty of room downstairs to store kayaks, surfboards, and other life-support systems. Thanks, too, to Kim Witherspoon and David Forrer at Inkwell Management. And Supurna Banerjee, Katy Hope, Rita Quintas, and the excellent copy editors and designers at Henry Holt.

Lastly, as has been the case for three books now, I am grateful to Jack Macrae, as fine a friend and editor as a writer could wish to find. In the case of this book, I want to particularly thank him for not stopping me from starting work on it so long ago, and then not allowing me to stop the work until it was the best I could make it be.

Index

About the Author

PAUL SCHNEIDER, the author of the highly praised and successful *The Adirondacks*, a *New York Times Book Review* Notable Book, and *The Enduring Shore*, lives in West Tisbury, Massachusetts.